TEXAS
ON THE HALFSHELL
TEX-MEX, BARBECUE, CHILI AND LONE STAR DELIGHTS

TEXAS
ON THE HALFSHELL

TEX-MEX, BARBECUE, CHILI AND LONE STAR DELIGHTS

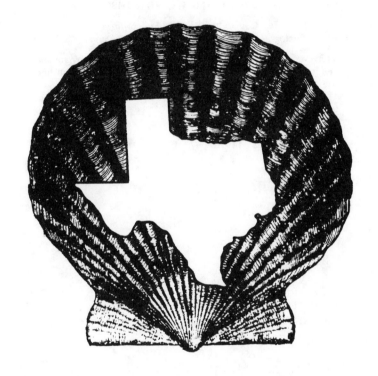

MAIN
STREET
BOOKS

DOUBLEDAY
NEW YORK LONDON TORONTO SYDNEY AUCKLAND

PUBLISHED BY DOUBLEDAY
a division of Bantam Doubleday Dell Publishing Group, Inc.
666 Fifth Avenue, New York, New York 10103

MAIN STREET BOOKS, DOUBLEDAY, and the portrayal of a
building with a tree are trademarks of Doubleday, a
division of Bantam Doubleday Dell Publishing Group, Inc.

PRODUCED BY DANIEL PRODUCTIONS

EDITOR: TERI TITCHENAL
ASSISTANT EDITOR: SUSAN KOSTER
PRODUCTION ASSISTANT: WENDY ROTHMAN
TYPESETTING: HORIZON GRAPHICS & TYPE CO.

TEST KITCHEN DIRECTOR: SUSAN KOSTER

ISBN: 0-385-17904-9
LIBRARY OF CONGRESS CATALOG CARD NUMBER: 81-4340-8

12   14   16   17   15   13   11

DEDICATED TO HAL JOHN AND JUDITH WIMBERLY — THANK YOU

As with any book project, its completion is the result of the collective efforts and contributions of many people. Here is our group of special people to whom we wish to extend warm and grateful "thank you's": To Mary Nell Reck whose *Cafe Moustache* in Houston epitomizes gourmet Texas cooking. Mary's sensitivities to the changing influences occurring daily in Texas are exemplified in her restaurant where she keeps one step ahead of the culinary pulse of the Lone Star State. Her contributions were invaluable. To Allegani Jani, your book *Mis Amigos* (My Hungry Friends) was a joy to receive. Copies of the book may be obtained by writing Jani at Box 954 - Hwy. 920 & Ranch Road 1, Stonewall, Texas 78671. To Mary Yturria and her wonderfully refreshing recipes — the Lower Rio Grande Valley will never be the same. To Ralph and Suzy Chacon, proprietors of *Señor Miguel's* in Boulder, Colorado, who came to our rescue when no one else could; we never found an enchilada sauce finer than theirs. To Joan Nobles, your peach cobbler we ate in *Gideons* (San Angelo, Texas) still haunts our memory — thanks for the recipes and your time. By the way, when are you going to cook us up that ranch dinner? To Sue Sims for willingness to share her knowledge with complete strangers late at night. To Hugh Alexander whose barbecued brisket is outta sight in Houston (Space Shuttle-wise). To Tex Schofield *the Divine* (The Mouth of the Chili World) and Helena *the Lovely* for their assistance, endless banter and Patron Club Packets. To Sam Lewis for human kindness; we can't think of a better Texan to have met first. To Eddie and Barb and Mom, your secret is safe with us. To John Raven (Bad McFad), your heart is gold — shine on. To Clyde and Mary Griffin for our initiation rites into Chilidom, and introducing us to Nat Henderson (of the *Austin Statesman*) who invited us to judge at the Taylor Barbecue. To LeBeast (Joe Aronson) who keeps his masterful fingers stirrin' and cookin' up a storm, and Admiral, his right hand man. To Shorty Fry who tirelessly carries Wick Fowler's Chili torch — thanks for the tour and a friendly face at the cookoffs. To Dr. Roy Nakayama, the capsaicin consultant extraordinaire. To Carol Risz — perseverance and dedication is her middle name. To Frank Tolbert who has bean around from the beginning. To Stubbs, sell that sauce and write on in Lubbock! To the *Cherokee Club Cookbook* folk of Longview, Texas. To the *Menard Bicentennial Cookbook* folk of Menard, Texas. To the *Texas Sheep and Goatraisers' Cookbook* folk of San Angelo, Texas. To the *New Del Rio Cookbook* folk of Del Rio, Texas. To the *Bounty of East Texas Cookbook* folk of Longview, Texas. To the *Sterling County's Treasure of Personal Recipes* folk of Sterling City, Texas. To the *Irion County Bicentennial Cookbook* folk of Irion, Texas. To *From the Trading Post* of Austin, Texas. To Ace Reid of Kerrville, Texas. To the folks of *A Hill Country Cookbook* in central Texas. To *Aunt Billie's Country Cookin'* of west Texas. To Phillip Morris, Inc. To Horizon Graphics of Boulder, Colorado, who typeset this book: thank you Jo, Deborah, Linda and Bryan, you literally bent over backwards to keep us on schedule day and night (mostly nights). To Wolf, aka Rocksteady Mercedes Lens, "Oh to live on Sugar Mountain." To T., your editorial editorializing expertise was inexpendable to us (never cry wolf, just kiss 'em). To Neil and Margaret McKenzie whose farm became a home-away-from-home. To Johnson & Johnson for dental floss. To SAAB for building front wheeled drive rocket ships, and a special "no thanks" to the Texas Highway Patrol who nailed us but good. To Terry Allan, we now know how hard the hard assphalt Amarillo Highway really is. To Hal John and Judith for warmth, hospitality, laughter, mamosa's, *Goat Gap Gazettes* and ability to impart "character" to a $250 hat. It's ten o'clock . . . do you know where your stet-Son is? And Heini, "Gee, I kinda feel like I should smoke a cigarette." To Doc Joe and Mother Mary who still can't believe we did this. To Janine and Wes for their eternal support. To Joe for fun and persistence and Phil for persistent fun . . . "Oh waitress!" To Sophie and Lina — we ate, slept and left all too soon — thanks so very much and dance on! To Clifford May, ace cub reporter, raconteur and the only guy in Manhattan willing to donate us floorspace (whether he liked it or not) so we could store our stuff and us . . . the check is in the mail. To Peter Galante, thanks for the assist, it was a point well taken. To Wendy for taking time off from her already "too many irons in the fire" schedule, submarine sandwiches, chocolate and telling us to "get the book done!" Thanks. To Coaster for her Suicide Test Kitchen, steady hand, wary eye, patience and astronomical-gastrointestinal expertise. If their is a misteak to be found, she'll find it. To the New Austin Motel, an excellent place to survive through a severe case of barbecue coma. To Marion Szurek of the San Angelo Chamber of Commerce. And finally to Lindy Hess, our editor at Doubleday and, alas, forever a "proper New York girl."

TEXAS ON THE HALFSHELL

BARBECUE - 12

From its incendiary past to its exalted present, the history of barbecue is explored from 'B' to 'Q.' You will also find directions on how to build an authentic Texas barbecue pit, what firewood to use and proper cooking and eating instructions. Included is a list of Texas barbecue joints mere mortals only dream about if they don't live in the Lone Star state.

CHILI - 42

We present in this chapter a brief history and a glimpse of maniacal madness known as "Chili Mania" that "plagues" the state of Texas. The ins and outs of the world of chile peppers are clarified as well as who's who in the World of Chili. A compendium of chili joints is provided for those of you puppilari untutored in the tutelage of epicurean gourmandizing and cibarious consumption of the proverbial bowl of Red.

TEX-MEX - 80

This chapter explains the origins of the culinary hybrid dubbed Tex-Mex, and offers an array of recipe which make a welcomed alternative to traditional American food (hopefully exciting the reader enough to enjoy the pleasures of frijoles at breakfast). Step-by-step instructions unravel the mystery of preparing tortillas and chilies, and detail the time-honored tradition of correct tequila drinking.

TRADITIONAL - 142

What is traditional Texas cooking? In a nutshell: steak, beans, cornbread and iced tea. Beyond that, the definition is up for grabs. So we have attempted to compile a representative group of recipes reflective of Texas' proud and independent heritage (from the days of the great trail drives to the present). You will find several "refreshingly humorous" ones, not found in "The Joy of Cooking," but as the saying goes . . . "Nowhere else But Texas."

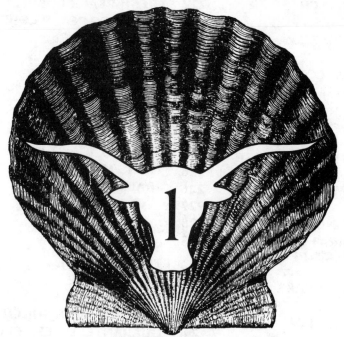

BARBECUE

Some claim a Paleolithic lightning bolt thundered to earth, frying some hapless saber-toothed tiger into a charred, but highly delectable, main dish which Cro-Magnon man dubbed "barbecue." Others, particularly Texans, defend the theory that barbecue originated in Texas, having been genetically imprinted onto their double helix right next to their inherent ability to breathe and tell tall tales. Whatever, the art of barbecue is deeply entrenched in the culinary heart of Texas and loved as fiercely as the Lone Star on the state flag.

The origin of the word barbecue remains vulnerable to smokey debates. Some claim the word comes from the French term "barbe de que" which connotated roasting a pig whole from barbe (chin) to que (tail). Others favor the "barbacoa" theory; barbacoa being a Mexican word describing a cooking frame suspended from posts; or, that the word came from an extinct Indian language, since early North American Indians were practicing the art of pit cooking before Columbus ever thought of discovering the New World. What is apparent is that no one really knows. Some things are best left shrouded in historical mystery.

What is known is that commercial barbecuing started in the back rooms of meat markets in Central Texas at the turn of the century. Butchers, averse to throwing out their less desirable cuts of meat and trimmings, began to feature Saturday afternoon barbecues. They took the unsold beef briskets and shoulder clods, made sausage from meat scraps, and then slow-smoked everything (in pits built behind the meat cases) to enhance the flavor of the poorer cuts. The custom caught on. Eventually the

Early barbecue masters (top) tending their pit. "Grills" were made from old Ford axles upon which the meat was draped. Lunchtime for Texas A&M students (bottom) encamped along the Rio Brazos. Venison haunches cook over a pit of smoldering mesquite coals in the foreground. Circa 1912. *Photos courtesy of The Institute of Texas Cultures.*

tradition of a combination butcher shop/barbecue pit became a Texas institution, complete with long lines of hungry customers.

Culturally speaking, barbecue is an obsession that has left a profound mark on Texas. Just about every state park and roadside table is graced with a BBQ pit. Many Texas politicians since the nineteenth century owe their stints in office to free barbecues they sponsored on the fourth of July. On the range, big ranches held barbecues as a device to reunite old hands, meet new friends and celebrate the past year's work. For example, the XIT Ranch, (at one time spanning ten million acres) still throws a pretty impressive whoop-de-doo. Come September thousands gather at Dalhart, Texas — home base for the XIT Ranch —the only place in the world where they barbecue with bulldozers, backhoes and dump trucks laden with animal carcasses. For a side dish (and side show) cowboys teeter atop 250 gallon stainless steel vats stirring ranch-style beans with stainless steel shovels.

When Lyndon Baines Johnson was elected to the Presidency in 1964, Texans rejoiced. They finally had a President who didn't speak with an "accent." LBJ probably did more to promote the popularity of barbecue by introducing the rest of the nation to his insatiable cravings for the smokey delicacy. When the bug bit and he found he couldn't quite get the desired "taste" from his White House kitchens, he thought nothing of packing visiting dignitaries and foreign officials into Air Force One, and flying to the LBJ Ranch to experience the taste of authentic Texas BBQ. King Faisal of Saudi Arabia, after sampling one taste of Texas barbecue, ordered ten thousand Texas cattle to satiate his royal cravings. Of course the Arabs, thinking as big as any Texas millionaire, took the original concept of roasting an animal whole one step further. They start with a chicken which is stuffed into the stomach of a lamb, the lamb into the stomach of a cow and then the cow is put into the stomach of a camel. After roasting for three days . . . voilá, Barbecued Barnyard Arabesque! The phenomena of barbecue mania has even permeated the entertainment industry in an episode of M*A*S*H. Alan Alda exemplified true fanatical barbecue panache when, after operating in Korea one meal too long, desperately picked up Radar's phone, dialed his favorite BBQ-pit in Chicago, Illinois and uttered these immortal words: "Do you deliver?" They did, and soon the M*A*S*H unit was elbow-deep in red sauce and ribs.

Today, with barbecue firmly embedded in the Texas environment, there are hundreds of cookoffs held to determine who cooks the best "Q" and even a monthly paper called the *Barbecue Times* keeping BBQ-bugs abreast of the latest culinary happenings. In paying homage to their favorite excuse for a social gathering upwards of 25,000 Texans gather yearly at the Taylor International Barbecue Cookoff held in Taylor, Texas. Amateur chefs, kitchen raconteurs and afficionados of the pit and spit display their finest culinary expertise as they vie for trophies and infamous notoriety. Everything from beef briskets, lamb haunches and quail breasts to soft shell turtles, rattlesnakes and armadillos are smoked to perfection at this cookoff. Contestants cook on a bizarre array of portable, hand-built kitchen rigs. Their designs vary from the simplicity of a washtub full of coals supporting a pitchfork grill, to the sophistication of a 20-foot long trailer — complete with a fifteen foot-long butane tank barbecue smoker, steak grills, deep fat fryers, sinks spouting hot and cold water, a beer tap, and a $40,000 price tag. The larger outfits are capable of dishing out enough food fit to feed a sit down orgy of 444 people. After the smoke clears and the awards are handed out, everyone returns home full-filled to digest the weekend's festivities . . . nowhere else but Texas!

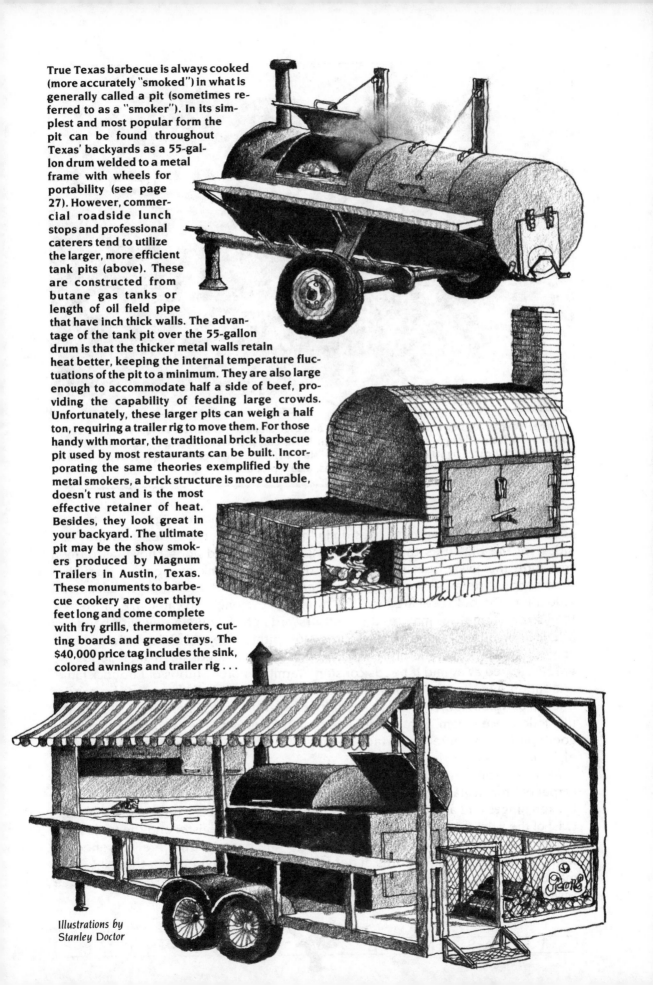

True Texas barbecue is always cooked (more accurately "smoked") in what is generally called a pit (sometimes referred to as a "smoker"). In its simplest and most popular form the pit can be found throughout Texas' backyards as a 55-gallon drum welded to a metal frame with wheels for portability (see page 27). However, commercial roadside lunch stops and professional caterers tend to utilize the larger, more efficient tank pits (above). These are constructed from butane gas tanks or length of oil field pipe that have inch thick walls. The advantage of the tank pit over the 55-gallon drum is that the thicker metal walls retain heat better, keeping the internal temperature fluctuations of the pit to a minimum. They are also large enough to accommodate half a side of beef, providing the capability of feeding large crowds. Unfortunately, these larger pits can weigh a half ton, requiring a trailer rig to move them. For those handy with mortar, the traditional brick barbecue pit used by most restaurants can be built. Incorporating the same theories exemplified by the metal smokers, a brick structure is more durable, doesn't rust and is the most effective retainer of heat. Besides, they look great in your backyard. The ultimate pit may be the show smokers produced by Magnum Trailers in Austin, Texas. These monuments to barbecue cookery are over thirty feet long and come complete with fry grills, thermometers, cutting boards and grease trays. The $40,000 price tag includes the sink, colored awnings and trailer rig . . .

Illustrations by Stanley Doctor

It's hard to pass by Louie Mueller's red, white and blue marquee in Taylor, Texas. Don't expect air conditioning inside though, he's never believed in it. His only priority is serving up perfect barbecue. Pitman Daddy Bruce (right) displays his famous "slab 'o ribs"; a product of sixty years of experience. He learned the "Art" from his father in Arkansas, also a pitman.

Yet despite the Texan's addiction to extravaganza, havin' a good ole time at cookoffs, traditional barbecue lives on in the small towns, roadside stops and "bad sides" of the big cities throughout Texas. Here, revered gods known as pitmen transform the lowly beef brisket — a tough, nasty hunk of meat — through a time-honored ritual, into a culinary masterpiece which demotes porterhouse and sirloin into the bologna category. The pitman is the one who can make or break a joint's reputation. He may tend his pit upwards of 16 hours a day with hands as grizzled and burned as the meat he turns. Most pitmen are real philosophers when it comes to talkin' "Q." "The pit is like the human face. It needs fresh air, it needs the grease cleared away and it needs constant warmth," notes Stubbs of Lubbock fame. "Attention must be paid constantly to your pit, good barbecue must be tender enough to drink. Hell, I get old folks without no teeth come in here and just suck at it like Jello or ice cream." Entrusted, like Prometheus, with the tending of the fire, a good pitman is more important to most Texans than having bought IBM at eight-and-a-half.

Most BBQ-pits are exactly that. The parking lot, if there is one, is littered with a carpet of broken glass and plastic fork shards. Rusted screen doors list to and fro on broken hinges and a patina of grease on the doorknob necessitates more than one twist of the wrist to open. Inside, a tackle box is the cash register and the tables are, more frequently than not, last week's garage sale bargain. The peeling veneered walls are papers with PR photos of defensive linemen who frequent the joint. They may be out of napkins and the soda machine is jetting hot, bubbly Dr. Pepper, but a wise tongue shouldn't judge this book by its cover.

At lunchtime the eating halls are filled to capacity with barbecue addicts. Regulars step through the aromatic blue haze to order meat by the pound. The carver deftly slices off brisket slabs, flopping the steaming meat onto sheets of dusty rose-colored butcher paper. The paper serves as cafeteria tray and plate. Seating, if available, is along tables arranged in what's called "friendship dining." At Kreuz's Market in Lockhart, Texas, knives attached to chains affixed to the table at ten foot intervals are available for the customer's "convenience."

Most pits also offer "extras" like thick slices of sweet white onions, pickles, hot peppers and stacks of white bread that pull double duty as napkins. And if you're looking around for barbecue sauce, at least

in Central Texas, forget it. There, masters refuse to blaspheme their smokey creations with the sugary red liquid. Instead they may provide a bottle of Tabasco or a similar spicy creation of their own making. They are of the belief that the magnificent taste of authentic Texas barbecue needs no sauce. The pitmen of East and West Texas may beg to differ, but regardless, there are lines of people outside of any good pit in Texas who will wait for hours, if need be, to get in — sauce or no sauce. They know that inside is a sixty-year-old pitman who's been cookin' there for most of his life and that only means one thing. Good Barbecue.

And this is what it's all about — turning a piece of meat "tough as a boot" into a delicacy that's the best you've ever locked your lips on." Along with the ever-present white bread, sweet onions, Tabasco sauce and a longneck brew this makes "larrupin' " good eating!

PEPSI

SAM'S - BAR - B - Q

WELCOME!
SAM'S
Bar-B-Que

BARBECUE PITS

To say that Texans love their barbecue is obvious, but to the Texas visitor seeking to taste the essence of that love, it may become confusing. In the Houston Yellow Pages there are over 180 listings for barbecue. In Dallas, 109. To alleviate disappointments (because there is *some* questionable barbecue to be found in Texas) and wasted travel time, the authors have compiled a list of their favorites. You are sure to find others, but then again, it's all a question of taste. Enjoy!

Angelo's Barbecue — A veritable barbecue mecca, Angelo's serves up the best mess of ribs and succulent beef found in the Fort Worth area. It's a "must stop and eat" place in Cowtown when the hungries hit. 2533 *White Settlement Road, Fort Worth,* (817) 332-0357 *Mon. thru Sat.* 11 A.M.-10 P.M., *Closed Sun.*

Kruez Market — No sauce, no trays, no plates, no forks . . . just the finest beef and sausage links to have ever passed between mortal lips. A classic barbecue featuring no-nonsense "friendship dining." Knives chained to wooden tables and a meat market reminiscent of the old-time barbecue tradition. 208 *South Commerce, Lockhart,* (512) 398-2361 *Mon. thru Fri.* 7 A.M.-6 P.M., *Sat.* 5 A.M.-7 P.M., *Closed Sun.*

Louie Mueller's — Operator Fred Fountaine keeps his briskets wrapped in paper after they're cooked. As a result, the meat stays so tender and moist you can cut it with a sharp look. His homemade spicy sauce is unlike any other found in Texas — sprinkled onto a steaming slice of brisket it creates a culinary match made in heaven. 206 *West Second, Taylor,* (512) 352-6206 *Mon. thru Sat. (ex. Thur.)* 7 A.M.-7 P.M., *Thur.* 7 A.M.-2 P.M., *Sun.* 7 A.M.-1 P.M.

Stubb's — This place does it all. Nightly music mingles with the aroma of sauce and smoke. When in Lubbock, make searching out this place a priority. It's always full at noon, so plan on lunch a little bit after the rush hour. Oh yes, you won't regret bringing home a quart of Stubb's famous barbecue sauce either! 108 *East Broadway, Lubbock,* (806) 762-9305 *Mon. thru Thur.* 11 A.M.-10 P.M., *Fri. and Sat.* 11 A.M.-2 A.M., *Sun.* 12 Noon-2 A.M.

Otto's — A businessman's favorite in Houston at lunchtime. Fast and efficient, Otto's can be consistently counted on for good barbecue ribs and beef, some of the best in town. 5502 *Memorial, Houston,* (713) 864-2573 *Mon. thru Sat.* 11 A.M.-9 P.M., *Closed Sun.*

Luling City Market — Not as large as Kreuz Market in Lockhart, it still serves up barbecue of equal excellence. Situated across from the railroad tracks paralleling Interstate 10, the Luling City Market is a mandatory stop when driving between Houston and San Antonio. 633 *Davis Street, Luling,* (512) 875-9019 *Mon. thru Sat.* 7 A.M.-8 P.M., *Closed Sun.*

The Hickory Hut — Everything from its tacky shingle exterior to the shinyl-vinyl interior is deceiving. But one taste of owner Eddie Jacobson's barbecued short ribs changes all that. Ask to look at his pit . . . it's a work of monumental art. 1501 *North Dallas, Lamesa,* (806) 872-2744 *Mon. thru Sat.,* 11 A.M.-9 P.M., *Closed Sun.*

Bill Barham's — Barreling down Highway 79, in the blink of an eye it's all too easy to miss the little town of Hutto. If you do, you will miss a ten-foot-long section of oil field pipe welded onto a Model 'A' frame, veiled in blue smoke. You will also miss some of the best barbecue found in Texas. This unpretentious roadside show is a barbecue addict's lifelong dream. Hutto, Texas — take your chances. *Highway 79 and East St. (on your left), Hutto,* (512) 846-9480 *Mon. thru Sat.* 11 A.M.-8 P.M., *Closed Sun.*

Sam's Barbecue (opposite) in Austin, Texas typifies pits found "off the beaten path." To find these gems, tucked away in most Texas towns, query five Texans at random. If two mention the same place, ask a sixth. If the sixth starts to say, "Wall sure that place is all rat, but thar's a newer place down the road . . ." get directions to the "all rat" place — three out of six Texans can't be wrong.

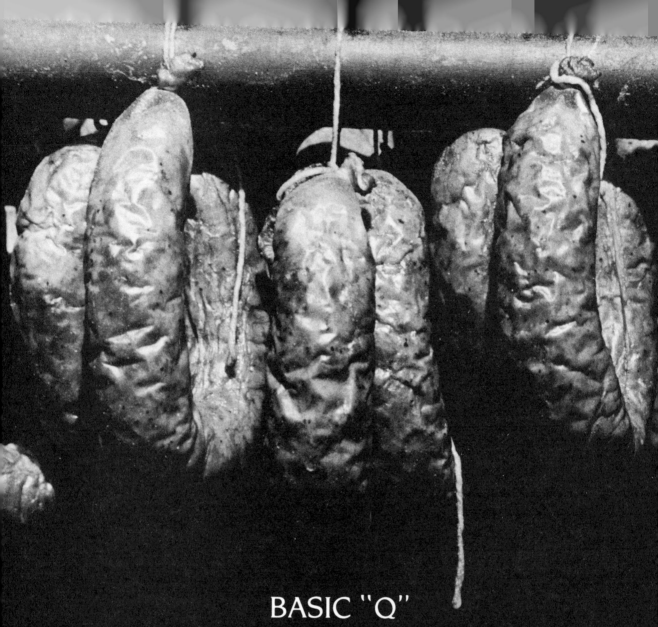

BASIC "Q"

"Barbecue" is actually a word used interchangeably to describe two different cooking styles. When most people want to barbecue, they fire up a grill, let the charcoal briquets glow white and slap on a piece of meat. The process is quick and efficient but does little to enhance the flavor or tenderize the meat. Although Texans utilize this method (substituting mesquite wood for briquets) for grilling steaks, they barbecue brisket, ribs and sausage links through an entirely different process. In Texas this style is called "pit" barbecue.

Pit barbecue is an art form. It requires patience, understanding and time to master but the rewards are well worth the trouble. The pit is an enclosed structure that cooks meats without the benefit of fiery coals directly underneath. It operates on the principle that the heat of the smoke cooks, not the fiery lick of flame. To achieve this, a fire is built at one end of the pit with a flue or smokestack at the other. The meat is set on a grill situated in between these two elements. By controlling the intensity of the fire and regulating the flue, the pitman cooks with indirect heat and smoke, trapped within the structure, in the manner of a modern convection oven. You will find that this method "chides and cajoles" even the most ornery piece of meat into

realms grilled sirloin will never venture. In the words of one dedicated pitman, "I refuses to let the 'lick of flame' desecrate the integrity of my meat . . . anyone who don't pit barbecue ain't barbecuing."

The most common mistake made by over-eager beginners is trying to cook too hot and too fast. The name of the game is cook "low" and cook slow; try and maintain a temperature of around 175 degrees for long periods of time — even a small brisket can take 10 hours. Remember, if your pit gets hotter than 212 degrees you literally boil the juices out of the food. This is a crime, so don't let it happen. You want to stabilize the temperature because radical heat changes will cook the food unevenly and dry it out. You want a slow fire that produces a steady volume of smoke, not a roaring inferno. A fire fueled to excess will only overimpregnate the meat with smoke, making it taste bitter and acrid, so stand by your pit and pay attention! Only through trial and error are the nuances and techniques of pit barbecue learned.

(Background photo) Sausages, also known as rings in Texas, are hand-tied and hung from racks for two hours of smoking at Kreuz Market. Owner "Smittie" imports the sausage casings from Switzerland, currently the only commercial source of cow intestines.

Wood was scarce for travelers on the Lone Prairie. This 1868 scene illustrates cooking over a "Prairie Coal" (cow chip) fire, the only fuel available in some regions of Texas. *Engraving courtesy of The Institute of Texas Cultures*. Cut post oak is stacked five feet high (background photo right) and sprawls over half an acre behind Kreuz Market in Lockhart, Texas. Pictured is a two-month wood supply to fuel pitman "Smittie's" pits. Inset photos show cross-sections of the most popular woods for barbecue (from top-to-bottom); mesquite, post oak, hickory.

WOOD

Choosing the right type of wood for smoking your barbecue is like trying to determine the difference between a Chateau Lafite Rothschild 1961 and Haute Brion '67 . . . it all boils down to a matter of taste. In Texas the preferred choice is mesquite, which the Cap Rock boys swear by and the authors are partial to because of the "balance" it strikes. The Cross Timbers and Hill Country folks feel scrub oak is just as good, but East Texans think it's a waste of time to cook with anything but seasoned hickory. Down in Southwest Texas, pecan wood will do because there is an abundance of it. The bottom line is to utilize a hardwood readily available in your area. Don't burn softwoods like pines or firs, because their high concentrations of sap will ruinously overpower the taste of the meat.

As for the best of the best, some feel that meat cooked over a post oak fire can't be beat. Post oak, which is cut during the winter months with the "sap's down" (in the roots), dries better and won't rot when cured. It produces the special flavor of mesquite and softer oaks, yet burns slower, radiating a steady heat.

However, many claim you can't taste the difference and barbecue is good even cooked over a pile of cow chips — which some do in a very serious way!

If you're not too much of a purist you can actually skirt the wood issue entirely. Sprinkle a handful of water-soaked — commercially available — hickory chips directly onto glowing charcoals just before the meat is set on the grill. This will give you the taste of Texas to an extent, without all the time-consuming commitment.

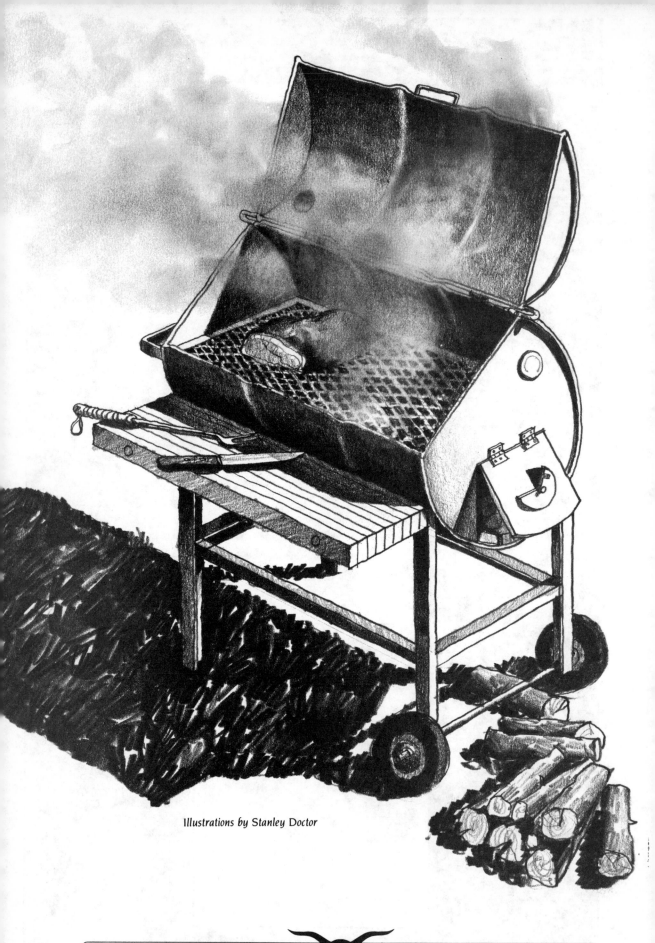

Illustrations by Stanley Doctor

BASIC PIT THEORY

You can make a barbecue pit out of just about any enclosed steel (or brick) structure — that includes oil field pipes, butane gas tanks and steel drums — as long as these principles are applied: the intake of fresh air at one end of the pit (which keeps the fire going) should be in harmony with the smoke exhaust exiting from the flue at the other end. Both openings should have valves to adjust the amount of intake airflow and exhaust. The trick to barbecuing meat with the heat of smoke is to regulate the intake vent to prevent the fire from either flaring up or extinguishing itself. In conjunction with the valve on the flue, you should be able to adjust both openings to trap the smoke from the fire to surround the meat, slow-cooking it in its own juices with the flavor of the smoke. A layer of sand and fire bricks, pictured in the illustration, prevents the fire from burning through the bottom of the pit and helps maintain the temperature of the pit at more constant levels. Unless you are grilling steaks, always place the meat away from the fire. Remember, you are barbecuing Texas style, not grilling American.

Illustrated at the lower right is the Weber grill which may be used in the same manner as a Texas barbecue pit. Instead of lining the entire grill with briquets, pile them over to one side. Set the meat away from the direct heat of the fire and place a small pan directly underneath to catch drippings for basting. Regulate the air/smoke flow by adjusting the two opposing vents for a proper cooking temperature. By closing the vents way down, it is possible to keep a dozen briquets smoldering all day long. In both cases (the 55-gallon drum and the Weber smoker) never scour out the carbon build-up on the inside walls. This is the mark of a well-seasoned pit that enhances the imparted flavor of the barbecue.

The most popular barbecue pit in Texas is the 55-gallon drum (opposite page). Anyone with access to a gas torch and an arc welder can build one of these for about $50, depending on how detailed the design is. If you decide to build one of these, check on the origin of the drum — make sure it was not used to store toxic wastes. Crude oil drums may be used; just wash them out thoroughly with an industrial detergent. All drums should be "burned out." Keep a fire burning in the drum for three to four days before attempting to cook food in a new pit. The two worst enemies of the drum are rain and fire. Keep the pit drum out of the weather to prevent rusting. A Number 9 steel mesh (available in steel yards) makes an excellent grill and lasts forever. For an exhaust flue, improvise. Go to a junkyard and scrounge up the tail pipe to a '57 Chevy or the smokestack from the D-9 Cat (just be sure to install a regulator valve in the flue to regulate the air flow). Cutting boards attached to the pit are handy but not necessary. One final note: we cannot stress enough the importance of using mesquite or oak as the fuel for your fire. These woods impart that special flavor that makes the Taste-of-Texas so unique.

BARBECUE

When it comes to barbecue in Texas, three types of meat predominate: brisket (the epitome of barbecue), ribs (pork or beef) and sausage. We offer these three classics plus a host of mouthwatering specialties.

TEXAS BARBECUED BEEF BRISKET

7 to 10 pounds beef brisket
dry rub (this is a mixture of equal parts salt, pepper and paprika)
1 barbecue pit fueled by burning mesquite or oak wood

Just about any brisket tastes better with a dry rub on it. Before cooking, rub a mixture of equal parts salt, pepper and paprika vigorously onto the meat. This helps to seal in the juices and enhances the over-all flavor. When handling the brisket in the pit, do not pierce it with a fork as this will allow precious juices to drain, ultimately drying out the meat. Use tongs or a set of quick fingers to turn while cooking. Some pitmen cook the brisket fatty-side down; others fatty-side up, so the juices permeate down through the meat. Experience will dictate a preference and turning the meat frequently is the best of both worlds. Always remember that the key ingredient in cooking a brisket is time. Lots of it. Cook with the heat of the smoke, never the flame, at about 150 to 175° for at least eight hours (twenty if you have the time, especially for a 7 to 10 pound brisket). The point of pit cookery is to tenderize tough meat, so the longer it cooks, the more the marbling breaks down.

If a tomato and sugar based sauce is used, daub it on during the last half hour of cooking time. Applied sooner, this type of sauce will caramelize, imparting a burnt taste to the meat. Non-sugar based sauces may be used during the entire cooking process. Drippings from the brisket may be collected in a shallow pan place directly under the meat. These can be used for basting continuously, with no danger of charring the meat. Some water added to the pan can help keep the moisture loss to a minimum.

We found that brisket is best eaten on the day of cooking. It has a tendency to lose its integrity if refrigerated overnight. Plan accordingly so it is served hot, directly from the pit, to awaiting hungry guests. Slice with the grain and serve with warmed barbecue sauce applied to taste. Leftover brisket may be wrapped up in butcher paper, set back into the pit (with low heat) and kept safely overnight. For those of you lacking the amenities of a backyard barbecue pit, brisket *may* be cooked in the oven (but it will never taste the same). Wrap the brisket in foil and bake at 250° for about six hours. Preferably (as a second choice to the pit, of course), place the brisket in a baking dish and pour a thin barbecue sauce that contains a teaspoon of liquid hickory smoke over the meat in hopes (vain) that it will impart that pit-cooked flavor. Bake, as before, in oven, basting often.

Donny Jacobson

BARBECUED PORK RIBS

3 sides spareribs
1 cup chili sauce
3 cloves garlic, pressed
1 cup tarragon vinegar
1 tablespoon Worcestershire sauce
1 tablespoon freshly ground pepper
1 cup tomato paste
1 cup brown sugar
1 bay leaf
1 teaspoon dry mustard
2 tablespoons lemon juice
1 tablespoon salt
1 cup red port wine
1/2 cup oil

Combine all sauce ingredients and bring to a boil. Simmer 15 minutes. Have butcher cut ribs into serving size pieces. Place ribs over charcoal; cook slowly (1-1/2 hours). Turn and baste ribs several times during cooking. Ribs may be cooked in a pit instead by slow smoking 3-4 hours, baste with sauce during final hour.

Lil Kothmann

SMITTY'S SAUSAGE

9 pounds assorted beef cuts
1 pound assorted pork cuts
1/3 pound cereal binder
sausage casings

"The secret to good sausage making is good meat. It's not what you put in it, but what you leave out." Smitty must leave out the right stuff because the sausages he sells at Kruez Market in Lockhart are some of the finest in the world. Here is his recipe as told to us: "The meat has to be good. Use a meat mixture of 90% beef and 10% pork. There should not be more than a 20% fat content overall. Sprinkle a liberal amount of salt and black and red pepper over the cut-up meat. For a 100 pound batch of sausages, add three pounds (3% of total weight) of commercial cereal binder (binder is made from flour, corn, wheat, rice, rye, etc. It is available from most butcher supply stores). Run the mixture through coarse ground hamburger plates twice. Stuff it into sausage casings and barbecue for about 45 minutes. Good luck."

"Smitty"

MUST EAT MORE BARBECUE CHICKEN

Joan Stocks Nobles was raised on an old Texas sheep ranch. Her family was well-known for their cooking. At the age of fourteen, she had to cook everything from scratch for the sixteen men who worked the ranch. Today she still loves to cook and you can taste Joan's expertise at her restaurant called "Gideon's" in San Angelo, Texas. She says, "I cook by taste, feel, smell and looks . . . I'm Texan enough to eat fried chicken and pork chops with my fingers." Her peach cobbler is one of the best in the West.

1 whole fryer, cut in half
1 cup vinegar
1/2 cup butter or margarine
juice of 3 lemons
6 tablespoons Worcestershire sauce
10 drops Tabasco sauce
2 teaspoons salt
1/2 teaspoon black pepper
1/2 cup apple jelly

Place chicken halves on coals which have been started one hour ahead of cooking chicken. Let one side begin to brown before brushing chicken with a sauce made from the remaining ingredients. Turn chicken frequently and baste, being careful not to let chicken burn. Takes approximately one hour to cook.

Joan Stocks Nobles

TEXAS-STYLE BARBECUED CHICKEN

two 3-1/2 pound chickens, split
juice of 1 large lemon
4 garlic cloves, minced
1/4 cup coarse salt
2 tablespoons sweet Hungarian paprika
2 teaspoons ground red pepper

Rub chicken with lemon juice and garlic. Combine salt, paprika and pepper and sprinkle over skin. Place skin side up on wire rack set over baking sheets and refrigerate uncovered at least 8 hours or, preferably, overnight. Preheat oven to 300°. Bake chicken 1 hour. Meanwhile, prepare charcoal. Transfer chicken to barbecue and grill, turning occasionally, until meat is done and skin is crisp, about 15 minutes per side. May be pit smoked instead for 3 hours.

Mary Nell Reck

CHICKEN BARBECUED IN A PAPER SACK

3 tablespoons tomato catsup
2 tablespoons vinegar
1 tablespoon lemon juice
2 tablespoons Worcestershire sauce
4 tablespoons water
2 tablespoons butter
3 tablespoons brown sugar
1 teaspoon salt
1 teaspoon dry mustard
1 teaspoon chili powder
1 teaspoon paprika
1/2 teaspoon pepper
3-pound chicken, cut up for frying

Make a sauce of all seasonings. Cook for a few minutes. Dip chicken in hot sauce. Put it in a paper sack that has been greased on the inside. Fold ends of sack down carefully. Do not open sack during cooking period. Slow smoke in large pit for 3 hours. Remember: cook with indirect heat method or else you've just created the first chicken cigarette. May be cooked in conventional oven by placing sack in a covered roaster. Bake for 15 minutes in preheated 500° oven; reduce heat to 300° and bake for 1 hour and 30 minutes.

Mrs. T. H. Graalmann

TEXAS PORK BARBECUE

1/4 cup vinegar
1/2 cup water
2 tablespoons sugar
1 tablespoon prepared mustard
1/4 teaspoon pepper
dash cayenne pepper
2 thick lemon slices
1 medium onion, chopped
1/4 cup butter or margarine
1/2 cup catsup
1-1/2 tablespoons Worcestershire sauce
3 cups cooked pork, finely diced
1 dozen barbecue rolls

Mix first 9 ingredients in quart saucepan. Simmer 20 minutes uncovered. Remove lemon slices. Add catsup and Worcestershire sauce; bring to a boil. Add diced pork. Simmer until thick enough to spoon on buns.

Mrs. O. G. (Andy) Rowland

CEDAR HILL RANCH FRESH PORK BARBECUE

4 to 5 pounds fresh pork roast
salt and pepper
2 medium onions, diced
2 tablespoons vinegar
2 tablespoons Worcestershire sauce
2 teaspoons salt
1 teaspoon paprika
1/2 teaspoon red pepper
1/4 teaspoon black pepper
1 teaspoon chili powder
3/4 cup catsup
3/4 cup water
1/2 stick margarine
2 tablespoons brown sugar

Season roast with salt and pepper. Cook on slow charcoal fire for about 5 hours. Meanwhile make barbecue sauce by mixing remaining ingredients in saucepan and let simmer 20 minutes. When meat is almost done, make slits in roast about 2 inches apart. Brush with sauce 2 or 3 times. Cook to desired doneness.

Mrs. Jerome (Margery) Felps

JOE BOB'S BARBECUED LAMB

1/2 cup of honey
1/2 cup red wine vinegar
2 tablespoons Worcestershire sauce
1 tablespoon dry mustard
1 tablespoon sweet basil
juice from 1 large lemon

Combine ingredients in sauce pan over low heat. Dip small thick cut pieces of lamb loin or thick cut lamb chops into hot sauce and slow smoke (after searing over hot coals) in pit for 1 hour.

a gift from the "Dawg"

BARBECUED FISH FILLETS

bass or trout fillets, rinsed in cold water and patted dry
lemon, thinly sliced
Glen's Fish Sauce (see sauces)

Brush fillets with sauce on both sides and allow to marinate for 20 to 30 minutes. In foil-lined shallow pan, arrange lemon slices and lay fish on top of them, about 3 slices to a fillet. (This keeps fish from sticking, in addition to adding zip.) Cook in pit on rack away from heat about 45 minutes, or until fish is flaky.

Mrs. Glen D. (Emma Lee) Hughes

TINY'S BARBECUED SHRIMP

Tiny is a veritable Master at the art of barbecuing. His chicken, pork, lamb and brisket have swept first place honors at cookoffs across Texas. He always cooks with mesquite wood and says his "secret ingredient is laughter." Well, he must put a lot of it in because one taste of his barbecue shrimp will make you howl for joy.

10 pounds large shrimp (about 30 of them)
1 teaspoon salt
1/8 teaspoon garlic powder
1 teaspoon paprika
1 teaspoon black pepper
1/4 cup fresh squeezed lemon juice
1 tablespoon Worcestershire sauce
5 dashes Tabasco
1/2 pound melted butter
1 tablespoon red wine vinegar
juice from two oranges

Peel and devein shrimp. Lay them out on a large sheet of aluminum foil with the edges slightly curled up. Mix salt, garlic powder, paprika and pepper in a bowl and sprinkle onto both sides of the shrimp. Set shrimp into refrigerator for two to three hours to absorb seasonings. Melt butter and add remaining ingredients for the basting sauce. Take the shrimp, still on the foil, and place in your smoker away from flame. Cook for ten to fifteen minutes, depending on the fire, in low heat, basting at least three times. Keep the pit closed. Serve with dry white wine or a light beer. This same recipe may be used for frog legs, just double the amount of lemon juice and baste more frequently because they will dry out too fast.

John "Tiny" Crenshaw

BROILED BARBECUED SHRIMP

If you don't have a barbecue pit, satisfactory results may be obtained by broiling the shrimp in the oven or setting them on a piece of foil over smokey charcoals (add soaked hickory chips to the coals). Baste frequently to prevent moisture loss.

Betsy Bee

BARBECUED SOFT SHELLED TURTLE

Ted Karkoska is a cook with Rose's Cantina Chili Team, and co-founder of the "Taylor Rio Grande Yeller Catters." The Yeller Catters are a group of Texans who love to fish and whose motto is: "We're livin' the way everybody else would like to." By the amount of fun they display at cookoffs, they sure do everything within their power to live up to that motto.

1 large freshwater soft shell turtle (the forequarters and hindquarters together should weigh about six pounds)
1 teaspoon garlic powder
4 heaping tablespoons salt
1 tablespoon black pepper
1 cup of lemon/lime juice
2 cans warm beer

The first thing you've gotta do is "ketch yourself a turtle" and dress him out. (If you don't know how to do this, find someone who does.) Use the water from your beer chest to wash off the meat. Put meat in an oval-bottomed dish and rub it down with lemon/lime juice. This acts as a tenderizer, breaking down the muscle tissue. Then rub in well a mixture of garlic powder and salt and pepper. Let it sit in a refrigerator for two hours, then pour a can of warm beer over it (save the marinade). Barbecue at a slow, low heat, around 225° for 5 hours. If a little bit of blood starts oozing, pour beer on the fire to slow the cooking down. When it's halfway done (when you can stick a fork into the meat easily and then meet resistance) put the meat on a sheet of aluminum foil. Add wet oak bark to the mesquite wood fire so the pit gets very smokey. Baste with the extra marinade and juices on the foil. Pay attention and don't let it dry out or cook too fast. Serve with pinto beans, homemade bread, lettuce and tomatoes.

Ted Karkoska

SAUCES

In Texas some of the barbecue is so good it serves as entree, main course and dessert all in one bite. Of primary importance to a barbecue hound is the sauce. A good sauce complements the meat's flavor rather than smothering it with an overbearing presence. Basically sauces fall into two categories: those that are sugar and tomato based and those that are not. Sugar-based sauces should not be applied to meats and fowl until the last twenty or thirty minutes of cooking. Prolonged exposure to heat caramelizes the sugar in the sauce, imparting a burnt taste to the food. In many barbecue joints this sauce is applied only after the meat is cooked, or served on the side so the customer may apply it at his own discretion.

The thinner non-sugar based sauces are good for marinades and basting since they don't burn. They can be spicy-hot like Tabasco, vinegary or so subtle you hardly know they're there.

MARCEIA'S OL' FASHION BARBECUE SAUCE

Ed Cernoch and his original ORIGINAL COOKERS barbecue team won the title of "Grand Reserve World Champion Barbecuer" at the Houston Astrodome in 1981. Here is the prize-winning sauce recipe courtesy of Marceia, Ed's wife.

1 stick butter
3 cloves minced garlic
1 chopped onion
1 diced lemon
1/2 cup Worcestershire sauce
1/2 cup brown sugar
4 cups catsup
1 large can tomato juice
1/4 cup chili powder
1/4 cup vinegar
1 large can V-8 juice
salt and pepper to taste

Saute garlic, onion and lemon in butter until tender, then add remaining ingredients. Simmer about 2 hours or until sauce thickens.

Mrs. Ed Cernoch

TEXAS BARBECUE SAUCE #1

1 cup vinegar
1 cup cooking oil
1/2 cup water or beer
3 tablespoons lemon juice
1 tablespoon Tabasco sauce
1/2 cup honey
1 tablespoon Worcestershire sauce
1 teaspoon pepper (or to taste)
1 teaspoon onion salt
1 teaspoon garlic salt
1 cup catsup (optional)

Bring ingredients to a boil and baste over any meat or chicken. Catsup may be added to mixture if tomato flavor is desired.

Rick Hodnett

BLACK JACK BARBECUE SAUCE

1 cup strong black coffee
1 cup Worcestershire sauce
1 cup catsup
1/2 cup cider vinegar
1/2 cup brown sugar
3 tablespoons chili powder
2 teaspoons salt
2 cups chopped onions
1/4 cup minced hot chili peppers
6 cloves garlic, minced

Combine all ingredients in a saucepan and simmer 25 minutes. Strain or puree in a blender or food processor. Refrigerate between uses. Makes 5 cups.

Philip Morris Inc.

EUEL'S BARBECUE SAUCE

1/2 gallon catsup
1 small bottle Worcestershire sauce
1/2 cup sugar
2/3 cup vinegar
2 to 3 cloves crushed garlic
Tabasco and/or mustard to taste

Mix and simmer. Add a dash of Tabasco and/or mustard for hotness till it tastes right. "Don't put it on the meat while cooking 'cause you will cause the sugar to caramelize and char. This used to be a secret but since I'm retired it makes no-never-mind. I makes more money now after I retired. If I knew I could make this much money as a retiree, I would have quit working when I was 20." (By "retired" Euel means he now runs a private catering company and cooks only for those who wisely seek out his skills.)

Euel Stribling

TEXAS BARBECUE SAUCE #2

1 pod garlic
5 medium onions, chopped
1 cup Wesson oil
2 bottles catsup
1/3 cup Louisiana Hot Sauce
2/3 cup Worcestershire sauce
2 cups vinegar
a fifth of sherry, if desired

Brown onions and garlic in small amount of oil. Add catsup, hot sauce, Worcestershire sauce, vinegar, and the rest of the oil. Blend well over slow fire. Remove from heat and add sherry. Mix well. May be refrigerated and used over and over.

Mrs. Byron Sherman

EDDIE'S BARBECUE SAUCE

1 gallon Worcestershire sauce
2 gallons catsup
10 pounds sugar
1 gallon 100 grain vinegar
1 cup of liquid smoke
1 cup paprika
1-1/2 cup salt
1 cup black pepper
1 cup red pepper (chili pepper)
3 chopped onions

Add enough water to the above ingredients to make 10 gallons of liquid. Simmer 2 hours.

Eddie's Hickory Hut

TEXAS BARBECUE SAUCE #3

1/4 teaspoon margarine
1 cup vinegar
4 teaspoons garlic salt
3 chopped garlic cloves
1 heaping tablespoon horseradish
4 tablespoons Worcestershire sauce
1 medium bottle catsup
1 bottle A-1 sauce
1 teaspoon salt
1-1/2 teaspoon Tabasco sauce
1/2 cup water
1 teaspoon dry mustard
1 teaspoon liquid smoke
1/2 cup packed brown sugar

Combine ingredients. Heat mixture until margarine melts.

Mrs. Dale Cox

GLEN'S FISH SAUCE

3 tablespoons catsup
1 tablespoon A-1 sauce
3 tablespoons chili sauce
3 dashes Tabasco
1 tablespoon Worcestershire sauce
1 teaspoon lemon juice

Mix well and use for barbecuing fish.

Mrs. Glen D. (Emma Lee) Hughes

SPRINKLE BARBECUE SAUCE

2 heaping tablespoons black pepper
6 heaping tablespoons salt
1-1/2 heaping tablespoons garlic powder
1 heaping tablespoon red pepper/cayenne
3 heaping tablespoons chili powder
4 heaping tablespoons paprika

Mix all the ingredients together in a bowl. Before barbecuing chicken, ribs, briskets, fish or pork chops, sprinkle on very heavy. This mixture serves as a "dry" barbecue sauce but makes a crust, sealing in juices.

Bill Maxwell

PLUM SAUCE FOR BARBECUE RIBS

1 (17-ounce) can purple plums
1 (6-ounce) can frozen lemonade concentrate, thawed
1/4 cup chili sauce
1/4 cup soy sauce
2 teaspoons prepared mustard
1 teaspoon ground ginger
1 teaspoon Worcestershire sauce
1/2 cup chopped onion

Drain plums, reserving syrup; remove pits and discard. Put plums and syrup in blender and blend until smooth. Add remaining ingredients and simmer uncovered about 15 minutes. Brush sauce on ribs when they are nearly done. Serve remaining sauce with ribs.

Barbecue Times

TEXAS BARBECUE SAUCE #4

2 medium onions
2 tablespoons salad oil
1 (12-ounce) bottle catsup
1/2 bottle Worcestershire sauce
1/2 lemon
1 small pod of garlic
1/2 (36-ounce) can tomato juice
1/4 can Ro-Tel green chiles
1/8 box brown sugar
dash of salt

Brown onions in oil; add remaining ingredients. Cook about 30 minutes.

Lillian Swanson

BARBECUE SAUCE FOR FOUR GOATS

1 gallon water, boiled
1 quart vinegar
1 pound sugar
1 small bottle Karo syrup
1 box red pepper
2 bottles hot sauce
2 bottles catsup
1 quart tomato juice
1 bottle chili powder
1/2 pint salt
Combine ingredients. Shortening, mustard, butter and Worcestershire sauce may be added to taste.

Mrs. Faye Bell Haska

CHILI

Texans are notorious for taking the ridiculous to the extreme. These "zealots" know no limits, especially when it comes to pursuing their favorite pastime . . . chili. They have successfully lobbied their legislature to enshrine chili as the Official State Dish. Some have gone as far as requesting "that the United States Congress should pass a law making it mandatory for all restaurants the world over to follow the Texas recipe for chili if they are to serve a bowl of Red." Ardent chiliheads tout chili's medicinal value, claiming "it's good for what ails you." They proudly cite documented examples where chili has cured everything from malaria to gastrointestinal disorders, as well as having saved more lives during the Depression than the Red Cross. Dedicated Crusaders for Texas Chili swear they will "never stop cooking chili until every man, woman and child on the face of the Earth, in the Galaxia of the Universe, has had the opportunity to sample a taste from the Bowl of Blessedness." In their own words, "There are not Seven Wonders of the World — only one — chili."

The public forum that has evolved to accommodate the ever-burgeoning chili mania is what is known as a cookoff. The cookoff is the culinary arena where thousands gather under the auspices of the Chili Appreciation Society International and the International Chili Society, to promote, partake and perpetuate all aspects of the Wonderful World of Chili. The focus of these competitions is twofold: to whip up the best damn bowl of chili ever made and have as much fun as humans are allowed to have doing it. As a result, chili meets are well-attended weekly traditions and have become an integral part of contemporary Texas culture.

Although Texans may boast more cookoffs in their state than any other place in the world, they cannot claim to have originated the idea. Cookoffs have been held since the days of the Greeks. Sardanapalus, the last Assyrian King of Greece, was obsessed with food, gluttony and sensual pleasures. He established the custom of cooking contests to satisfy his appetite. Cooks with winning sauces were rewarded with prizes and gold pieces for their gourmet treats. The king's insatiable love for food and his scorn for life's drudgery eventually prompted him to erect a monument with this enduring inscription: "Sardanapalus the King . . . In one day he built Anchiale and Tarsus. Eat, drink and love, the rest's not worth this!"

In a similar vein, the Aztec King Montezuma was also a true gourmand who demanded an array of unique dishes at each meal. His royal palate refused to sample the same flavor twice; consequently, cooks were continually recruited to devise a never-repeated presentation of foods for their king. Proficient chefs were rewarded with their lives and a position in the king's retinue — until the day arrived when they could not come up with a clever new dish and they were quickly "disposed of."

Cookoffs were revived in the twentieth century when the Pillsbury Company launched the National Bakeoffs in the Fifties. These contests were well-attended by women, but in 1959 a barbecue contest was announced with a ten thousand dollar first prize. That prompted many men to suddenly display a keen interest in cooking. Fueled by the Hawaiian luau craze and the growing popularity of outdoor cooking, more and more men "began" to cook in the Sixties. Concocting chili was a perfect vehicle to promote the Art of Masculine Cookery, for as one bemused bystander pointed out, "Any man smart enough to steal a horse can whip up a passable batch of chili."

In 1967, the first chili cookoff took place. "Chili Wars" gained national recognition when humorist and New York resident H. Allen Smith issued this brazen declaration: "Nobody knows more about chili than I do. No living man can put together a pot of chili as ambrosial, delicately, zestfully flavored as the chili I make. This is a fact so stern, so granitic that it belongs in the encyclopedia as well as in all the standard histories of civilization." The impact of this statement was incendiary to Frank X. Tolbert, a loyal Texan and Dallas newspaperman, who found Smith's "idle" boasting hard to swallow. He immediately arranged a cookoff between Mr. Smith and Wick Fowler. Fowler, another newspaperman, was the obvious choice.; his favorite hobby, chili cooking, naturally made him Texas' "leading authority" on the subject. The culinary proving ground for determining who made the best chili was Terlingua, Texas, a dusty ghost town along the Tex-Mex border. The showdown ended in a tie with promoter Tolbert muttering that non-Texan Smith's chili was a "chili-flavored, low torque, beef and vegetable soup!" and that he had "the blasphemous gall to add canned pinto beans!" (In some circles, especially in Texas, the addition of beans to chili is sacrilegious. A chorus of the National Chili Anthem puts it this way: "If you know b e a n s a b o u t chili,

you know that chili has no beans.") Despite cries of foul play because one of the judges did not vote, having succumbed to an incapacitating mixture of sun and beer, the two contestants parted amicably. Frank Tolbert inadvertently founded a tradition that has blossomed into a Cowboy Woodstock a.k.a. The Wick Fowler Memorial World Championship Chili Cookoff, the top chili cookoff in Texas. Fowler also went on to successfully market his secret recipe called Wick Fowler's 1, 2 and 3 Alarm Chili Mix.

As a result of the first chili cookoff, renewed interest was sparked among chilicrats to investigate the true origins and evolution of chili. What came to light was a hodgepodge of information that only further fueled the controversial fires surrounding chili history.

"Nobody knows more about chili than I do . . . I wrote the book on chili," says Frank Xavier Tolbert, author of the definitive chili thesis: A Bowl of Red. After organizing the legendary chili confrontation between H. Allen Smith and Wick Fowler at Terlingua, Frank went on to own two world-famous chili parlors in Dallas. Frank Tolbert's Texas Chili Parlor and Museum of Chili Culture, located on Main Street, is a repository for archival chili documentia and mania no chilihead should miss. Most recently Frank is pictured as the "Chili Expert" on nationwide television commercials for Dennison's canned chili (yes, we've noticed it does have beans in it). Frank is pictured here in front of the restaurant that chili built.

There are as many "we made chili first" allegations as there are chili recipes. Mexicans argue that chili originated in Mexico (of course!) pointing out that the chilipiquin pepper was widely cultivated by the ancient Aztecs and Mayans. Chili is the Aztec word for the chile plant. American Indians vigorously claim that, "Our fathers harvested wild chile peppers before the first Mayan calendar was ever chiseled." Texans pooh-pooh both theories, asserting that chili originated in the jails of San Antonio in the mid 1800's. Supposedly it was made from the rankest cuts of meat and enough chili pepper to kill any bad taste. Even so, Jailhouse or Chain Gang Chili was reported to be so good that ex-cons, unable to find a comparable bowl of Red on the outside, broke parole to be recommitted.

Credit must also be given to the Mexican lavanderas (washerwomen), the original Chili Queens of San Antonio, according to Western historian and chili cook, Mel Marshall. In 1835, when the Republic of Texas was mobilizing a military force in San Antonio, officers employed the lavanderas to cook for the embryonic army. Facilities for mass feeding were nonexistent so the women were called upon to stew vats of beef and dry chili peppers in the next best thing available — their huge washtubs.

What is certain is that chili originated in the Southwest because of the abundant supply of meat and chilipiquins, little fiery chilies that grow wild. Indians pounded together jerked meat and chilies into what became known as the "pemmican of the Southwest." The strips kept well and made excellent trail food. Eventually, on the wagon trains heading West and along the cow trails North, range cooks took the Indian concept one step further and pounded the meat and chilies into dried chili bricks. The chili bricks were soaked in water during the day. By nightfall they were soft enough to be cooked up with garlic and cumin and served as a savory dish "hot enough to cure a six-week hangover."

Cowhands in particular developed a real taste for the stuff. Working hard all day from "can't see to can't see," there was nothing more satisfying and nutritious than a steaming hot bowl of Red. Ex-chuck wagon cooks and cowboys, aware of the penchant for chili and foreseeing the end of the cattle drives, opened up chili joints in towns along the cow trails.

Western historian John Hendrix describes an old-time chili joint as "about 25 feet wide, half that in length with a small space in the rear partitioned off to screen the cook stove and hide the lack of sanitation." The whole thing probably cost $100 to grubstake, including the sign scrawled on the front that unpretentiously proclaimed "CHILI."

The chili joints became very popular. Trail-weary customers would stop in a chili joint to "stave off the hungries" before they slickered up to get a fancy meal in the higher-priced food emporiums down the street. Hungry men found that they could get a hearty meal that filled the drinks in their stomachs for a nickel. A generous

The Chili Queens of San Antonio established a tradition that Mexican fast-food chains have capitalized upon — they offered up quick meals of chili, burritos, tacos and tamales. Originally the glow of the lavanderas' lamps illuminated the Military Plaza until the wee hours of the morning. Open-air picnic tables functioned simultaneously as counters and kitchens until the 1930's when canvas tents and electric lightbulbs began to add a touch more sophistication to these pioneering Tex-Mex restaurants. By the 1940's, the Health Department and food shortages created by WW II forced their unceremonious closures. Each year the Chili Queens and their stands are resurrected at the San Antonio Folk Life Festival. Stands fill the Plaza, reminiscent of the old days, dispensing a staggering array of ethnic dishes. Each stand represents an aspect of Texas' multi-cultural communities. *Photos courtesy of the Institute of Texan Cultures.*

supply of soda crackers and water quelled the burning fires. After the second bowl they had lost all interest in a big Texas steak.

The first chili joints may have actually been a natural outgrowth of the tradition established by the lavanderas in San Antonio. In the mid 1800's San Antonio was a hub of military activity, playing host to armies from Mexico and America, as well as being an outpost of the Texas Rangers. The lavanderas washed soldier uniforms by day, but found that at night they made more money as chili vendors. They set up stalls in the military plaza, quite often selling chili from big tubs used earlier in the day for dirty laundry. These stands endured until 1946 when War rationing and health inspectors forced their closure for sanitary reasons. Today the San Antonio Chili Queens and their stands are gone forever. In their wake they spawned a legacy that has made chili a favorite dish the world over, and has secured it a permanent position in the culinary repertoire of the American palate forever.

To fully comprehend the scope and impact chili has had on Texas, one must experience, in its totality, a modern Texas chili cookoff. Only after two days of sensory immersion in a chili festival can the foreigner (anybody not from Texas) begin to appreciate the importance of chili mania to the state as a whole.

When the call goes out for chiliheads to unite and stir up a batch of their favorite brew, people driven by chili-pang-passion will flock to a cookoff like moths to a flame. All over Texas thousands gather in parks, on river banks and at baseball fields to cook, carouse and have a good old time.

Wizards of the Capsicum Art come from the world over to compete. They arrive toting smoke-blackened cauldrons, dented Coleman stoves and little brown bags of secretly blended ingredients. Their hats and hair festooned with bright red peppers, the chiliheads (true lovers of chili) and chiliholics (normally stable individuals who attain an inebriated high at the mere mention of chili) kibitz and argue over its merits. Praises like "nice afterbite," "too scary" and "definitely high torque" are traded over steaming vats of "God's gift to Texas." Gathered under an Army surplus sun tarp, members of the Houston Pod (pod is another name for team) swear an oath of allegiance: "I pledge allegiance to the Houston Pod of the Chili Appreciation Society International, camaraderie for which it stands; one comestible indigestible, with heartburn and gas pains for all; so help me Chiligula (the god of Chili)." Meanwhile, members of the Schplitz Chili Team — an all-girl gymnastic group from San Marcos — display their athletic prowess by back-flipping and cartwheeling in front of their aromatic chili pot.

Some Texans at a chili cookoff will make chili from any type of meat that isn't obviously poison. Riding high atop their whims of culinary inspiration, they will cook with wild boar, bear, rattlesnake, raccoon, armadillo and nutria (nutria is an animal that has a body like a beaver and a tail like a 'possum). This creative cookery once prompted Carroll Shelby, co-founder of the International Chili Society, to observe, "One man's chili is another man's axle grease. If a guy wants to toss in an armadillo, I don't argue with him — I just don't eat with him!"

Vying for showmanship awards and the title of Chili Maker Supreme, contenders represent a surprising cross section of humanity. Cookoff teams include competitors from as far away as Hawaii, Guadalajara and Anchorage. Doctors, lawyers and politicians join in the fun dressed in diapers, tuxedos and hula skirts, and carry fire extinguishers just in case some poor soul exceeds the jalapeno limit. One Texas-based Japanese chili team sports head-to-toe Samurai war dress and takes particular delight in stirring their brew with a four-foot Japanese sword, à la John Belushi.

Bad McFad Daredevil, otherwise known as John Raven, likes to call himself "a living legend in my own time . . . it's not easy being a memory." He is notorious for blowing himself up while straddling homemade "rocket ships" or sitting in his field office (a portable outhouse). Recently the Chilympiad Committee honored McFad with the coveted Don Russell Appreciation Award for chiliheads who have gone above and beyond the call of duty to promote chili to the world. Besides making "Jes' a damn good bowl of Chili," he has also helped found the *Goat Gap Gazette*, the definitive tabloid of the chili world. The *Goat Gap Gazette* is published by Hal John and Judith Wimberly who "Hope nothing serious is included in its columns." To subscribe, send $11 for "eleven ravishing, delectable copies" to' Goat Gap Gazette c/o Wimberly, 5110 Bayard Lane #2, Houston, Texas 77006 or call (at your expense) (713) 523-2362. Today McFad publishes the *Barbecue Times*. To subscribe or become a member of the Texas Barbecue Appreciation Society, send $15 (American) to The Texas Barbecue Appreciation Society, 1914 South Seventh, Temple, Texas 76501.

Chiliheads like to name their chili, here are a few favorites: Chicken Lips Chili, Peanut Butter - No Jelly Chili, Boiled Cigar Butts and Sheep Dip Chili, Scorpion Breath Chili, Brother Willy & Sister Lilly's Traveling Salvation Army Chili, Hillbilly Chili, It's Not Chili, D.J.'s Ulcer Scorcher & Manuary Gland Builder Chili, Dr. Tabasco & Nurse Heartburn's V.D. Chili, Happy Heine Chili, Last of the Red Hot Lovers Chili.

Mariachi, bluegrass and country western music can be heard filtering through the crowds, while self-proclaimed, gun-toting ministers dressed in top hats and tails perform weddings on request. The young at heart take part in everything from chicken flying to face-making contests. Moseying and Great Falling Down events are also popular, providing you have the time and patience. And then, for the diehards, there is the Hot Chili Pepper Eating Contest. Paragons of asbestos-tongued virtue sweat it out as peppers are munched in ascending order of hotness, starting with the milder anaheims, graduating up to the devilish santakas and bahamians that are grown in the pits of hell and can fry the taste buds with the ferocity of a nuclear meltdown. The losers are carted away on stretchers, while the winners (or should we say "survivors") gratefully accept their prizes — boxes of Maaloxes.

Dedicated chili purists opt for simplicity. They stand vigil by their pots, passionately adding a little bit of this and little bit of that, carefully stirring their "celestial delight" when the force moves them. A folding table supporting a pot of chili simmering on a portable stove is their whole show. The chili gets top billing. These virtuosos know that when the moment of truth arrives, it's not what's cavorting around the pot that counts but what's inside it, i.e. the masterful blending of ingredients through subtle chemical transmutations creating a bowl of blessedness fit to be eaten by the Great God of Chili, Chiligula himself! Top honors at a chili cookoff always go to he (or she, as any chili libber is quick to add) who can concoct the definitive bowl of Texas Red.

Although the festivities and chili attract the greatest attention, one other reason cookoffs have proliferated is that they are prime occasions to raise funds for charities. At most cookoffs proceeds from entry fees, gate admissions and concessions go directly to needy coffers. The town of San Marcos, a giant in the fund raising field, hosts the Greek equivalent of the Olympics of Chili, called the Chilympiad. In 1981, for example, seventy thousand chiliheads watched 316 chili teams cook up a storm — $179,000 was taken in with proceeds going to aid hospitals, schools and youth organizations in the city. Other chili cookoffs may not operate on such a grand scale, but in towns like Marble Falls or Terlingua, bowls of the first place chili have been auctioned off for up to thirty-five thousand dollars . . . all for charity, of course.

The phenomenon of the Texas Chili Cookoff is a delightful and needed celebration of the human spirit. In trying to decipher its ramifications, Frank Tolbert once put it this way: "Chili mania is an international subculture with thousands of chiliheads all striving to promote one simple culinary idea with its infinite variations." That may be an oversimplification of a very significant social happening, but regardless, no other group of people has elevated such a lowly dish to such lofty heights and has had such a good time doing it.

You are never too old or too young to participate in a chili cookoff. Dedicated chiliheads, those born with greasy wooden spoons in their mouths, enter competitions at an early age. Ten-year-old "Chief Joseph" (upper left) patiently attends his creation for approval in the Junior Division. When asked what his secret ingredient was, he deftly removed a bottle of Gatorade from sight and said, "Nuthin' special." Ray and Estel Shade (The Shady Bunch) from Lubbock, Texas, travel the chili circuit, but prefer to enter the Showmanship Division because Ray likes to play music so much he doesn't have time to cook chili. An elite panel of judges sample chili entries, during the finals at Chilympiad, from Styrofoam "tasting" cups (each cup is marked on the bottom with the contender's entry number). It is their job to select three winning chilis from upwards of 300 submitted. To help clear palates after each "taste" are plates heaped with chopped celery, carrots, crackers and endless mugs of cold beer.

CHILI PARLORS

Texas chili parlors have gone the way of the original Texas longhorns. At one time they could be found all across Texas; today only a handful remain. Most of these parlors showcase chili, but, for the sake of financial survival, supplement their menus with barbecue, hamburgers and the like.

This is not to imply that in Texas chili is only available in chili parlors. Quite the contrary. A bowl of Red is a permanent fixture in most cafes and restaurants. If it's homemade, try it out. But remember, half the fun in being a chili addict is the unexpected discovery of an authentic chili parlor, a vanishing breed worth the search.

The Texas Chili Parlor features chili in three stages of hotness, from mild to hot. Their menu claims "The best bowl of Red in the state of Texas and the Southwest . . ." Supposedly you must sign a "release" absolving the "Parlor" from any responsibilities when ordering XXX (obviously the hottest) chili. 1409 *Lavaca, Austin,* (512) 472-2828 *Mon. thru Sat.* 11 A.M. - 2 A.M., *Sun. Noon* - 2 A.M.

Crazy Ed's is champion chili-maker Ed Paetzel's place. Besides his own brands of prize-winning chili, hamburgers, ribs and excellent fajitas are available. *Sugar Creek Shopping Center at Highway 59 and South, Houston,* (713) 464-1268 *Mon. thru Sat.* 11 A.M. - 9 P.M., *Closed Sun.*

Frank Tolbert's **Native Texas Foods and Museum of Chili Culture** is one of two parlors run by a man who wrote the book on chili. Tolbert's downtown location offers chili graced by tender chunks of meat with a good balance of spices. A good homemade hot sauce can be added to enhance the taste. No meal is complete without a stroll through the chili museum. 802 *Main Street, Dallas,* (214) 742-6336, *Mon. thru Fri.* 11 A.M. - 3 P.M., *Closed Sat.-Sun.*

Tolbert's Texas Chili Parlor is the branch parlor of Tolbert's downtown location. 3802 *Cedar Springs, Dallas,* (214) 522-4340 *Mon. thru Thurs.* 11 A.M. - 11 P.M., *Fri. and Sat.* 11 A.M. - *Midnight, Sun. Noon* - 11 P.M.

The Texas Roadside Diner has one of the finest neon signs found in Texas that admirably reflects its good chili, German foods and desserts. Excellent barbecue on the patio Saturdays and Sundays. Owner Le Beast and head chef the "Admiral" specialize in Texas-style home cooking. *Located on Highway 16, Fredricksburg,* (512) 997-2229 *Mon. thru Sat.* 11 A.M. - 10 P.M.

Highland Park Cafeteria has specials all week long. On Wednesday and Friday it's chili. They use toasted cumin seeds, giving the chili a distinctive taste. 4611 *Cole, Dallas,* (214) 526-3801 *Mon. thru Sat.* 11 A.M. - 8 P.M., *Closed Sun.*

Chili's Hamburger Bar and Grill can be found in Dallas, Houston, Denver and San José. These chains serve authentic bowls of Texas Red, chili-burgers and regional dishes. 7567 *Greenville Avenue, Dallas,* (214) 361-4371 *Mon. thru Thurs.* 11 A.M. - 11 P.M., *Fri. and Sat.* 11 A.M. - 1 A.M., *Sun.* 11 A.M. - 11 P.M.

Sol's in El Paso is more oriented to the New Mexican and Mexican style of chili verde than the traditional bowl of Red, but it's still delicious. Excellent barbecue. 601 *North Stanton, El Paso,* 10 A.M. - 3:30 A.M., *7 days a week.*

Tucked under the protective shadow of the Texas State Capitol building in Austin, the Texas Chili Parlor features bowls of Red: "The Official State Dish of Texas" sanctified by the Texas legislature. Unfortunately, not everybody was satisfied with the legislature's choice, especially the avid supporters of barbecue. Barbecue hounds howled "foul play" when chili lobbyists, headed by Robert "Yeller Dog" Marsh, cooked up the "World's Largest Pot of Chili" for the members of congress. It wasn't just the 259 gallons of chili (weighing over 2500 pounds) that put a political burr under the barbecue lobby's saddle, but the 24 cases of free beer which they claimed ultimately swayed the decisive votes in favor of chili. The controversy rages on. The next time you visit Texas, sample both dishes . . . you be the judge.

CHILI SPICES

In any cookbook, terminology can be confusing. Even the dictionary is of little help in nailing down the exact definition and spelling of chili — the dish, versus chile — the vegetable; the terms are interchangeable and their pluralities vary depending on what part of the country you are in. For clarity's sake, chili powder (with an "i") is a blend of spices that may include onion, cumin, garlic and chile powder. Chile powder (with an "e") is just chile peppers ground coarse or fine, and nothing else. When you purchase a chili mix, like Wick Fowler's 2-Alarm Chili or Ed Paetzel's Championship Chili Mix, you usually get separate packets of pre-mixed chili powder (that includes the secret seasonings) and pure ground chile powder (that may be added to the pot of chili for extra hotness). To further confuse the issue, Texans will label blends of ground chile peppers as chili pepper.

Many spices used in Tex-Mex cooking and chili preparation present a similar problem. Cumin, a spice brought over from the Canary Islands in the eighteenth century, and probably the most popular flavoring in Tex-Mex dishes and chili, is also known as comino. Coriander is often called cilantro, depending on who you talk to. One reliable source claims coriander is the seed of the cilantro plant and what is called cilantro is the leaves. Regardless, this is an extremely pungent spice that may easily overpower any dish if used incorrectly. Paprika is another spice whose definition appears up for grabs. In its most common form, paprika is produced from ground red bell peppers or mild red chilies. It does come hot, but the milder form is favored because the pigmentation properties intensify the red color of any dish without upping the hotness factor. And finally, cayenne. It, too, is known as a red chile, but is generically labeled "Red Pepper" in some spice racks. Whatever form cayenne takes, it also imparts a rich, red color to a dish, but packs a good deal more punch.

BASIC CHILE THEORY

The stem should be curved and firm, not shriveled. A healthy stem is indicative of a good meaty pod.

As a general rule, the broader the shoulder, the milder the pepper. Grouped in the broad shoulder category are the poblanos, ana-heims, sandias, fres-nos, and New Mex big jims, collectively known as "long green chilies." They grow up to a foot long, are thick skinned, and contain more vita-min C than citrus fruits. Utilized in their green stage these chilies are pureed for sauces, diced up into chili pots and cooked whole as chile re-llenos. Upon maturity, these peppers turn red to brownish-black and are dried and ground into chile powders.

The meat of the chile pepper, rich in vitamins A and C, is what supplies the delicious chile taste — providing that the devilish capsaicin has not singed your taste buds in-to oblivion. As a pepper ma-tures, starches in the meat wall convert to sugars, imparting a paradoxi-cally sweet/hot flavor. Oleoresins in the meat produce a pigmenta-tion coloring the pep-per red.

The yellow-orange seed clusters attached to the ribs are where the greatest concentra-tion of the chemical capsaicin is found. Capsaicin is the oily compound responsible for the pepper's fiery nature.

The veins or ribs are where the fiery heat originates.

The milder long green chilies have a tough, thick outer skin. For some dishes, like chile verde, the skin is heat-blistered and then peeled off, revealing the tender, green meat. The epidermis of the short, but hotter, green chile is thin, eliminating the need for peeling. Pepperheads can munch these easily . . . that is, until the heat flares up.

Sharp pointed tips are characteristic of the shorter, hot chile peppers like the serranos (green bullets from Hell), cay-ennes and the infernal habaneros from Yucatan.

CHILIES

Pequin Chilies   These small chilies, found growing wild in South Texas, really pack a wallop. Cowboys, and other brave souls, used to carry pockets full of these belly busters, munching on them like beer nuts. They are also called chile petin, tepin and chilipiquîn. Pequin chilies are used in salsas and ground into pastes to make dried beef jerky and pemmican.

Serrano   Grown worldwide, these little green bullets from Hell, one to four inches long, are prized for their pungent flavor. They are the "hot" in Louisiana Hot Sauce, Tabasco and Chile Escabeche. Chile Escabeche is a potent concoction of serranos pickled in vinegar and oil. The spicy liquid is sprinkled onto any dish that needs a little "kick." Chopped serranos are used in machacado — a dish made with scrambled eggs and dried beef. The dried serrano is known as a japone, an essential ingredient used liberally in Szechuan Chinese cooking. Other variations of these little devils are santaka, hontaka, Bombay cherry, cayenne and the hottest of the hot, arbol and habanero.

Jalapeno   The jalapeno is the perfect pepper for all seasons. Blending the best of both worlds, this chile has the punch of the little pequins and meaty bulk of the long greens. The versatile jalapeno commands stage center atop nachos, makes salsas adventuresome, and is the heart and soul of a good bowl of Red. This chile is also the star of such taste treats as jalapeno wine, lollipops, jellybeans, corn bread and ice cream. When picked red and dried, the jalapeno is called chilpotl, the basis for a very exciting chili powder. Dedicated hotheads enjoy the jalapeno sliced on a bread and butter sandwich or batter-coated, deep fat fried and eaten like a potato chip.

Anaheim or Long Green   Unquestionably, the tough-skinned, long green chilies are the preferred cooking peppers. Cultivated throughout the Southwest, these chilies grow to a length of twelve inches. The anaheim is a favorite long green for sauces, chile verde and chile rellenos. Other varieties like New Mex Big Jim, Fresno and Sandia are used similarly. All of the long greens, when used whole, are usually heat-blistered and peeled to remove their tough, outer skin. Long greens, when mature, turn red. They are dried and strung up on decorative strings and into Christmas wreaths. Commercial growers grind the dried red chilies into powders and flakes to be sold as pre-packaged chili mixes like Wick Fowler's 2-Alarm Chili Mix.

Poblanos   The broad-shouldered poblano looks very much like the bell pepper but has a richer flavor and a bit more bite. In the green stage, it's used for chile rellenos and mild sauces. When the poblano matures, turns a brownish-black and dries, it is referred to as an ancho (when the bell pepper turns red, it is called a pimiento). The flavorful ancho is the main ingredient for Mexican red sauces.

Caribe   The caribe pepper is also known as the yellow hot wax pepper in some part of the country. They are about finger-length in size and similar in shape to the jalapeno, but have a richer flavor and more succulent meat. Because of their bright yellow color, the caribe is a favorite to visually spice-up sauces, as well as other dishes.

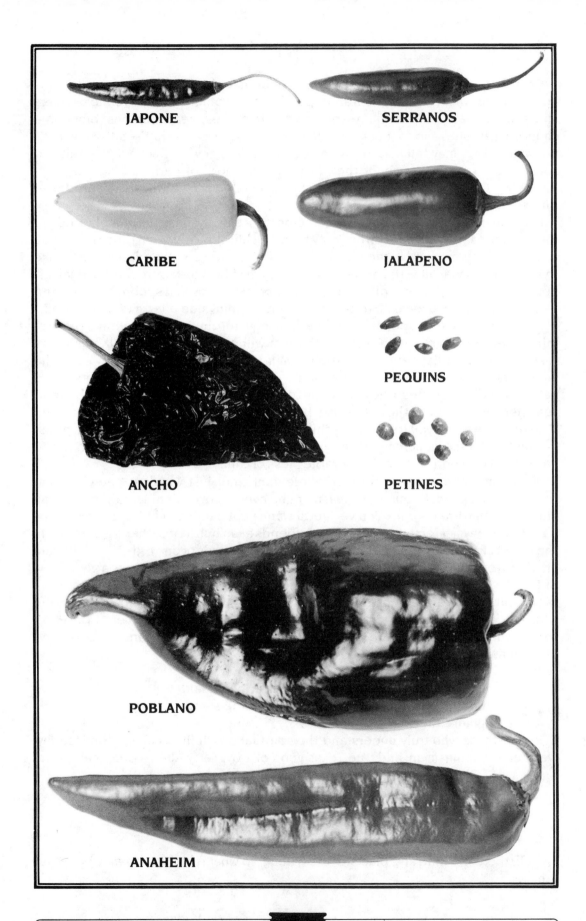

JAPONE

SERRANOS

CARIBE

JALAPENO

PEQUINS

ANCHO

PETINES

POBLANO

ANAHEIM

CHILI

Chili is a deceptively easy dish to make. It lends itself to versatility since everything about it is optional. Basically it is any type of meat in conjunction with chile peppers and spices. That's it. From there you can put tomatoes, beans, onions, pineapple chunks, cigar ashes and/or nuts and bolts into it and still call it chili — although that's not what others may call it. Chili can be eaten straight or with crackers. The salt and sugar in crackers can augment the most decrepit bowl of Red, making it at least palatable. Chili can be served over pasta (as a chili mac) with rice or poured over pinto beans.

It's a dish that, if you follow the recipe too closely, may ultimately end up disappointing. There *is* no "correct" way to make chili. It's a personal process and you can't tell someone how it should be done. Chilihead C. V. Wood says that's like trying "to tell a man how to part his hair." Cooking chili is the sport of individualists. Let the whims of culinary exploration guide your taste buds and spoon; keep in mind — always — that you eat chili to counteract the harmful side effects of health foods.

Step one in cooking a pot of basic "medium high torque" chili is to attain peace of mind. Step two is get a cold beer . . . the rest will be no problem at all. In a heavy cast-iron pot or skillet, render out about a half-inch of grease from kidney suet. The suet imparts a sweet flavor and some claim the iron in the pot leaches into the grease neutralizing "bad" tastes. Cut up any kind of meat available into half-inch cubes and sear them until brown in the hot grease. Lower the heat, add the chili powder and stir. (The purists will tell you to use fresh chilies ground in a molcajete, but that's a purist for you.) Add some garlic, cumin, paprika for color, water and other stuff and voilá, you have got a very good and highly tolerable mess of chili.

It's a combination of environmental elements, not just what's in the chili, that makes it taste good. If your attitude isn't right, even a prize-winning bowl of Red can "taste like third-rate swill." You've "gotta wanna eat chili" for chili to taste good. A hard day of physical activity or jawin' with friends at an outdoor gathering puts one in the perfect frame of mind for craving the stuff. In the words of one old-time chilihead, "It's how you put your spoon into it and crumble the crackers that makes a good bowl of Red."

Of course, there are those poor, misguided souls who don't always see the ritualistic act of chili-eating for what it is. Ex-Texas governor, Allan Shivers, in an effort to help chili-cultists gain some rational perspective on their chili mania, once offered his own recipe for chili:

> **"Put a pot of chili on the stove to simmer.**
> **Let it simmer. Meanwhile, broil a sirloin steak.**
> **Continue to simmer the chili and eat the steak.**
> **Ignore the chili."**

But for those who truly understand the spiritual possibilities of chili philosophy, we offer artist/musician, and true Texas good ol' boy, Terry Allen's personal recipe:

> **"Git yourself a big black pot.**
> **Turn the stove on 'High'.**
> **Set the pot on the stove.**
> **Wait 'till the black pot glows red,**
> **Stick your head inside . . . and Dream."**

Well, there is a time and place for everything, so what is chili today may be better tamale.

FRANK TOLBERT'S QUINTESSENTIAL CHILI

3 pounds mature lean beef or venison
beer
1/8 pound kidney suet
2 to 4 jalapeno or ancho chile pods
2 tablespoons crushed cumin seeds
1 tablespoon salt
1 tablespoon cayenne
1 teaspoon oregano
garlic cloves

In his own words: "The main vehicle in the formula is three pounds of mature beef or venison and we usually call for lean beef when we can get it. At the start, we marinate the beef in beer and keep this liquid in the cooking process. Cut the meat into thumb-size pieces or put it through a grinder at the coarsest setting. We sear the beef until it is grey in rendered beef kidney suet, which adds a sweet flavor, but you will probably do the searing in vegetable oil. Vegetable oil is okay. The searing will seal in meat flavors and solidify the beef for the cooking process, same as you would sear a steak. I use about an eighth of a pound of rendered kidney suet, and a like amount of vegetable oil would do. Many old-time chili cooks sprinkle some chopped-up onions on the meat while it is being seared. Go ahead if you think it'll suit your taste. Chile peppers, such as sun-dried anchos or jalapeños, can be obtained in most Mexican food stores. For mild chili, use two average-sized chile pepper pods for each pound of beef. For "elevated" chili, use four pods. Put chile peppers in a blender along with enough water to make a puree, transfer to a large pot along with the beer marinade and meat, and cook the seared meat, first bringing it to a boil and then simmering for about thirty minutes. Take the pot off the stove for awhile. Add fresh garlic to taste, two level tablespoons of crushed cumin seeds or powdered comino, one level tablespoon of salt, one level tablespoon of cayenne pepper and a few pinches of oregano. We go very slow with the oregano. Too much oregano can give a spaghetti sauce flavor. If you use yellowish, greenish, or purplish chili peppers you can sprinkle in some paprika to add a reddish hue to the chili. It won't affect the taste. Wick Fowler, one of the greatest of chili cooks, put 15 ounces of tomato sauce in a recipe calling for three pounds of meat. He said it adds color and thickening and most of the tomato flavor surrenders to the more powerful spices.

With the spices in there, put the pot back on the stove, bring to a boil, and then simmer about 45 minutes, stirring some but keeping the lid on as much as possible. This last time for simmering isn't arbitrary. Cook the meat till it's tender and has the taste you're looking for. Keep the chili in the refrigerator overnight to seal in the spices. This also makes it easy to spoon off any grease at the top which you don't want in your chili. Actually, a little grease helps the flavor.

If you want pinto or red beans with your chili, for God's sake cook the beans separately, and there's no need to make the beans highly flavored. I'm constantly running into people who cook beans in with the meat in making chili con carne. These people flunked chemistry."

Frank Tolbert

TEXAS CHILI

4 pounds coarse ground beef
1 pound suet (beef)
4 tablespoons ground chili
1 teaspoon cumin
1/2 teaspoon oregano
1 onion (to make 3/4 cup, ground)
2-3 cloves ground garlic
salt to taste

Use large heavy kettle, cast iron or aluminum. Slice suet thin and fry out in kettle until about 3 to 4 tablespoons fat are in bottom of kettle. Crumble rough ground beef into hot suet and stir until meat has changed color. Do not brown meat. It will turn gravy dark. Add chili powder to meat; stir. Allow to simmer slowly for a few minutes. Add garlic and onion and other spices. If necessary, add small amount of HOT water from time to time but chili should cook thick. Simmer for 2 to 3 hours stirring and adding water as needed. Cornmeal may be added in water for additional thickening if desired.

Woody Barron

HOT PANTS CHILI

Allegani Jani Schofield is a woman for all seasons. When denied entrance to the "males only" Texas State Championship Chili Cook-Off in San Marcos, she and other irate chili-libbers formed the Hell Hath No Fury Susan B. Anthony Memorial Women's Chili Cooking Group. They retaliated (giving the male-oriented chili world a bit of a taste of their own chauvinism) and staged the First Annual Texas State Championship Ladies Only Chili Bust held in Luckenbach, Texas . . . This historic event helped pave the way for equality among chili cooks and virtually eliminated sexual discrimination at the male-dominated cookoffs. Allegani went on to become the first woman ever to win the title of World Champion Chili Maker at Terlingua, in 1974, for her Hot Pants Chili. Texas writer, Sam Huddleston, had these observations on her accomplishment, "Allegani Jani wore a set of hot pants which move planned parenthood back ten years. One spoonful of her chili would get an hombre spastic with happiness." As Allegani accepted her awards, she left the formerly all-male chili world with this poignant remark, "The hand that rocks the cradle will rule the chili world."

4 pounds stew meat, ground once
3 onions, chopped
2 tablespoons oil
salt and pepper to taste
2 heaping teaspoons comino seeds
6 garlic pods, smashed
1 can tomatoes
1 teaspoon sugar

1/2 can beer
3 tablespoons chili powder (or 1 small pack Vanco chili powder)
OR:
1 teaspoon red pepper flakes
2 tablespoons ground coriander
2 tablespoons ground cumin
4 tablespoons paprika
2 teaspoons salt
4 teaspoons oregano
2 tablespoons dried onion flakes
1 teaspoon dried garlic flakes
1/4 cup cornstarch
1/2 teaspoon ground black pepper
3 teaspoons molé paste
1 teaspoon Tabasco
1 teaspoon salt
1 quart water
4 jalapeno peppers (remove seeds before chopping if you don't like hot chili)
1/2 cup masa flour

Brown meat and onions in oil. Season with salt and pepper to taste. Using a molcajete, grind comino seeds and garlic with a little water. Add to meat. In blender, combine tomatoes, sugar, beer, chili seasoning and powder. Add to stew along with molé paste, 1 teaspoon each Tabasco and salt, and 1 quart water. Add chopped jalapenos. Cook for 2-1/2 hours, stirring well from time to time. At end of cooking time, make a thin paste of masa and water and add to stew while stirring fast. This will thicken the stew, but stir fast or it will be lumpy. Cook 1/2 hour more to thicken.

Allegani Jani Schofield

GOAT CHILI

8 pounds goat meat, chili ground or in 1/4-inch cubes
5 tablespoons chili powder
2 garlic cloves, crushed
1 teaspoon red pepper
2 tablespoons salt
1 beer

Cook meat in heavy skillet until lightly browned. Add dry seasonings and stir. Pour in beer. Cook uncovered for 45 minutes. Serve with a side of beans, corn bread and onion slice.

"Stick"

HORNADILLO CHILI

Hondo Crouch lived in Luckenbach. He was a poet, musician, artist and friend of the earth. Only after visiting Texas will the curious begin to understand the legacy this loved man left behind. Hopefully, Hondo's chili recipe, as told to Allegani Jani, will begin to express the particular warmth and joy Hondo had towards any endeavor he chose to undertake.

1 medium armadillo (save the shell)
green food coloring
Ysleta red chile pods
3 comino seeds
1 jigger tequila
pinch of salt
slice of lime
1 egg (2, if they're cheap)
olive oil (if you can borrow some)
green onion tops
finely ground cedar bark
green spinach or fresh watercress

Dice armadillo into chunks, do not grind. Next, dye them pea green to produce the color for green chili. Use only Ysleta red chile pods, grown only in Ysleta because the soil is peculiar. Grind comino seeds vigorously. Add jigger of tequila, pinch of salt, slice of lime. (May be either taken internally or added to chili.) For chili thickening, put in a raw egg — two, if their cheap. And if you can borrow some, add olive oil. It's too expensive to buy. Add green onion tops and finely ground cedar bark. Sprinkle with green spinach or fresh watercress and serve on the half shell.

Hondo Crouch

$20,000 PRIZE-WINNING CHILI

Bill and Becky Pfeiffer are winners of the 1980 World Championship Chili Cookoff. Here's a chance to try a prize-winning recipe.

2-1/2 pounds lean ground chuck
1 pound lean ground pork
1 cup finely chopped onion
4 cloves garlic, finely chopped
1 (12-ounce) can Budweiser Beer
1 (8-ounce) can Hunt's tomato sauce
1 cup water
3 tablespoons chili powder
2 tablespoons ground cumin
2 tablespoons Wyler's Beef-Flavor Instant Bouillon (or 6 cubes)
2 teaspoons oregano leaves

2 teaspoons paprika
2 teaspoons sugar
1 teaspoon unsweetened cocoa
1/2 teaspoon ground coriander
1/2 teaspoon Louisiana Red Hot! sauce, to taste
1 teaspoon flour
1 teaspoon cornmeal
1 tablespoon warm water

In large saucepan or Dutch oven, brown half the meat; pour off fat. Remove meat. Brown remaining meat; pour off all fat except 2 tablespoons. Add onion and garlic; cook and stir until tender. Add meat and remaining ingredients except flour, cornmeal and warm water. Mix well. Bring to a boil; reduce heat and simmer covered 2 hours. Stir together flour and cornmeal; add warm water. Mix well. Stir into chili mixture. Cook covered 20 minutes longer. Serve hot. Makes about 2 quarts.

Bill & Becky Pfeiffer

OLD FOLKS CHILI

4 pounds coarse or chili grind beef chuck, remove gristle
1 pound onions, coarsely chopped
1 clove garlic, put through garlic press
1 cup boiling water
1 (7-ounce) can tomato paste
3 ounces chili powder
3/4 tablespoon cumin seed, ground
5 ounces flour
salt to taste

Place meat, onions and garlic in heavy pot and cook over medium heat until onions are transparent. For grease-free chili, remove from fire and strain juices into another pan. Cool until grease layer can be peeled off and discarded. Recombine juice and meat with 1 cup boiling water. Add tomato paste, chili powder and cumin. Simmer 2 hours, stirring occasionally. While this is cooking, sift flour into shallow pan and place in preheated 350° oven. Stir about every 20 minutes until golden brown. This should take about 1-1/2 hours. When chili has cooked 2 hours, add parched flour and sufficient boiling water to bring to desired thickness. Add salt to taste. Cook 2 more hours stirring occasionally and adding boiling water to maintain thickness desired. Serves 8.

Alfred O. Saenger

GORDO'S MAD DOG CHILI

Gordon Lish, who describes himself as a "wonderful food writer," held the title as the "World's Greatest Chili Maker" until the 1977 International Houston Invitational Chili Cookoff. In that "sad year" Gordo lost to a young Texas teen named Kim (Gordo refers to her as a "sneaky brat") who toppled Lish's reputation with her entry, "Kim Paetzel's Punk Kid Chili."

12 pounds beef brisket, cubed
bacon drippings
beer
6 tablespoons chili powder
10 tablespoons cumin seeds
4 tablespoons oregano
2 tablespoons marjoram
3 tablespoons ground coriander
1 tablespoon woodruff
1 tablespoon gumbo filé
2 tablespoons lemon juice
2 tablespoons sugar
4 tablespoons salt
2 teaspoons ground chile pepper
1 tablespoon cayenne
2 tablespoons Dijon mustard
1 tablespoon Worcestershire sauce
3 teaspoons Louisiana Hot Sauce
14 minced garlic cloves
4 bay leaves
2 teaspoons cinnamon
1 small can tomato paste
3 tablespoons paprika
3 teaspoons MSG
2 tablespoons masa harina
3 onions, finely minced

Trim and cube brisket. In a large, heavy pot sear meat in bacon drippings and drain. Add enough beer to cover top of meat by one inch. Simmer over low heat. Add remaining ingredients. Cover and let simmer for no less than 6 hours, for as long as 12 hours if convenient, stirring now and then. One hour before completion, add 2 tablespoons of masa harina and 3 finely minced onions. Remove bay leaves before serving.

Gordon Lish

MOVIN' ON CHILI

3 pounds lean ground round
garlic salt
salt
pepper
meat tenderizer
3 large yellow onions, chopped
6 (12-ounce) cans red kidney beans
2 (12-ounce) cans tomato paste
cumin seeds
chili powder

Season meat with garlic salt, salt and pepper and meat tenderizer. Let sit for 2 hours. Brown onions in oil. Add beans and tomato paste and simmer. In a 9-inch pie pan, put a double layer of cumin seeds and roast on a low burner until brown. Add to pot and stir through. Simmer about 8 hours, adding water as needed. Gradually add chili powder until it smells good and continue to simmer about 4 more hours or until ready to serve.

Texas Country

ARMADILLO CHILI BY ENRIQUE

*Enrique hangs his armadillo meat in a cooler for a few days to cure it. This is a necessary first step for armadillo meat.

5 pounds cured armadillo meat*, ground fine
salt to taste (about 1 teaspoon)
3 pods garlic, ground
1/8 teaspoon cumin
1 jalapeno or serrano pepper
3 ounces chili powder
1 cup flour
1-1/2 cups boiling water

Brown meat in a little oil until meat is medium-well done. Salt to taste while cooking. Grind garlic, cumin and peppers (seeds and all) in a molcajete. Add to meat. Add chili powder. Sprinkle flour over meat and stir. Stir in boiling water gradually. Simmer about 40 minutes, keeping the pot loosely covered.

Allegani Jani

SAM LEWIS' CHILI

This is basic chili at its best. No chocolate, banana chunks or yak meat.

2 pounds beef suet
4 pounds lean beef chili meat
1 large onion, diced
3 whole jalapeno peppers (for normal people)
6 garlic cloves
1/2 teaspoon ground cumin
1 teaspoon cumin seed
1 tablespoon red cayenne pepper

Render suet in heavy skillet. Lightly stir-fry diced onions in suet. Add meat and enough water to cover the meat. Cover skillet and simmer until meat is cooked. Add spices 30 minutes before serving chili. "If you leave spices in too long, it gets bitter." For a winning pot of chili: Boil a pot of beans. Strain the juice and use the juice instead of water in your chili.

Sam Lewis

C. V. WOOD'S UNDENIA-BULL WORLD CHAMPIONSHIP CHILI

C.V. Wood is a co-founder of the International Chili Society, the West Coast's answer to Texas' Chili Appreciation Society International. C.V. has since won the ICS Cookoff two years in a row and retired as an undefeated World Champion Chili Cook.

1 (3-pound) stewing chicken, cut up
1-1/2 quarts water
1/2 pound beef kidney suet
4 pounds flank steak
5 pounds thin, center-cut pork chops
1/4 cup finely chopped celery
7 cups peeled, chopped tomatoes
2 teaspoons sugar
6 long green chilies, anaheim greens or New Mexico No. 6
8 ounces good light beer, preferably Mexicali
3 teaspoons ground oregano
3 teaspoons ground cumin
1/2 teaspoon monosodium glutamate (optional)
3 teaspoons fine black pepper
4 teaspoons salt
5 tablespoons chili powder
1 teaspoon chopped fresh cilantro
1 teaspoon thyme
2 cloves garlic, finely chopped
2 cups onion, cut into 1/4-inch pieces

2 cups green pepper, cut into 3/8-inch pieces
1 pound Jack cheese, grated
1 large lime

Simmer chicken in water for two hours. Strain off broth and save chicken for other dishes. Render suet to make 6 to 8 tablespoons of oil. Throw out fat and save oil. Trim all fat from flank steak. Cut into 3/8-inch cubes. Trim all fat and bones from the pork chops. Cut into 1/4-inch cubes. In a two-quart saucepan mix celery, tomatoes and sugar. Simmer 1-1/2 hours until tender. Blister green chilies over open flame. Remove skins and boil in water for fifteen minutes. Remove seeds and cut up into 1/4-inch squares. Put oregano, cumin, monosodium glutamate, black pepper, salt, chili powder, cilantro and thyme into 8 ounces of light beer and stir until lumps dissolve. Add the tomato mixture, the cut up chilies, the beer mixture and garlic to chicken broth in a two-gallon pot. Stir with a wooden spoon and bring to a low simmer. Brown pork in a skillet with 1/3 of the oil from the kidney suet. The pork should become white on all six sides and fully separate — do not overcook. Add the pork to the two-gallon pot and bring to a low boil for thirty minutes. With balance of oil, brown the beef, let it get white on all six sides — do not overcook. Add beef to the pot and cook for one hour, low boil. Add chopped onions and peppers and continue to cook for 2 hours at a low boil. Remove chili from stove, let cool for one hour and set in refrigerator for 24 hours. This allows the spices to permeate the meat without breaking down the texture. Five minutes before serving, add one pound of grated Jack cheese; stir until melted. About one minute before serving, add juice of lime, stir with wooden spoon and serve.

C. V. Wood

RON'S CHILI RECIPE

4 pounds choice shank meat (tough) run through chili grind
1 pound suet (kidney is best) ground
4 rounded tablespoons chili powder
2 tablespoons cumin (heat seed before grinding)
1 teaspoon ground cayenne, or more to taste
2 large garlic cloves, shredded

Place suet in skillet and render out until clear. Put meat in a large pan, barely cover it with water and cook it 1-1/2 hours. Add cooked suet to meat and add remaining ingredients. Cook 1/2 hour more. If beans are desired, serve them separately.

Ron Wilson

MOUTH OF HELL CHILI

1 large onion, chopped
2 tablespoons oil
2 pounds lean chili meat
1 large can tomatoes
2 small cans tomato sauce
1 teaspoon sugar
2 teaspoons ground comino
2 teaspoons paprika
1 large clove garlic
1 can beer
2 fresh jalapeno peppers
5 tablespoons chili powder
salt and cayenne pepper to taste (hotness of chili depends on how much cayenne)
2 cups cooked pinto beans (optional)
1 tablespoon tequila (at least 150 proof)

Sauté chopped onion in oil. Add chili meat and stir until grey. Add remaining ingredients except for tequila and beans. Cook until thick, about 1-1/2 hours. At this point, if you like beans in your chili, add the two cups cooked pinto beans . . . but make sure there aren't any Texans around. When ready to serve, put into a large bowl, pour tequila over and light. Chili Flambé, for all you gourmets.

JoAnn Horton

EDERNALES RIVER CHILI

LBJ loved to eat chili. Unfortunately, after his first heart attack, his doctor put him on a fat-free diet. Chili was not on the menu, until this virtually fat-free recipe evolved, made from lean venison meat.

4 pounds cubed or chili-ground venison
1 large onion, chopped
2 cloves garlic, minced
1 teaspoon ground oregano
1 teaspoon cumin seeds
6 teaspoons chili powder or to taste
2 cans Ro-Tel tomatoes
2 cups hot water
hot pepper sauce to taste

Sear meat, onions and garlic in large heavy boiler or skillet until lightly browned. Add seasonings, tomatoes and hot water. Bring to a boil. Lower heat; simmer about 1 hour. As chili cooks, skim off fat.

Mrs. Lyndon B. Johnson

CHAMPIONSHIP SUPERCHILI

6 to 8 pounds choice round steak
15.7 ounces unsweetened tomato paste
2.8 heaping teaspoons salt
51.2 ounces hot water
1.3 chopped white onions
medium hot powdered red chile (pure chile - not chili mix)
one bottle of Fred McMurry's Superchili Mix (see recipe below)
6 ounces premium beer (the rest of the 6-pack to be taken internally while
    cooking)
3.3 jalapenos, diced
1.2 anchos, diced
1.1 anaheim greens, diced
2.4 Harris County reds, diced
1 fresh green bell pepper
1 fresh red bell pepper (for color)
masa harina

SUPERCHILI MIX (ingredients only, proportions are still secret!)

pre-mixed comino
thyme
oregano
coriander
prickly pear cactus leaves (optional)
garlic
exotic Texas herbs
6 species of dried peppers
Midland mesquite beans

Remove all fat and gristle from steak so that you have exactly 5 pounds after trimming. Chill the 6-pack to 1°C. Chop the meat into small bite-size pieces. Never grind beef for chili — this is a sure sign you are: a) lazy, b) using tough meat, or c) a carpetbagger. Stir in tomato paste, salt, water, onions, red chile powder, Fred McMurry's Superchili Mix, 6 ounces of chilled beer (the rest being taken internally while cooking, remember?), and the peppers. Simmer 349 minutes, stirring with mesquite spoon. Taste and make minor adjustments as necessary (depending on size of peppers, altitude, age, emotional state, aroma, color, distance from Houston). Thicken as needed with masa mixed with hot water to form thick, smooth liquid. Refrigerate overnight if possible (chili is always better is allowed to cool 21 hours or more). Serve with hot peppers, cold beer, guitar music, conversation and, if you like, separately cooked pinto beans (in no case may they ever be cooked in with the chili — that's illegal in Texas; immoral and unsafe anywhere).

Fred McMurry

MPS MIND-EXPANDING THERAPEUTIC CHILI VERDE

5 pounds top round steak (trimmed)
3.8 heaping teaspoons salt
1.1 heaping teaspoons garlic
3.9 heaping teaspoons powdered comino
3.1 heaping teaspoons MPS (optional)
3.1 heaping teaspoons oregano
2 large white onions, diced
7 chopped jalapeño peppers
6 chopped serrano peppers
25.6 ounces water
2 prickly pear cactus leaves, de-follicated and slivered
1 dozen pasilla chile peppers, blistered, peeled, deveined and chopped
1 dozen anaheim greens
4 large bell peppers (only soft green meat)
2 more onions
5 large tomatoes, chopped
1 can beer
24 ounces water
masa harina

Sear trimmed meat and add salt, garlic, comino, oregano, 2 onions, jalapeños, serranos, 25.6 ounces water and prickly pear leaves. Cook in pressure cooker for 46 minutes at 10 pounds of pressure. Add other peppers, the other 2 onions, tomatoes, beer and water. Simmer for 28 minutes. Thicken as needed with masa harina mixed with warm water to form thick, smooth liquid. Serve with yellow hominy and/or pinto beans, added to bowl of chili according to individual taste.

Allegani Jani

GENUINE TEXAS RED CHILI (RIO LLANO VARIETY)

3 to 3-1/2 pounds lean beef or venison, coarse ground
6 ounces Pearl or Lone Star beer
3 ounces tomato paste
2 tablespoons freshly ground cumin seeds
1 tablespoon freshly ground oregano (or marjoram) leaves
3 medium cloves garlic, crushed
1 medium onion, finely chopped
1 tablespoon salt
6 to 9 long red chile pods (depending on pungency)
masa harina
cayenne or Tabasco (optional)

In a large stew pot put meat, beer and 2 cups water. Simmer meat until light grey in color; add tomato paste. Stir and simmer for a few minutes, then add spices (which have been ground in perfectly dry blender at high speed) garlic, onion and salt. Stir thoroughly and remove from heat. Remove stems and seeds from chile pods and boil in covered saucepan with 3 cups water for 15 minutes. Remove peppers and water to blender and blend into thick sauce. Add sauce to meat and simmer 2 hours. If chili needs thickening, up to 1 tablespoon masa harina (corn flour) may be added. This adds a unique Mexican flavor. If chili is too thick, additional water may be added, but add slowly and cautiously. For low calorie or greaseless chili, use very lean meat and never add suet. If additional "caliente" is needed, while chili is simmering, add ground cayenne pepper or Tabasco sauce.

SUPERB X CHILI

This recipies Wick Fowler's original scratch recipe from which he evolved his Wick Fowler 2-Alarm Mix, available in supermarkets. It was given to Allegani Jani Schofield, the first woman to ever win at Terlingua and author of *My Hungry Friends*, from which we gratefully pass it along. It's hot, so have plenty of margaritas or buttermilk on hand to help neutralize the burning sensation.

3 pounds chili grind meat
15-ounce can tomato sauce
1 cup water
1 teaspoon Tabasco
3 heaping tablespoons chili powder
1 heaping tablespoon oregano
1 heaping teaspoon comino (seeds or powder)
6 garlic cloves, chopped
1 teaspoon salt
1 teaspoon cayenne pepper
1 level teaspoon paprika
1 dozen red peppers (whole dried jalapeños)
4 or 5 chilipiquins
2 heaping tablespoons flour

Sear the meat in a large skillet until grey in color. Put the meat into a chili pot, with the tomato sauce and enough water to cover the meat by 1/2 inch. Add the remaining ingredients, except the whole pepper pods, and stir. Then put in the chile pods whole, careful not to break them, because they are for flavor. Eating them is left up to the individual. Simmer for one hour and 15 minutes. Skim off excess grease. Add thickener made of 2 heaping tablespoons flour and water and simmer for additional 30 minutes (or overnight . . . it can't hurt).

Wick Fowler

ED PAETZEL'S WORLD FAMOUS 4-K CHILI

Ed Paetzel will tell anyone willing to listen that it was he who should have won Terlingua in 1974, not Allegani Jani. He vehemently swears, "The drunken judge mistakenly put my chili into Jani's judging cup. She won because I made the best chili!" Regardless, Ed went on to take top honors at Terlingua in later years. Today Ed markets his secret blended chili mix and runs "Crazy Ed's" in Houston, specializing in chili, ribs and fajitas.

5 pounds lean meat (chili grind or small cubed chuck)
1 package Ed Paetzel's Championship Chili Mix
1 (15-ounce) can tomato sauce
1 can beer
16 ounces water
2 tablespoons ground cumin
2 tablespoons New Mexico ground red chile
1 teaspoon paprika
1 teaspoon ground black pepper
1 teaspoon Accent
2 teaspoons salt
4 cloves garlic, finely chopped
1 large white onion, finely chopped
1 large jalapeno pepper, chopped with seeds - canned or fresh (for hotter chili add 2 or 3 more)

Brown meat in large chili pot. Brown onion, garlic and jalapeno together in skillet. Before adding liquid, mix onion, garlic, jalapeno, chili mix and spices to meat and stir in well. Let stand for one hour without cooking. Return pot to stove, add tomato sauce, beer and water. Stir well. Cook chili ground meat in pot for at least 2 hours. Hand-cut meat should be cooked 3-4 hours.

Ed Paetzel

CHILI CHA CHA

4 pounds top round steak, cubed in 1/4-inch pieces
2 to 4 tablespoons cooking oil
10 tablespoons instant minced onion, soaked in 1/4 cup tomato juice
2-1/2 tablespoons celery salt
4 tablespoons ancho chile pepper or 3 tablespoons of a standard brand
1/2 teaspoon curry powder
1/2 teaspoon garlic powder
1/2 teaspoon powdered thyme
5 (6-ounce) cans tomato paste
3 to 4 cups tomato juice
1 (27-ounce) can diced green chilies (fire-roasted and peeled)
4 to 6 ounces Mexican chocolate or American sweet milk chocolate

Grind together 1/2 teaspoon each:
allspice
bay leaf
coriander
cumin
ginger
marjoram
oregano
paprika
red pepper
sage

Brown meat in cooking oil. Add onions, spices and remaining ingredients except chocolate and simmer for 90 minutes. Add the chocolate and continue cooking for 30 minutes adding 3-5 more cups tomato juice for desired thickness. Stir frequently. Randolph J. Jouno won the 1979 International Chili Championship with the above recipe.

Randolph J. Jouno

H. ALLEN SMITH'S PERFECT CHILI

H. Allen Smith was one of the two original culinary combatants at the first chili cookoff held at Terlingua, Texas in 1967. This is a recipe, published shortly before his death in 1976, called "The Perfect Chili."

4 pounds carefully trimmed sirloin or tenderloin tips, coarse grind
olive oil and/or butter
2 (6-ounce) cans tomato paste
1 quart water
3 or 4 medium onions, chopped
1 bell pepper, chopped
10 cloves garlic, chopped
1 tablespoon oregano
1/2 teaspoon basil
1 tablespoon cumin seeds or ground cumin
salt and black pepper to taste
3 tablespoons chili powder or more
2 cans pinto or pink beans

Cook meat in olive oil and/or butter until grey. Add tomato paste and water. Stir in remaining ingredients except beans. Simmer covered for 2 or 3 hours, stirring occasionally. Taste and correct seasonings as needed. Add one or two cans of beans ten to fifteen minutes before serving time.

H. Allen Smith

OREHOUSE CHILI

Carol Risz is a chili cook's chili cook. She will go anywhere in the state to compete, as long as it's for charity. She has cooked at three different cookoffs in one weekend, and in 1979 placed first five times in a row. Carol's dedication to chili is humbling. In a valiant display of chilimania, while stricken with a case of heatstroke, Carol wrapped herself in wet blankets and called out cooking instructions to sympathetic bystanders from the back of her V.W. bus. It's hard to keep a good chili cook down. Her advice to aspiring chiliheads is to "stand by your pot. Never leave it. Fiddle with it. Love it. Pay attention to it." With bowls of her chili being auctioned off for up to ten thousand dollars a bowl, her words of wisdom should be heeded.

5 pounds beef shoulder and/or butt (trimmed and coarse ground)
whole jalapenos to suit taste
1-1/2 cups diced onions
2 cloves garlic
8-ounce can Hunt's tomato sauce
1/2 can water
1 tablespoon seasoned salt
1 tablespoon chili per pound of meat
1 teaspoon cumin powder per pound of meat

Brown meat in chili pot and drain off juices. Add onions which have been finely diced so that after cooking they are unrecognizable. Mash garlic in a press and add along with tomato sauce, chili powder, cumin powder and enough water to just cover the meat. Slit and de-seed jalapenos, put into chili mixture and remove after cooking.

Carol Risz

"MY RECIPE" CHILI

Stubbs, among other vocations, was a mess sergeant during the Korean War. He has written a book called "We Were Few, But We Were There," the story of Black Americans' contribution to the war effort. He comes from a family of cooks and is a firm believer in "never over-ingredienting" a dish. His no-nonsense chili recipe subscribes to this belief and reinforces the "KISS" Rule: Keep It Simple, Stupid.

3 to 4 pounds rough-ground chili meat
6-ounce jar chili powder
1 tablespoon salt
1/2 teaspoon black pepper
2 medium garlic cloves, chopped
1 tablespoon ground cumin
6-ounce can tomato paste
2 tablespoons flour
water as needed

Put just enough water to cover the bottom of a large chili pot. Turn the heat on high; when the water steams, add the meat and stir fry until lightly browned. Mix together all the dry ingredients and add to the browned meat. Add tomato paste and water as needed to thicken as desired. Season to taste and simmer 45 minutes.

Stubbs

RED BARON (CONFEDERATE) CHILI

This is a favorite chili of the Texas Confederate Air Force. The Air Force is a group of vintage war plane collectors who assemble yearly at the Luckenbach World's Fair. On the opening day of the fair, precisely at nine o'clock, the Confederate Air Force lines up on the outskirts of the little town of Luckenbach. They proceed to "Not Fly Over" Luckenbach until it has been determined the whole air fleet has "Not Flown Over" Luckenbach (it's a great "Non–Fly Over Event" no one should "not" miss).

3 pounds lean round (chili grind)
1 tablespoon oil if needed
black pepper to taste
1/2 cup chili powder
2 teaspoons salt
1-1/2 cups bell pepper, chopped
1 cup finely chopped onions
3 to 4 cloves garlic
2 teaspoons ground cumin
1 teaspoon paprika
1 teaspoon red pepper
2 teaspoons oregano
2 cups beef bouillon (dissolve cubes in water)
2 to 3 magnolia (bay) leaves
12-ounce can tomato sauce
1/2 cup Masa Harina
4 cups water

Brown meat, using oil if necessary. Work in all spices and simmer for 30 minutes. Add 12-ounce can of tomato sauce and 4 cups water. Simmer 3 hours. Make a thin paste of 1/2 cup Masa Harina and water. Add to chili and cook for 30 minutes more. Taste occasionally; stir frequently. Correct seasoning as needed. Keep pot covered, except while tasting or stirring.

Col. Wm. Von Maszewski

FLAMING PUERTO RICAN CHILI

1 pound suet (beef fat)
2 onions, chopped
3 cloves garlic, chopped
2 pounds coarse hump meat from a Brahma bull (flank steak)
4 tomatoes, chopped
2 teaspoons sea salt
6 native hot red peppers, chopped
2 teaspoons cumin
1 teaspoon cayenne pepper
1 quart rain water
2 cans red beans
1/2 fresh pineapple, cut in chunks
1/2 cup 151 proof Puerto Rican rum

Chop the suet finely and fry until most of fat is rendered; fry onions, garlic and meat until onions are transparent and meat is brown. Add remaining ingredients up to beans and simmer for 2-3 more hours (stirring occasionally) or until meat is tender. If mixture thickens, add more water. Add beans 15 minutes before serving. Just before serving, top with native pineapple chunks, heated 151 Rum and ignite.

Allegani Jani

TEXAS CHILI #2

2 tablespoons vegetable oil
2 pounds stewing beef, cubed
1 cup chopped onions
1 green bell pepper, seeded and chopped
1 clove garlic, minced
1 (12-ounce) can tomato paste
2-1/2 cups water
2 pickled jalapeno peppers, rinsed, seeded and chopped
1-1/2 tablespoons chili powder
1/2 teaspoon crushed red pepper
1/2 teaspoon salt
1/2 teaspoon dried oregano
1/2 teaspoon cumin
1 (15-1/2-ounce) can pinto beans, drained

In a large heavy pan, heat oil, and brown beef cubes on all sides. Add onions, bell pepper and garlic, and fry them with beef for about 5 minutes. Add all the remaining ingredients except beans and simmer the chili for 1-1/2 hours or until the meat is tender. Add beans and simmer 30 minutes longer.

Lone Star Brewing Company

CRAIG CLAIBORNE'S NO-SALT CHILI

1 tablespoon peanut or vegetable oil
3 medium onions, finely chopped
1 green bell or sweet red pepper, cored, seeded, and finely chopped
1-1/4 pounds veal, beef, or pork, coarse chili grind
2 medium cloves garlic, finely chopped
2 tablespoons ground hot red chile
1 tablespoon ground mild red chile
1 teaspoon ground cumin
1 teaspoon dried oregano
1 bay leaf
1/2 teaspoon freshly ground black pepper
4 cups fresh or canned unsalted tomatoes
1 tablespoon red wine vinegar
1/4 teaspoon chile caribe, or to taste

Heat the oil in a deep skillet over medium heat. Add the onions and green pepper and sauté until the onions are translucent, about 3 minutes. Sprinkle the meat with the garlic, ground chile, cumin, and oregano. Stir to blend. Add the meat to the skillet. Break up any lumps with a fork, stirring occasionally until the meat is evenly browned. Add the bay leaf, pepper, tomatoes, vinegar, and caribe. Bring to a boil, lower the heat and simmer 1 hour, stirring occasionally. Taste and adjust seasoning.

Craig Claiborne

VENISON CHILI

4 pounds venison
1 pound kidney suet
2 tablespoons comino seeds
6 pods garlic
6 dried chilies, seeded
2 cups water
crackers
salt
pepper
1/2 teaspoon cayenne pepper

Grind the venison and suet together. Roast the comino seeds in the oven, being careful not to burn them. Crush them with the garlic. Boil the chilies in 2 cups water until tender. Mash through strainer, retaining all the water in which the chilies cooked. Roll enough crackers to make 3/4 cup crumbs. Brown the meat in a heavy pot. Add all other ingredients. Salt and pepper to taste and add 1/2 teaspoon cayenne.

Beulah Mulkey

BUZZARD'S BREATH CHILI

Tom Griffin started cooking chili in April, 1977. By November of that same year, to the stunned amazement of chiliheads, he took first place at the World Championship Cookoff in Terlingua, Texas. They called him a "flash in the pan," a "freak of nature"; but for one year they had to call him "Champ." His original prizewinning recipe called for dead cow meat, dried red ants and cigar ashes. If you don't like dried red ants in your chili, substitute black ones and up the amount of cigar ashes.

8 lbs. beef (U.S. choice boneless chuck)
3 (8-ounce) cans tomato sauce
2 large onions, chopped
5 gloves garlic, crushed and chopped
2 jalapeno peppers
5 tablespoons chili powder
2 teaspoons cumin, ground
1/4 to 1/2 teaspoon oregano
salt to taste
1 to 2 teaspoons paprika
cayenne pepper (to taste)
masa harina (as needed)
1 quart beef stock

Take meat and chop into 3/8" cubes, removing all gristle and visible fat. Brown in an iron skillet (about 2 pounds at a time) until grey in color. Place in a large, cast-iron chili pot, adding tomato sauce and equal amounts of water. Add chopped onion, garlic, jalapeno peppers, and chili powder. Simmer for 20 minutes, then add cumin, oregano, salt and cayenne pepper to taste. As moisture is required, add homemade beef stock until amount used, then add water if needed. Simmer covered until meat is tender (about two hours), stirring occasionally. Then add masa harina to achieve desired thickness if needed. Add paprika for color. Cook 10 additional minutes, correct seasoning to taste, discard jalapenos and serves. A small additional amount of cumin enhances aroma when added in last ten minutes.

Tom Griffin

TEX-MEX

From the 889-mile-long border that separates four Mexican states from Texas comes a culinary hybrid called Tex-Mex Cooking. Today this is actually an "umbrella" term under which falls several cooking styles, i.e. authentic Mexican cooking, Texas' interpretation of authentic Mexican cooking and the adulterization of Mexican and Tex-Mex cooking by the fast food chains.

To extract a precise definition of Tex-Mex is difficult, because the cultural and culinary intermingling of peoples along the border has blurred the distinctive lines between traditional Mexican cookery and its offspring — Tex-Mex. If you ask the locals to characterize the differences in the two styles, their conflicting opinions only add to the confusion. Some will claim Tex-Mex is "high-class Mexican cooking using lots of beans, lard and meat raised only in Texas." "It's hotter . . . no, it's milder — but the salsas are hotter." "The sauces are thicker." "They are not!" And on it goes. One border cook put it this way, "Authentic Mexican cooking has thousands of dishes. Because of the varied geography of Mexico, a greater selection of foods are available. You'll find peanuts, chocolate, squashes, pumpkins and pineapples in the regional dishes. Tex-Mex is less "exotic," but still good."

Corn has been grown in Mexico since 6000 B.C. It appears in a variety of colors: yellow, red, blue and purple. White corn was most commonly used for tortillas. Tortilla making was an everyday, back-breaking job but, as the saying goes, "If a girl doesn't know how to make tortillas, she isn't ready to have a boyfriend." The boiled corn kernels are ground daily into masa (corn flour) between a stone slab called a metate and a grinding stone called a mano. The masa was mixed with water, patted into thin pancakes and cooked on a comal (a grill) over an open fire. The tortilla was the main dietary staple of Old Mexico and figures prominently in Tex-Mex cooking. "The Tortilla Makers" by Julio Michaudy Thomas, 1848. Courtesy of the Institute of Texas Cultures.

Like the modern-day lunch truck (minus the wheels), tamale vendors in the nineteenth century walked the streets of "old San Antone" hawking their wares. The tamales were kept warm in pots cradled in a bed of hot coals. Painting courtesy of the Wittey Museum.

So, generally speaking, Tex-Mex is the "Texification" of Mexican foods. It encompasses such dishes as tacos, tamales, enchiladas, nachos, tostadas, chile con queso, guacamole, rice and beans.

Unfortunately, its reputation has suffered in the hands of insensitive restaurateurs looking to make a quick buck rather than a good dish. What distinguishes real Tex-Mex to the American palate is that it's made from scratch using only the freshest of ingredients. Chile peppers, for example, are probably the most essential (and abused) ingredients in Tex-Mex cooking. Most restaurants, in an effort to "streamline" their operation, will substitute commercially ground chile powder in place of fresh ground chile pulp. If you haven't tasted an enchilada sauce made from fresh ground ancho chile pulp, you haven't tasted enchilada sauce — or real Tex-Mex cooking. Commenting on

the sorry state of the art, Mary Yturria (one of the finest Tex-Mex cooks in the Lower Rio Grande Valley) told *Town & Country Magazine*, "Tex-Mex has been commercialized and corrupted to the point of utter crudeness. What with all the frozen dinners, chains and restaurants claiming to serve real border cooking, people just don't know the difference anymore." Mary goes on to illustrate her point with frijoles and tamales: "When we prepare beans at home, we use fresh garlic and coriander, carrots and onions, ham hocks and jalapeno for zip, but in the restaurants they'll just dump in a lot of bacon grease and — if you can imagine it — catsup! It's a disgrace. Or take these tamales, which are pure Texan. Much of their flavor comes from the soaked corn husks. Well, just like down in Mexico, most people use so much masa and chili powder, you can't even taste the meat and would you believe that lots of the tamales you find today are bound with some sort of paper instead of corn husks?"

A paper-wrapped tamale isn't the only culinary "crime" patrons of Tex-Mex are subjected to. Afficionados cringe at being served meat that has been machine ground instead of hand-shredded. And when it comes to sauces, there is no greater affront besmirching the good name of Tex-Mex than canned chile gravies and commercially bottled salsas. And yet, factory-made tortillas deal the ultimate blow. These horribly thin, glutinous, miserable excuses for a tortilla pale in comparison to the taste of a fresh handmade ground corn tortilla. Commercial tortillas do little to fulfill and complement the flavor of authentic Tex-Mex cuisine. Just about the only recourse for the connoisseur is to go home and cook his (or her) own (which more and more people are doing).

Probably the earliest example of Tex-Mex cooking was found in San Antonio during the mid-1800s. There the same chili queens who set up booths in the Military Plaza hawking chili, added tamales, tacos and burritos to the menu offered to passers-by and hungry soldiers visiting the open-air markets. The popularity of this particular

Mexican-influenced food grew. Soon fonditas, family-run inns, began to spring up in Mexican communities all across Texas, usually at the behest of friends and neighbors. A woman renowned for her mouth-watering Mexican dishes would set up a few tables and serve her specialties. Range hands and locals would patronize these makeshift restaurants and the fonditas' fame grew. "Felix's" in Houston is one such fondita that started just this way. Mrs. Felix Tijerina says "My mother ran a fondita for hungry gringos at the turn of the century," and from there the art was passed down.

In 1893 at the Chicago World's Fair, the world got its first taste of border cooking from a booth called the San Antonio Chili Stand. In 1898, William Gebhardt, a German from San Antonio, produced the first commercially available chili powder mix, and by 1908 followed with the first can of Gebhardt's canned Eagle Chili Con Carne. San Antonio was indeed becoming known as the birthplace of Tex-Mex cooking. The rest is history. The world began to discover what Texans had known for years: Mexican cooking, Texified, is a delicious and welcome alternative to conventional American dishes. The financial powers-that-were began to take notice of the long lines queueing up at established restaurants like "El Fenix" and "El Choico" in Dallas and "La Posta" in Mesilla. Soon there were enough "Taco Times," "Taco Ticos," "Taco Johns," "Taco Huts" and "Tippy's Taco Houses" to give "McDonald's" a run for their money. America began eating Tex-Mex foods in unprecedented numbers. In 1966, there were six "Taco Bell" restaurants. By the late seventies, the Mexican chain had over 800 locations and was grossing over 200 million dollars.

Although these chains serve foods that bear little or no resemblance to authentic Tex-Mex cuisine, they have helped expose a nation otherwise oblivious to the possible delights of border cooking. For those who have become jaded by combo dinners served on yellow plastic cafeteria trays (in less than a minute) and who flinch while eating within the confines of illusory adobe walls, Tex-Mex home cookery is a welcomed alternative. In some cases it may take a lot of time to prepare and ingredients may be difficult to obtain, but the savory results speak for themselves.

Tomatillos, (opposite, upper right) are the best of both worlds. Known as the "Mexican tomato," this hybrid combines the juice and pulp of a tomato with the flavor and sting of a medium hot chile pepper. Because of their popularity and versatility tomatillos are becoming widely available (just be sure to peel off the paper, lantern-like shroud that encompasses the fruit before using). Napolitas — young, succulent cactus leaves — are a popular ingredient used in seafood, omelets, jellies and candies. They are available in jars in supermarkets, but if you prefer to harvest your own, remove the prickly spines (wear heavy gloves!) with a paring knife under water. Boil until tender and slice into strips. The molcajete, a Mexican mortar and pestle, is made from volcanic stone and is used to grind up chile peppers and spices into pastes or powders.

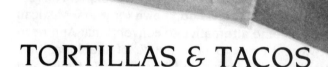

TORTILLAS & TACOS

If rice is the staff of life in the Orient, then corn tortillas are the backbone of Mexico. Having migrated North across the Rio Grande into Texas, the tortilla was integrated as the workhorse of Tex-Mex cookery. In parts of Texas, it can be found on the breakfast, lunch and dinner table as well as being the basis for all snacks in between. The tortilla is rolled up, deep fried, dipped and used as a general all-purpose tool for soppin' up. It's been called the "Mexican Lunchbox" because virtually anything edible may be put inside this flexible frisbee — and later consumed. When eaten with beans the innocuous tortilla becomes a nearly perfect food, insuring the health of those whose diet lacks meat. The amino acids found in both corn and beans complement each other, making a well-rounded protein that the ancient Aztecs and Mayans built their empires upon.

Traditionally, tortillas are handmade, requiring about fifty pats to per tortilla. If you walk the streets of Mexico, the rhythmic patting of hands making tortillas can still be heard. "It was a three o'clock in the morning job," as one tortilla maker put it, "and if, in the old days, a woman couldn't make tortillas, her chances for marriage were grim." This ancient art form requires patience and practice.

The tedious tortilla-making process began by boiling parched corn kernels in limed water. The lime loosened the skins (and, coincidentally, enhanced the usable protein value and taste of the tortilla. It is speculated that this phenomenon was discovered accidentally when some charcoal from the fire or pieces of limestone rocks — used to contain the fire — found their way into the pot). After the skins were removed, the blanched kernels were hand-ground into a paste between a metate (a flat stone surface) and a mano (a type of stone rolling pin). The resulting flour, called masa, was mixed with water until pliable and rolled into two-inch balls. Flattening the balls by gently tossing them from hand to hand rapidly, a tortilla maker, like a pizza dough thrower, stretched the ball into a disc. The finished product was then placed on a comal (a stone grill) and cooked briefly.

Today, tortilla factories found throughout the Southwest and Texas have stream-lined the task of tortilla making. Frozen, canned and fresh-made tortillas are now available on most grocers' shelves. But to obtain that truly fresh-made taste, tortillas are best made at home. Fortunately, the tortilla press and Masa Harina flour (a

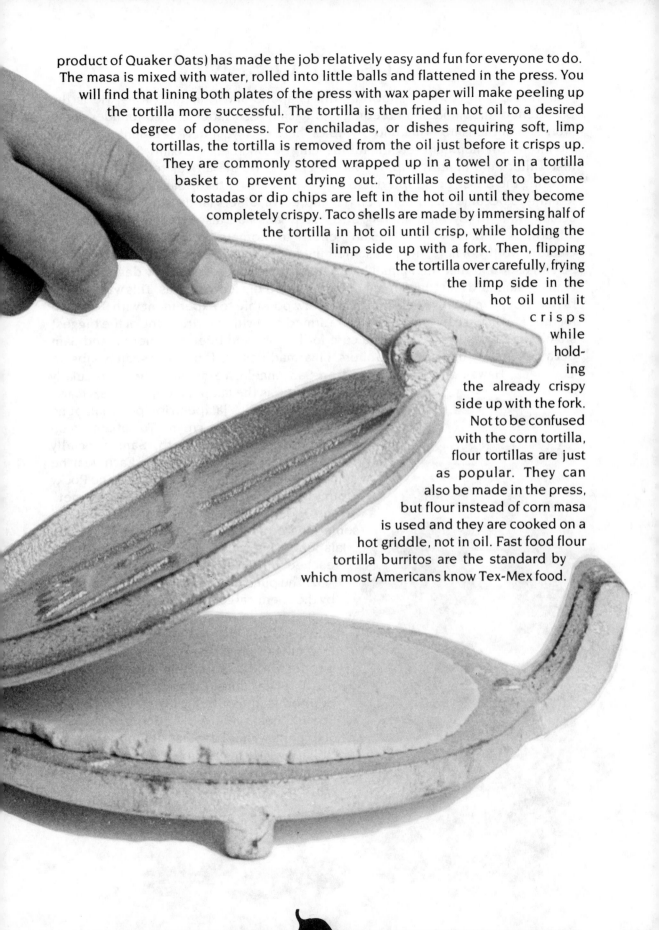

product of Quaker Oats) has made the job relatively easy and fun for everyone to do. The masa is mixed with water, rolled into little balls and flattened in the press. You will find that lining both plates of the press with wax paper will make peeling up the tortilla more successful. The tortilla is then fried in hot oil to a desired degree of doneness. For enchiladas, or dishes requiring soft, limp tortillas, the tortilla is removed from the oil just before it crisps up. They are commonly stored wrapped up in a towel or in a tortilla basket to prevent drying out. Tortillas destined to become tostadas or dip chips are left in the hot oil until they become completely crispy. Taco shells are made by immersing half of the tortilla in hot oil until crisp, while holding the limp side up with a fork. Then, flipping the tortilla over carefully, frying the limp side in the hot oil until it crisps while hold- ing the already crispy side up with the fork. Not to be confused with the corn tortilla, flour tortillas are just as popular. They can also be made in the press, but flour instead of corn masa is used and they are cooked on a hot griddle, not in oil. Fast food flour tortilla burritos are the standard by which most Americans know Tex-Mex food.

JALAPENO SAM

In Texas, Sam Lewis is known as the Jalapeno and Armadillo King. He is the president of the Armadillo Breeding and Racing Association and co-founder of the World Championship Armadillo Olympics (held each year in New Braunfels, Texas). His interest in thoroughbred armadillo racing began when, as a child, Sam caught his first 'diller on a hunting trip. He was fascinated by the articulated leather armor covering the beast; he adopted it for the summer. Eventually Sam's initial curiosity led him to become an authority on the subject of 'dillers (at the time very little was actually known). By the mid-1960's research labs had also become interested in armadillos, in part because of Sam's efforts to promote the odd little animal as a creature worthy of note, not just something to be crushed unmercifully on the road. Scientists found that the animal had a body temperature just a few degrees lower than humans and that ten percent of them carried the leprosy virus. This was a major breakthrough in leprosy research. It was now possible to experiment with a vaccine for the skin disease by innoculating the armadillos with the virus. One of the biggest stumbling blocks in discovering a cure for leprosy had been conquered, and Sam became one of the main suppliers of armadillos to leprosy research labs in Louisiana, Hawaii and China. Based on San Angelo, Texas, his other particularly unique "hobby" is the jalapeno pepper. He's made a new career selling jalapeno lollipops, jalapeno jelly and jalapeno ice cream. To satiate President Reagan's sweet tooth, Sam specially created the jalapeno jellybean. Each year he hosts The Great Jalapeno Lickoff and The Rocky Mountain Oyster Fryoff; both are "gourmet" events not to be missed. If you ever need something promoted, sold or talked about, the Jalapeno King will do it in style. Sam can be reached in San Angelo, Texas at (915) 658-1432. The punch in Sam's lollipops is delivered by the chemical compound capsaicin (the hot stuff founds in peppers that puts your taste buds on red alert and makes them able to leap tall buildings). Intelligentsia of the chile pepper world calibrate this "torque factor" in Scoville heat units. For example, a jalapeno pepper is rated between 2000 and 3000 Scoville heat units. A mild poblano is about 500 units. The jalapeno lollipops rate a titillating 1000 heat units — so small children are advised to lick with jurisprudence. The jelly beans? A bit hotter . . .

TEQUILA

Tequila is distilled from the agave (a species of yucca) plant. There are light and gold tequilas, and an infamous variation called mezcal that has a little worm in the bottle. The working man's drink in Mexico, tequila has been readily adopted as a favorite in the Southwest and Texas. It's usually served in shot glasses, with a saltshaker and a plate of limes or lemons on the side. The ritual that accompanies the drink is as follows: lick the space between your thumb and forefinger, or a spot on the back of your hand. Sprinkle a little bit of salt onto the moistened skin. "Shoot" a shot of tequila, bite into a lime wedge and lick some of the salt from your hand. Repeat the procedure until you can't. And remember . . . ancient legend promises that if, when you reach the bottom of the bottle, you also eat the worm, you will be elevated to a higher level — one rarely visited by those North of the border!

APPETIZERS

A red salsa and tortilla chips (to tantalize the taste buds) start off any Tex-Mex meal, sometimes followed by a small salad (guacamole) or side dish. Here is a collection guaranteed to whet your appetite for the main course.

JALAPENO EGGS

1 onion, sliced and broken into rings
3/4 cup white vinegar
jalapenos, sliced
pimientos, sliced (optional)
3/4 cup jalapeño juice
8 eggs

Bring the eggs to a rolling boil. Cover and turn off burner. Let sit for about 20-25 minutes. Meanwhile, slice jalapenos and onion. Peel eggs while hot. Do not cool them, except just enough to handle. Place in a wide mouth salad dressing jar alternating with layers of jalapenos, onions and pimientos. Bring vinegar and jalapeno juice to a boil in a small saucepan. Pour over eggs immediately. Cover and refrigerate about 2 weeks. If you want to fix more than 8 eggs, remember that the liquid must always be half jalapeno juice and half vinegar. Do not use water. If you don't have enough jalapeno juice, use more vinegar. Work fast and keep eggs as hot as you can because it makes the eggs tough when they are pickled cold.

Emma Whitehead and Betty Moon

JALAPENO APPETIZER

1 (6-1/2-ounce) can tuna, drained and mashed
1 hard boiled egg, grated
1/4 cup celery, minced
2 tablespoons onion, grated
1/4 cup Miracle Whip
1/2 teaspoon Worcestershire sauce
1/2 teaspoon seasoned salt
dash Tabasco
10 mild jalapenos
paprika

Mix thoroughly all ingredients but jalapeños and paprika; set aside. Rinse jalapenos, cut in half and scrape out seeds. Rinse again, drain and pat dry with paper towel. Pile tuna stuffing on jalapeno halves. Garnish with paprika. Chill before serving. For variety, add 1/2 ground nuts and 2/3 cup grated cheese.

Betty Davis and Richie Bell

FRIED JALAPENO PEPPERS

1 egg
1/2 cup milk
1/2 teaspoon Savory salt
1/2 teaspoon garlic salt
2 tablespoons Salad Supreme (this is an all-purpose seasoning made by Schilling)
2 cups any pancake mix
2 dozen jalapeno peppers
deep fat or vegetable oil

Combine egg, milk, and Salad Supreme. Beat well. Combine Savory salt, garlic salt and pancake mix in a separate bowl. Dip peppers into liquid, then flour. Repeat. Fry in deep fat or vegetable oil until golden brown.

Ray Moore

JALAPENOED MUSHROOMS

1 can jalapenos
1 jar mushroom caps

Drain "escabeche" (pickling juices) from jalapenos. Heat to boiling point and pour over drained mushroom caps. Let mellow in refrigerator through the day to serve in the evening. The longer they sit, the hotter they get.

Dorothy Gurley

JALAPENO CHEESE LOG

3/4 cup grated very sharp Cheddar cheese
3/4 cup creamed pimiento cheese
3/4 cup creamed English cheese
5 ounces cream cheese
1 tablespoon grated onion
3 canned jalapeno peppers, chopped
1 clove garlic, crushed
1 cup chopped pecans

Leave sharp cheese and cream cheese at room temperature until each is soft. Blend all ingredients well, except the nuts. Stir in nuts last and form into a loaf. Seal in wax paper and refrigerate for 2 days. Remove from refrigerator 3 hours before time to serve. Select a wooden tray or cheese board to serve log with assorted crackers.

Harry Hutchens

PICKLED JALAPENO PEPPERS

jalapeno peppers to fill pint jar
1 cup apple cider vinegar
1/4 cup water
1/4 cup olive oil
1 teaspoon salt
1 teaspoon mixed pickling spices

Wash peppers and pack tightly in sterilized jars. Heat remaining ingredients to boiling and pour over peppers. Seal. Process in boiling water 10 minutes. Remove jar from water and set in draft-free place to cool. This amount of liquid should cover 2 pints.

Mrs. Roy (Eva) Oberman

QUESO

1 pound of white melting cheese such as Monterey Jack, Mozzarella or Havarti
3 tablespoons oil
1 large yellow onion, chopped
1/2 cup sweet bell pepper, chopped
1 pound mushrooms, sliced
1/2 cup heavy cream
flour tortillas

Grate the cheese and place it in a large, shallow oven-proof dish. You may use any white cheese that melts and becomes stringy or you may use a combination of those suggested above. Place the cheese in a preheated 200° oven to slowly melt for 10 minutes. If it is allowed to become too hot, the cheese will separate and become rubbery. Meanwhile, heat the oil in a large frying pan. When hot, sauté the onions and bell pepper for 3-4 minutes over a moderate flame. Stir in the sliced mushrooms and continue cooking over a high flame for 4-5 minutes or until they become moist looking and darken slightly in color. Remove the cheese from the oven. It should look three-quarters melted. Gradually stir in the cream. Add the sauté mixture little by little including the liquid remaining in the pan until all ingredients are thoroughly blended. Serve immediately by spreading on hot, fresh flour tortillas.

Mary Nell Reck

OSINAGA EMPANADAS

3 medium onions, finely chopped
2 ripe tomatoes, chopped
2 green bell peppers, finely chopped
1 can peeled green chilies, finely chopped
1 pound ground beef
2 tablespoons flour
2 tablespoons capers
1 teaspoon sugar
2 cloves garlic, smashed
salt to taste
Tabasco or chili powder to taste

PASTRY DOUGH:
3 cups flour
2 teaspoons baking powder
3 tablespoons sugar
1/2 teaspoon salt
1/2 cup shortening
1/2 cup milk

Fry vegetables in oil in a large skillet. Add meat and brown. Stir in flour, capers, sugar and seasonings. Cook for 15 minutes. Chill to thicken. For pastry dough, mix and sift dry ingredients. Fold in shortening and enough milk so dough doesn't fall apart. Roll out to 1/8" thickness on slightly floured board. Cut out circles 3 to 4 inches in diameter. Place about 1 tablespoon of filling onto the middle of each pastry round. Fold and press edges with a fork. Fry in deep fat until golden brown. Drain on paper and serve. For a variation, fill with apples and sugar or fruit filling instead of meat mixture. Serve as a dessert.

Emma Perez

CHILIGULA CHEESE BALL

1/2 cup chopped pecans
8 ounces cream cheese, softened
3 to 4 garlic cloves, crushed in a garlic press
garlic salt to taste

Mix cheese, crushed garlic and garlic salt well, tasting as you mix. The cheese should be hot with garlic and have a strong flavor. Shape cheese into a ball and press onto serving tray. Cover the cheese ball with chopped pecans and press them in well. Chill thoroughly. Serve as a spread with crackers.

Carol Anne Banning

QUESADILLAS

3 chopped jalapeno peppers
1/2 pound Monterey Jack cheese, grated
1/2 cup chopped parsley
approximately 2 cups masa tortilla dough

Cut the peppers in half lengthwise. Remove the seeds and finely chop the peppers. With a fork, combine chopped peppers with the grated cheese and chopped parsley. As each tortilla is flattened in a press, place two teaspoons of filling in the center of each. Fold over and seal the edges. Water may be needed if the dough is beginning to dry out. Fry the quesadillas in hot oil for about 2 minutes.

Mary Nell Reck

GUAC A WAY

Children love and can easily make this

4 ripe avocados, peeled (soft, not mushy)
1 medium ripe tomato, chopped
1/4 cup sour cream
1/8 cup red onion, chopped fine
1 teaspoon lemon juice
1/4 teaspoon (or to taste) salt
1 level tablespoon chili powder

Put all ingredients in a bowl, tomatoes last, and combine. Serve with corn chips or as an appetizer.

Wendy B. Rothman

JELLIED GUACAMOLE PHILLIPS

3 avocados, peeled and mashed
1 tomato, peeled, seeded and chopped
1 onion, finely chopped
2 tablespoons mayonnaise
2 tablespoons lemon juice
1 teaspoon salt
dash of Tabasco
2 cups cold chicken broth
3 envelopes gelatin
1/2 cup cold chicken broth

Combine avocados, tomato and onion. Add seasonings. Stir in 2 cups cold chicken broth. Sprinkle gelatin over 1/2 cup cold broth to soften. Set the pan over simmering water and stir until it is completely dissolved. Stir the gelatin into the guacamole mixture thoroughly and pour it into a 2-quart ring mold. Chill.

Ann Chreitzberg Sheppard

GUACAMOLE ROBINSON

6 soft avocados (8, if small)
6 minced fresh green onions
1 (4-ounce) can chopped green chilies or 4 fresh green chilies, chopped
garlic salt
pepper
squeeze of fresh lemon
2-3 tomatoes, sliced (optional)
lettuce leaves
tortilla chips

Blend avocados, onions and chilies together, seasoning with garlic salt, pepper and lemon juice to taste. Serve on sliced tomatoes and/or lettuce leaves with tortilla chips as salad.

Mrs. Charles W. (Joan) Robinson

GUACAMOLE (AVOCADO DIP)

2 tablespoons finely minced white, mild onion
1 to 2 chilies, serranos
2 sprigs cilantro
salt to taste
2 medium avocados
1 medium tomato, skinned, seeded, chopped

In a molcajete or blender grind together the onion, chilies, cilantro and salt to a smooth paste. Mash the avocado flesh roughly with the chile paste in the molcajete. Stir in the chopped tomato and onion. If the guacamole is to be served as a dip, put it on the table in the molcajete.

Mary Nell Reck

JELL-O GUACAMOLE

1 box lime Jell-O
boiling water
1 large peeled, pitted and mashed avocado
1 tablespoon grated onion
2 tablespoons grated celery
1/4 teaspoon red pepper or Tabasco
1/2 cup mayonnaise
1 cup sour cream

Dissolve Jell-O in boiling water and set aside. In a large mixing bowl, combine the remaining ingredients and blend well. Add the hot Jell-O. Stir until smooth. Chill. Some like this with 1/2 cup finely chopped nuts.

Sue Sims

SPANISH SALAD

1/2 cup salad oil
1/4 cup cider vinegar
1 teaspoon salt
1 teaspoon garlic salt
juice of 2 lemons
lettuce, torn into pieces
1 avocado, chopped
1 purple onion, sliced
2 tomatoes, quartered

Mix oil, vinegar, salt, garlic salt and lemon juice together two hours before serving. Toss vegetables together and add the dressing.

Joan Stocks Nobles

SAUCES & CONDIMENTS

Sauces are a wonderful addition to any Tex-Mex dish. They may be served on the side for dipping tortilla chips or poured onto an entree to help spice it up. Even straightforward American foods like eggs, omelets, hamburgers and vegetables profit from a spoonful of salsa. All the sauces in this section may be canned, which make them convenient to use on the spur of the moment, but sauces made daily have a freshness and zest sometimes lost in the canning process.

SUSANA'S SALSA SABROSA

This is an excellent all-purpose salsa . . . pour it on everything.

1 cup chopped fresh jalapenos (10 medium jalapenos)
1 cup chopped onions (2-1/2 very large onions)
3 cups chopped tomatoes (6 medium tomatoes)
1/4 cup vinegar
1 clove minced garlic
1 tablespoon fresh chopped cilantro leaves
1/2 tablespoon crushed cumin seeds

Use freshest vegetables possible and chop very fine. Combine all ingredients in glass jar and refrigerate 2 days before using. Salsa will keep refrigerated 2 to 3 weeks and freezes well.

Susan Koster

ALLEGANI'S SALSA PICANTE

5 medium to large fresh tomatoes, chopped
1 bell pepper, de-seeded and chopped fine
1 medium onion, chopped fine
4 fresh jalapenos, de-seeded and chopped
salt and pepper to taste
3 garlic cloves, smashed or chopped fine
1/2 teaspoon cumin seeds or powder (grind seeds before using)
2 tablespoons wine vinegar
1 teaspoon Tabasco

Blend all ingredients slightly in a blender so that the texture is mushy but still chunky.

Jani Schofield

SALSA

1/2 cup cold water
5 small fresh green chilies, finely chopped
2 small fresh red chilies, finely chopped
2 garlic cloves, minced
1 medium tomato, finely chopped
1 medium onion, finely chopped
1 teaspoon salt

Combine all ingredients and mix well.

Mary Nell Reck

CHILE CARIBE SAUCE

Keep a jar handy in the icebox. It serves as a good pre-mixed base for enchilada sauce or chili sauce.

1 cup "chile caribe grind" (coarse) red chile
1-1/2 cups cold water
1 large garlic clove, cut in large pieces
1 teaspoon salt

Blend all ingredients in electric blender for 15 to 20 seconds.

Margaret G. McKenzie

PICO DE GALLO

Pico de Gallo means "peck of the cock." It's a mild sauce with just enough spice to let its presence be known on meats or chalupas.

8 long green chilies, roasted, peeled, deveined and chopped
2 small yellow chilies, roasted, peeled and chopped
5 green onions, chopped (including tops)
5 medium tomatoes, peeled and chopped
1/4 cup chopped, fresh cilantro leaves
2 tablespoons salad oil
1 tablespoon vinegar (red wine)
salt to taste

Combine all ingredients and chill. Will keep at least 2 weeks in refrigerator.

ALL-PURPOSE CHILI SAUCE

2 tablespoons bacon drippings
2 tablespoons flour
3/4 cup pure ground medium hot chile powder (substitute 1/2 cup ground ancho
chile pulp for enchilada sauce)
2 cups beef bouillon or water
3 heaping tablespoons finely chopped onions
4 ounces tomato sauce
1/2 teaspoon salt
2 garlic cloves, crushed
1 pinch oregano
1 pinch ground cumin
dash ground coriander

Heat bacon drippings in a saucepan over medium low heat. Add flour and stir until slightly browned. Add 1/2 chile powder and all the beef bouillon or water. Stir, taste and add remaining chile powder to taste. Put in remaining ingredients and stir constantly. Taste, and adjust seasonings. Simmer for at least ten minutes to leach out flavor. May be used over eggs, meats, enchiladas and tacos.

"P.B."

SALSA RANCHERO

2 tablespoons oil
1/2 cup finely chopped white onions
1/2 clove garlic, crushed and chopped
3 medium tomatoes, peeled, seeded, and finely chopped
1/4 teaspoon sugar
1/2 teaspoon salt
black pepper to taste
1 tablespoon chopped cilantro
2 chile serranos, finely chopped

Heat the oil in a saucepan. Stir in the onion and sauté gently for about 2 minutes. Add the garlic and cook another 2 minutes. Stir in the tomatoes, chilies, sugar, salt, and pepper. Bring the mixture to a boil; reduce to a simmer and continue cooking uncovered for 10-15 minutes (stirring occasionally) or until most of the tomato juices have evaporated and the sauce is a thickened puree. Stir in the cilantro. Taste for seasoning and serve over the warm eggs. This sauce may be refrigerated and served later. It is delicious with tacos, refried beans, or roasted meats. It may also be frozen successfully.

Mary Nell Reck

HOT CHILE SAUCE

4 quarts peeled, chopped tomatoes
2 cups chopped onions
1 cup chopped sweet green pepper
8 hot chile peppers, roasted, peeled and chopped
1 tablespoon finely chopped garlic
1/4 cup sugar
2-1/2 cups vinegar
3 tablespoons celery seeds
1 tablespoon mustard seeds
1 stick cinnamon
1 bay leaf
1 teaspoon whole cloves

Mix vegetables, salt, sugar and spices (tied in a cheesecloth bag). Bring to a boil slowly and simmer until boiled down to half the original volume, stirring frequently. Add vinegar and boil rapidly for 5 minutes, stirring constantly; reduce heat and simmer 5 minutes. Pack into hot, sterile jars and process in boiling water 10 minutes.

Margaret G. McKenzie

HOT CHOW-CHOW

2 quarts cabbage
1 quart green tomatoes
1-1/2 pounds onions
1 pound bell peppers (use mix of
  green and red)
1/4 cup canning salt
3 pounds jalapeno peppers, chopped
1-1/2 quarts white vinegar
2-1/2 cups sugar
2 tablespoons mustard seeds
1 tablespoon celery seeds
1 tablespoon allspice

Chop first 4 vegetables coarsely—measure cabbage and tomatoes after chopping—mix well with salt in a large stone crock or non-metallic container. Let stand overnight in cool place or in refrigerator. Next day, drain but do not rinse. Add jalapeno peppers and mix well. Combine vinegar, sugar, mustard seed, celery seed and allspice in large enamel pan and simmer 20 minutes. Add the vegetable mixture and simmer for 10 minutes, stirring occasionally. Pack quickly into sterilized jars to within 1/2 inch from top, cover with liquid and seal.

Mrs. Thomas H. (Lillian) Hill

JALAPENO PEPPER SAUCE

5 onions, chopped
2 bell peppers, chopped
12 to 14 small ripe peeled tomatoes, chopped
6 garlic cloves, chopped
3/4 cup jalapeno peppers, chopped
1 cup sugar
1 cup vinegar
1 cup cooking oil
1 cup water
4 tablespoons salt
4 teaspoons black pepper

Combine all ingredients and cook 2-1/2 to 3 hours until thick. Pour while hot into sterilized fruit jars and seal.

Jim Heller

CREMA FRESCAS

1 cup sour cream
1 cup whipping cream

Combine sour cream and whipping cream in small bowl and blend well. Cover surface with plastic and let stand at room temperature about 8 hours, then chill until thick, about 24 hours.

Mary Nell Reck

SALSA DE LEGUMBRES FRESCAS

2 large tomatoes, peeled and diced
1 cucumber, peeled and diced
1/2 cup diced green chiles
1/3 cup fine chopped onion
2 tablespoons brown sugar
1/3 cup vinegar
1 teaspoon salt
1/2 teaspoon celery seeds
1/2 teaspoon black pepper

Combine all ingredients and refrigerate in tightly sealed container for several hours

Barbecue Times

TOMATO SAUCE WITH GREEN CHILIES

1 medium onion, minced
1 clove garlic, minced
2 tablespoons vegetable oil
2 cups tomato sauce
1 (4-ounce) can whole green chilies, drained, seeded and minced
1/4 teaspoon salt
1/4 teaspoon dried whole oregano
1/4 teaspoon ground cumin

Sauté onion and garlic in oil in a medium saucepan until tender. Stir in remaining ingredients; simmer, uncovered, 20 minutes, stirring occasionally. Serve warm.

Ella C. Stivers

NINFA'S GREEN SAUCE

12 green peeled Mexican tomatoes (tomatillos)
cilantro leaves
salt
2 chilies (little green ones)
1 onion, chopped
4 avocados
sour cream

Boil tomatoes and chilies 10 minutes. Drain and grind with cilantro and onion. Season with salt and let cool. Peel avocados and add to the sauce. Blend in sour cream to taste.

Mary Nell Reck

PEPPER RELISH

18 red peppers, stemmed and seeded
12 green sweet or bell peppers, stemmed and seeded
12 medium-sized onions, peeled
2 cups vinegar
2 cups sugar
3 tablespoons salt

Grind peppers and onions. Cover with boiling water and let stand 5 minutes. Drain. Add vinegar, sugar and salt and boil 5 minutes. Pour into sterilized jars and seal.

Mrs. Bent (Grace) Laune

JALAPENO JELLY

4-6 large jalapeno peppers
4 green bell peppers
1 cup apple cider vinegar
5 cups sugar
1 (6-ounce) bottle of pectin
green food coloring (optional)

Seed and devein all peppers and chop fine. Liquify in a blender 1/4 of peppers with 1/4 cup of vinegar. Repeat until all are liquified. Mix liquified pepper/vinegar mixture with sugar and boil slowly for ten minutes in a 2-quart kettle. Add one bottle of pectin. Boil hard for five minutes, stirring. Remove from heat. Skim foam with a metal spoon (add an optional few drops of green food coloring). Put in sterilized jelly jars and seal with wax.

Margaret McKenzie

PRICKLY PEAR JELLY

ripe cactus fruit
1 package (1-3/4 ounces) powdered
** fruit pectin**
4 cups sugar
1 teaspoon lemon juice

Using tongs to hold cactus, remove spines by scraping with paring knife under running water. Cut each fruit into several pieces. Place in saucepan. Add water to cover completely. Boil for 15-20 minutes, then strain through jelly bag. In a saucepan, combine 3 cups of the strained liquid and the pectin. Bring to a hard boil. Add 4 cups sugar and the lemon juice. Bring to a rolling boil (one that may not be stirred down) and boil for 5 minutes. Skim and pour into prepared jelly glasses.

Nell Walker

ON THE SIDE

Refried beans and rice are probably the most well-known companion dishes for Tex-Mex entrees, but there are others. In many of the finer restaurants, a host of soups and prepared vegetables expand the scope of this cooking style.

FRIJOLES (REFRIED BEANS)

Frijoles is a Mexican term for any type of cooked beans. The most common variety used to make frijoles is the pinto bean, but kidney beans, navy beans and black beans are also used. Refried beans are slightly mashed frijoles mixed with melted lard and "fried" until a smooth consistency is reached. Frijoles can be served whole, slightly mashed or puréed. Spices may be added to them or they may be cooked just "as is." This versatile bean paste may be used on tostadas and chalupas, in tacos, burritos and enchiladas. It's a standard side dish to any Tex-Mex entree.

1 pound pinto beans
1 small can tomato sauce (optional)
1 large onion, chopped
grated Longhorn cheese to taste
4 tablespoons pure lard

Wash and clean beans. Let beans soak overnight in four quart pot. Cook slowly until tender, adding boiling water if necessary (cold water darkens beans). When beans are done, drain and save the broth. Mash up beans to desired consistency and pour in 4 tablespoons of smoking-hot lard. Mix well, pour reserved broth back in, mix again and stir over low heat. Cover with optional tomato sauce, a layer of finely chopped onions and a generous layer of grated cheese. Cover pot and heat until cheese melts. Serve as a dip with tortilla chips or on Huevos Rancheros or chalupas.

Rudy Gonzalez

MEXICAN BEAN SOUP

1 tablespoon bacon drippings
2 green onions, cut in 1-inch lengths
2 cloves garlic, minced
1 medium green pepper, coarsely chopped
1/4 cup tomato, peeled, seeded and chopped
1 cup cooked pinto beans, cooked in water with garlic
3 cups bean broth
1 teaspoon dried coriander, crushed
salt to taste
Garnishes:
1/4 cup chopped onions
1/2 cup grated Monterey Jack cheese

Sauté onions, garlic and green pepper in drippings until slightly soft, 3-5 minutes. Add tomatoes, beans and broth, coriander and salt. Bring to a boil and boil briskly, uncovered, 10 minutes.

Linda Ryan Butter

PECOS BEAN SOUP

1 pound dry pinto beans
2-1/2 quarts water
1/2 cup chopped onion
1 clove garlic, minced
1 large piece bacon rind
1 tablespoon chili powder
1/2 teaspoon oregano
1 (4-ounce) can peeled, seeded, diced green chile peppers
2 teaspoons salt

Wash beans and soak overnight in cold water; drain. Put beans in a large kettle, add 2-1/2 quarts water and simmer 1 hour. Add onion, garlic, bacon rind, chili powder, oregano and chile peppers. Cover and simmer 2 hours, adding salt the last hour.

Philip Morris, Inc.

SPANISH FRIED RICE

3 small cloves garlic
1 teaspoon comino seeds
1-1/2 cups uncooked, not enriched, rice
1 medium onion, chopped
1/8 cup cooking oil
1 tomato, diced
1/4 teaspoon salt
1 cup water

Crush garlic and comino seeds in a molcajete with a little water and set aside. Sauté dry rice and onion in oil until light brown in color. Stir constantly while frying. Add tomato, salt, garlic mixture and water. Cover. Cook slowly for about 20 minutes. Do not stir.

Dana Lilly

MONTEREY RICE

1 cup uncooked rice
2 (4-ounce) cans green chilies, chopped
2 cups sour cream
3/4 pound Monterey Jack cheese

Preheat oven to 350°. Cook rice according to directions on package. Mix chopped chilies with sour cream. Spoon thin layer of rice in buttered casserole, approximately 10 x 10 inches; add layer of sour cream mixture followed by layer of sliced Jack cheese. Repeat layers, finishing with rice on top. Bake 30 minutes. Parmesan cheese may be sprinkled over top the last 5 minutes of baking.

Mrs. Bent (Grace) Laune

REALLY THICK GAZPACHO

1 clove garlic
2 teaspoons salt
1/2 cup chopped fresh mushrooms
4 tablespoons olive oil
1 cup finely chopped onions
2 cups finely chopped tomatoes
1-1/4 cups finely chopped green peppers
1 cup finely chopped celery
2 teaspoons chopped chives
1 tablespoon chopped parsley
1 teaspoon freshly ground black pepper
1 teaspoon Tabasco
1 teaspoon Worcestershire sauce
1/2 cup tarragon or wine vinegar
3 cups tomato juice
croutons

Crush garlic in 1 teaspoon salt. Sauté mushrooms in olive oil until lightly browned. Combine mushrooms and garlic with remaining ingredients in glass bowl. Cover and chill several hours before serving. Serve with croutons. Do NOT chop vegetables in blender as this is good with fresh vegetables in small pieces rather than pureed. This is better for you than an apple a day.

Mrs. John A. (Nancy) Greenway

GAZPACHO

1/4 cup oil
2 tablespoons lemon juice
6 cups tomato juice (1 large can)
2 cups beef bouillon (2 cubes in 2 cups water)
1 cup minced onion
1 cup minced celery
1 cup minced green pepper
1 cup diced tomato
2 tablespoons Worcestershire sauce
1 tablespoon salt

Beat oil and lemon juice together. Add all other ingredients. Refrigerate at least 3 hours before serving.

Billie Cawley

VERA CRUZ TOMATOES

3 strips bacon; reserve 2 tablespoons drippings
1/4 cup chopped onion
8 ounces fresh spinach, snipped
1/2 cup sour cream
1/4 teaspoon hot pepper sauce
4 medium tomatoes
1/2 cup shredded Mozzarella cheese (2 ounces)

Preheat oven to 375°. Cook bacon until crisp. Drain. Crumble bacon and set aside. Cook onion in reserved drippings until tender. Stir in spinach and cook covered until tender, 3-5 minutes. Remove from heat. Stir in sour cream, bacon and pepper sauce. Cut tops from tomatoes, remove centers, leaving shells. Drain. Salt shells and fill with spinach mixture. Place in 8 x 8 x 2 inch baking dish. Bake 20-25 minutes. Top with shredded cheese. Bake 2-3 minutes or until cheese is melted.

Mrs. Ralph (Martha Lee) Smith

PAPAS CON CHORIZOS

1/2 pound California potatoes, diced
1/2 pound chorizos (Mexican sausage)
1/2 cup chopped yellow onion
2 long red peppers or 2 fresh jalapeno peppers
4 tablespoons frozen peas
1 bay leaf
1/4 cup chicken stock
1/4 cup tomato sauce
salt and black pepper to taste

Peel and dice the potatoes. Rinse them well under cold water and set aside to drain. Crumble the chorizos and cook over moderate heat, stirring to break up. Cook them slowly for 10-15 minutes until brown and the fat cooks out into the pan. Remove the cooked meat with a slotted spoon. Coarsely chop the onion and place it in the frying pan with the oil from the sausage. Cook it over moderate heat until it becomes soft and translucent. Add the drained potatoes and cook them, stirring, for 7-8 minutes or until they are just beginning to become tender. Return the chorizos to the skillet. Stir in the chopped peppers, peas, bay leaf, chicken stock and tomato sauce. Bring to gentle boil and simmer, uncovered, for 10-15 minutes or until most of the moisture has evaporated. Place the potatoes on a serving plate and garnish with thin slices of avocado and crumbled white cheese.

Sra. Aurora Martinez

AVOCADO SOUP

1 large avocado, peeled and diced
1-1/2 cups chicken broth
1 clove garlic, crushed
2 cups light cream

Put avocado, chicken broth and garlic in electric blender and blend 15 seconds at high speed. Remove small part of cover to blender and add cream while blending. Chill well. Serve with chopped chives and paprika on top.

Mrs. Ashley (Molly) Denton

PUEBLA STEW

2 pounds pork cubes
1-1/4 teaspoons salt
1/2 cup water
1 can tomatoes, undrained

1 teaspoon chili powder
2 tablespoons shortening
1 clove garlic
1 cup onion, chopped
1 teaspoon oregano
dash of cayenne
avocado, sliced
small raw potatoes

Brown pork cubes on all sides in 1 tablespoon shortening in a heavy skillet over moderate heat, turning pieces as needed to brown evenly. Add 1 teaspoon salt, minced garlic and water. Cook, covered, slowly until pork is tender, 1 to 1-1/4 hours. Meanwhile, pan-fry onion in remaining shortening until tender, but not brown. Add tomatoes, oregano, chili powder, 1-1/2 teaspoons sugar, cayenne and the remaining salt. Cook until flavors blend, about 15 minutes. Add to pork; add small raw potatoes and cook until done. Serve topped with avocado slices.

Pablo Albores

CALABACITAS CON CREMA

1-1/2 pounds zucchini
1/2 cup chopped yellow onion
1/2 teaspoon salt
1/4 teaspoon black pepper
4 sprigs cilantro
2 sprigs fresh mint
1/2-inch stick cinnamon
4 whole cloves
2 whole chilies, serranos
1/2 cup half-and-half

Wash and trim the zucchini; cut it into large chunks. Chop the onion. In a sauté pan, combine the zucchini and onion with all the remaining ingredients. Stir to combine. Cover and simmer over low heat for about 30 minutes. You will need to scrape the bottom of the pan from time to time to prevent sticking. If the pan becomes dry, it may be necessary to add a little water. When the vegetables are cooked, the liquid should be completely evaporated. Remove the chilies, cloves and cinnamon. Serve hot, garnished with a few sprigs of fresh cilantro.

Mary Nell Reck

MENUDO

3 to 4 pounds cleaned tripe, preferably white and thick
water
1-1/2 teaspoons salt
1/2 teaspoon whole black peppercorns
1 to 2 pork knuckles or pork feet
1 bay leaf
1/2 teaspoon comino seeds
1 cup chopped onion
2 pods garlic, minced
1 large can golden hominy
1 to 2 whole, imported Japanese hot peppers
1/3 cup chili powder

Dice tripe into bite-size pieces and place in large boiler. Cover with cold water and bring to a boil. Boil rapidly for 10 minutes. Drain tripe, throw water away and start all over again. This time add salt and peppercorns. Add pork knuckles or pork feet and boil for 4 hours or until tripe is tender. Add water if necessary to keep a soupy mixture. Add remaining ingredients and simmer for 45 minutes. Add 1/3 cup chili powder and boil for another 15 minutes. This soup is famous in Mexico for its restorative powers.

Frankie Lee Harlow

JALAPENO CORN BREAD

1 cup buttermilk
1 cup cornmeal
1 cup flour
3 tablespoons sugar
1 teaspoon baking powder
1/2 teaspoon soda
2 eggs
4 tablespoons melted shortening
1 cup cream-style corn
1 cup grated Cheddar cheese
3 diced jalapeno peppers or 1 can diced green chile peppers
1 (4-ounce) jar sliced pimientos

Combine buttermilk and cornmeal, let stand 30 minutes. Preheat oven to 375°. Add remaining ingredients. Mix well. Pour into 9 x 12-inch greased pan and bake 30 minutes.

John Sheldon

MEXICAN CORN BREAD

1 cup cornmeal
1 cup cream-style corn
1/2 teaspoon soda
1/2 teaspoon salt
1/2 cup salad oil
2 cups grated cheese
2 eggs
1 small can green chilies, cut fine

Mix all ingredients and pour into hot, greased pan or into muffin tins. Bake at 400° for 45 minutes.

Bergine Gatlin

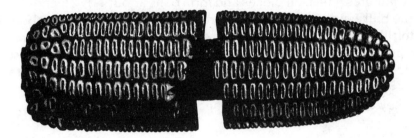

THE CLASSICS

You will find that the dishes you have been paying top dollar for in restaurants are deceptively easy and inexpensive to make at home. Some take a little time to prepare (like the chilies rellenos) but the finished products are affordably rewarding.

MEXICAN CORN TORTILLAS

2 cups Quaker masa harina
1 cup warm water

Combine masa harina and water; knead to blend well. (If necessary, add a little more water to hold dough together.) Shape into 12 balls. Roll out or press each ball between 2 sheets of waxed paper in a tortilla press, or pat out by hand to form a 6-inch circle. Fry on hot, lightly greased griddle until lightly browned (30 seconds to 1 minute per side). Tortillas should be soft and pliable. Makes 12 tortillas.

Quaker Masa Harina

TORTILLAS DE HARINA DE TRIGO (FLOUR TORTILLAS)

1/2 cup shortening
1 pound all-purpose flour, at room temperature
2 teaspoons salt
1 cup warm water

Sift the flour into a large mixing bowl. Cut the shortening into 1-inch pieces and place into the bowl of flour. Using your fingers, rub the shortening well into the flour until it has a uniformly coarse texture. Dissolve the salt in the cup of warm water. The water should be about 115°. Add the water to the flour mixture. Knead the ingredients together in the bowl until they form a solid mass. Place the dough on a lightly floured surface and continue kneading about 3 minutes. The dough will not be smooth. Cover and set the dough aside for 2 hours at room temperature. Knead the dough again for about a minute. The second kneading will make it smooth. Cover again and let stand for about 10 minutes. Pinch off pieces and form balls about 1-1/2 inches in diameter. Press out the ball evenly on a floured board and roll to a diameter of about 7 inches. Place the tortillas on an ungreased griddle over medium-high flame. There should be a slight sizzling sound when they first touch the griddle. Cook for about 20 seconds on the first side and 10 seconds on the second side. Stack them and cover with a napkin. Just before serving, place them in a steamer for about 5 minutes to reheat and re-soften. They can be made well in advance and reheated successfully.

Mary Nell Reck

TACOS CON POLLO

1 (three-pound) fryer
1 carrot, cut in quarters
1 onion, cut in quarters
1 stalk celery, cut in quarters
1 clove garlic
1 bay leaf
1 tablespoon salt
1 teaspoon white peppercorns

Place the chicken and all the seasoning ingredients in a stockpot. Cover with water. With the lid off, bring to a boil. Reduce the heat until the water simmers. Cover and cook gently for about an hour or until the chicken is tender. Let the chicken cool. Using your hands, remove the meat from the bones. Return the bones to the broth and continue simmering another two hours. Strain the broth into jars and freeze for using in soups and sauces.

11 to 18 fresh corn tortillas, uncooked
2 cups cooked chicken
1 cup grated Monterey Jack cheese
oil for frying

Place about 1/4 cup of cooked chicken in each fresh tortilla. Sprinkle with about 2 tablespoons of grated cheese. Roll the tortilla carefully. Place in the frying pan with about 1/4 inch of hot oil. Fry the tacos until golden, turning to brown evenly on all sides.

Mary Nell Reck

TERLINGUA TACOS

1 pound ground meat
1 small onion, chopped
1 small tomato, diced
1/2 teaspoon comino seeds
1 package Lawry's Taco Seasoning
1 cup water
garlic salt to taste
1 package corn tortillas
1 pint sour cream

Brown meat and onions in skillet. Add tomato, seasonings and water. Simmer for 25 minutes. Soften tortillas one at a time in a small amount of butter or oil in another skillet. Lay softened tortillas on plate. Fill with meat mixture and 1 tablespoon sour cream. Fold over and serve. Option: Chop jalapenos (fine) and blend into sour cream.

Glen Young

BREAKFAST TACOS

There is no defined recipe for Breakfast Tacos. Their creation is dictated by the state of mind of the breakfast cook and the availability of leftovers. To make a Breakfast Taco, take a flour tortilla and lay it out flat. Put a mixture of eggs (any style) meat (hamburger, bacon, ham, Mexican sausage, etc.) browned potatoes, stir-fried vegetables, diced green chilies or what have you. Sprinkle on some salsa. Roll up and eat. With a few alterations of ingredients, the highly adaptable Breakfast Taco can become the Lunch Taco, the Dinner Taco and the Midnight-Snack Taco. According to Le Beast, who gave us this non-recipe, the Breakfast Taco is theoretically a perpetual motion machine "because you can take leftover Midnight-Snack Tacos, dice 'em up, and put 'em into Breakfast Tacos which can be diced up into Lunch Tacos which can be diced up . . ."

Le Beast (Joe Aronson) is a master cook from Austin, Texas, who has catered all the Willie Nelson Fourth of July Picnics, serving barbecue to 60,000 concert-goers.

Le Beast

HUEVOS RANCHEROS

4 to 6 tablespoons corn oil
6 small tortillas
6 eggs
Salsa Ranchera, warmed (see Sauces)
jalapeno or poblano for garnish

Heat 2 tablespoons of oil in a frying pan. Fry the tortillas lightly on both sides (they should not become crisp). Drain them on paper towels and keep them warm in a 170° oven. Add additional oil to the frying pan. When it is hot, fry the eggs over moderately-high heat until the whites are set and the yolks are still soft. Remove the eggs with a spatula and place an egg on each warm tortilla. Surround the egg with the Salsa Ranchera and garnish with a thin strip of jalapeno or poblano.

Mary Nell Reck

CHILIQUILLES

10 to 12 tortillas, cut into strips about 1/2 inch wide and 2 inches long
1 large onion, chopped
4 tablespoons butter
1 dozen eggs, beaten
1/4 cup milk
1/2 teaspoon garlic juice
salt and pepper to taste
1 can green chilies, chopped
1/2 cup grated sharp cheese
1 tomato, peeled and chopped

Sauté tortilla strips and chopped onion in butter until soft. Beat eggs, add milk, garlic juice, salt and pepper. Pour mixture over tortilla mixture. Cook, stirring until soft scrambled. Add green chilies, cheese and tomato. Stir until cheese melts.

Mrs. Charles (Bette) Bowen

CHALUPAS (BEAN)

corn tortillas
cooking oil
lettuce, shredded
tomatoes, diced
sharp cheese, grated
refried beans
tomatilla sauce

Fry a package of tortillas in cooking oil until crisp. Let drain on paper towels. Bean chalupas are made by spreading beans on top of the fried tortillas, then topping with lettuce, tomatoes, cheese and tomatillo sauce.

Anna Medina

FAJITAS

Fajitas are to Texans what Coney Island hot dogs are to New Yorkers. Fajita means "belt." Butchers know it as beef skirt or skirt steak cut from the rib area. The meat is sometimes marinated, always charbroiled, sliced into strips and rolled up in flour tortillas with a few dashes of meat sauce. It sounds like a humble dish, but fajitas are rapidly becoming one of the most popular foods in Texas.

several pounds of skirt steak (preferably the inside skirt, it's more flavorful)
Burgundy
onion, chopped
bell pepper, chopped
Italian dressing
red and black pepper
paprika
garlic powder
salt
flour tortillas
barbecue, pico de gallo or picante sauce

Trim excess fat off meat. Marinate meat in mixture of Burgundy, onions, bell peppers and dressing (in quantities to taste) overnight in refrigerator. Wrap meat in aluminum foil and cook over coals for 1 to 2 hours, after met is well-steamed, remove foil, season with red and black pepper, paprika, garlic powder and salt. Grill meat unwrapped for 10 to 15 minutes over coals and hickory chips (for smoke flavor). Slice meat in thin strips, place some in a flour tortilla, sprinkle on favorite barbecue, pico de gallo or picante sauce and roll up. Fajita purists shun marinating and steaming the meat. They will instead cook the skirt steak like a brisket in a pit. When almost done, they will charbroil meat over hickory chips, slice thin and serve rolled up in flour tortilla with sauce.

Terry Kelly

PETANA

1 tenderized round steak
1 medium onion
2 small bell peppers
1 stick butter or margarine
salt
pepper
8 flour tortillas

Cut meat into finger-sized pieces. Season with salt and pepper to taste and set aside. Slice onion thick and cut slices in half. Cut bell peppers into strips, discarding seeds. Melt butter or margarine in medium-low heated skillet and sauté onions and peppers for about 5 minutes. Remove vegetables from skillet and brown steak slices in remaining grease. Return vegetables to skillet and stir together. Cover and reduce heat to low or simmer for about 30 minutes. Stir occasionally. Remove to a warm platter or serve directly from the skillet at the table. Lightly butter and salt warm flour tortilla. Place spoonful of meat and vegetables on tortilla and roll. You may dip your petana in the drippings for even more flavor.

Kay Bates

TAMALES

30 to 36 green or dried yellow corn husks
2 cups shortening or lard
8 cups masa harina
3 cups chicken broth or water, heated to lukewarm (95°)
2 tablespoons baking powder
1 tablespoon salt
Picadillo (recipe follows)
salsa (optional)

If using dried corn husks, soak overnight in enough cold water to cover. Beat shortening in large bowl of electric mixer until light and fluffy, about 5 minutes. Gradually add masa harina alternately with chicken broth, adding the broth in slow, steady stream. (If broth is too warm, dough will separate. If dough does separate, refrigerate before adding remaining masa and broth.) Stir in baking powder and salt. Drain corn husks and dry between 2 dish towels. Place in single layer on work surface. Divide dough among husks, spreading on wider half of each and leaving 1-inch border on one long side. Spoon 1 to 2 tablespoons picadillo down center of dough. Fold in long sides of husk, then fold narrow half over to make packets open at one end. Arrange tamales upright in steamer. Cover with dish towel, then steamer lid, and steam over gently boiling water until done, 1-1/2 to 2 hours. Transfer to platter and serve with bowl of salsa.

Mary Nell Reck

PICADILLO

2 tablespoons vegetable oil
1 medium onion, chopped
1-1/2 pounds lean ground beef
1 (16-ounce) can tomatoes, undrained
1 (6-ounce) can tomato paste
1/2 cup raisins
2 tablespoons vinegar
2 tablespoons chili powder or to taste
1 teaspoon cinnamon
1 teaspoon ground cumin
1 teaspoon sugar
pinch of ground cloves
2 cups sliced mushrooms
1/2 cup toasted chopped almonds
2 to 3 jalapeno peppers, seeded and finely chopped

Heat oil in Dutch oven or large saucepan over medium heat. Add onion and sauté until softened, about 5 minutes. Increase heat, add beef and brown well. Add remaining ingredients except mushrooms, almonds and jalapenos; cover and simmer 1 hour. Stir in mushrooms and simmer another 30 minutes. Blend in almonds and peppers.

Mary Nell Reck

NACHOS

corn torilla chips
1/4 pound Monterey Jack cheese
1 or 2 jalapeno peppers, diced fine

Lay chips out on a cookie tray. Place a small piece of cheese on each chip. Top with a small piece of pepper. Broil in oven until cheese melts.

Nana

YOUR BASIC CHEESE ENCHILADA

1 pound Monterey Jack cheese, cut into 1/4" cubes
1-1/2 cups onion, chopped
1/2 cup green chile strips (optional)
2 cups All-Purpose Chile Sauce (See Sauces)
18 corn tortillas
yellow cheese
cooking oil
toothpicks

Prepare cheese and onions. Heat 1/4-inch of cooking oil until just smokey hot in a small skillet. Gently place a corn tortilla in oil and fry briefly (1 to 2 seconds on each side) until limp. Don't let the edges crisp up because you will break the tortilla when it's rolled. Remove, and drain excess grease on paper toweling. Place a generous portion of cheese and onions (and optional green chile strips) along the diameter of the tortilla. Fold one edge of tortilla over mixture, roll up and pin the seam shut by inserting a toothpick all the way through. Place rolled tortillas seam-side down, side by side, on a 9 x 12-inch baking dish. Pour sauce over all, making sure entire dish bottom is also covered with sauce. Sprinkle with remaining onions and cheese, and some grated yellow cheese for color. Bake in preheated oven at 350° for about 15 minutes or until cheese melts. Serve hot, topped with sour cream; and frijoles and rice on the side.

"P.B."

SOUR CREAM ENCHILADAS

2 tablespoons cooking oil
2 pounds lean ground beef
1 onion
1 green bell pepper, finely diced
salt and pepper to taste
2 tablespoons picante sauce (see Sauces)
1 tablespoon chili powder
1/2 teaspoon cumin powder
1 tablespoon garlic powder
4 drops Tabasco sauce
1 tablespoon Worcestershire sauce
1/2 cup rice sliced, pitted olives
12 corn tortillas
1/4 cup picante sauce
2 cups water
1/4 pound butter
4 tablespoons flour
1-1/2 cups milk
1 pint sour cream

1 pound grated mild Cheddar cheese
1/2 cup whole, pitted ripe olives

In heavy skillet, heat oil; then brown beef. Add onion and bell pepper, cooking until soft. Add salt, pepper, 2 tablespoons picante sauce, chili powder, Worcestershire sauce, Tabasco and sliced ripe olives. Simmer for 5 minutes. Blend 1/4 cup picante sauce in 2 cups water. Place tortillas in water and soak for a few minutes. Melt butter and stir in flour. Add milk and cook until thickened. Blend in sour cream and heat 1 minute. Select a large casserole dish and grease lightly. Drain each tortilla slightly and fill with 2 tablespoons of meat mixture. Sprinkle some cheese (reserving 1/2 pound) over meat and fold over enchilada style. Arrange in dish and top with sour cream sauce. Sprinkle with cheese. Bake 25 minutes at 375°.

Becky Hodges

CHICKEN ENCHILADAS WITH SOUR CREAM

1 pound chicken breasts (fresh or frozen)
1 small carrot
1 sprig parsley
4 tablespoons olive oil
1 clove chopped garlic
1-1/2 cups canned green chilies (3-4 ounce can)
5 ripe tomatoes, skinned and chopped
2 medium onions, chopped fine
1 pinch oregano
1/2 pound grated Cheddar cheese
12 tortillas
1 pint sour cream
fat or lard for frying

Place chicken breasts, parsley and the chopped carrot in a pot; salt lightly and cover with water. Bring to a boil and cook until tender (about 45 minutes). Remove the chicken and let cool. When it is thoroughly cool, remove skin and bones and shred meat into a bowl. Fry the garlic in olive oil lightly, and add the chilies, tomatoes, onions, the oregano and a pinch of salt. Cover with water and cook over low heat until thick. To the shredded chicken breasts add the grated cheese and sour cream. Fry tortillas, one at a time, until soft (only a few seconds). Dip each tortilla in the chili sauce, fill with the chicken mixture and roll. Place in flat casserole or baker, cover with the remaining chili sauce and bake at 350° until thoroughly heated, about 10-15 minutes. Put dab of sour cream on each, surround with chopped lettuce.

Alice Cauthorn

CHIMICHANGAS

1 quart water
1 cup dried kidney beans
1 medium onion, chopped
1 dried hot chile pepper, seeded and minced
1 tablespoon shortening
1 clove garlic, minced
1 bay leaf
1 teaspoon salt
1/4 cup plus 1 tablespoon shortening
1 medium onion, minced
3 cloves garlic, minced
tomato sauce with green chilies
1 (4-ounce) can whole green chilies, drained, seeded, and minced
1 tablespoon chili powder
1 teaspoon ground cumin
1/3 cup (1-1/3 ounces) shredded Monterey Jack cheese
10 (8-inch) flour tortillas
vegetable oil
1/2 cup (2 ounces) shredded Monterey Jack cheese
sour cream

Combine first 7 ingredients in a Dutch oven; cover and simmer 2-1/2 hours, stirring occasionally. Discard bay leaf. Stir in salt and refrigerate beans overnight, partially covered. Melt 1/4 cup plus 1 tablespoon shortening in a medium saucepan; add onion and garlic, and sauté until tender. Stir in 2/3 cup tomato sauce with green chilies, minced chilies, chili powder, and cumin; simmer 3 minutes. Mash beans. Stir sauce into beans, and cook 8-10 minutes or until thick. Add 1/3 cup cheese, stirring until melted. Cool. Spoon 1/3 cup of bean mixture on center of a tortilla. Fold the edge nearest bean filling up and over filling, just until mixture is covered. Fold in opposite side of tortilla to center; roll up. Secure with wooden picks. Repeat with remaining bean mixture and tortillas. Fry burritos in deep hot oil (375°) 2-3 minutes or until golden brown, turning once. Drain well on paper towels. Remove wooden picks. Arrange burritos in a 13 x 9 x 2-inch baking dish. Sprinkle with 1/2 cup cheese. Broil 30 seconds or until cheese melts. Serve with sour cream and remaining tomato sauce with chilies.

Ella C. Stivers

CHILIES RELLENOS DE PICADILLO

Most first-time chile relleno cooks find skinning chilies a frustrating experience, so they resort to using canned chilies. That's unfortunate; canned chilies just don't compare to the subtle flavor of fresh-peeled ones.

4 tablespoons oil
1 cup finely chopped onion
3 cloves garlic
1 pound lean ground pork
1 pound lean ground beef
2 teaspoons salt
1/2 teaspoon pepper
4 cloves
1/2-inch stick cinnamon
4 tablespoons raisins
4 tablespoons chopped almonds
2 tablespoons flour
2 large tomatoes, peeled and seeded

Heat the oil in a large frying pan. Stir in the onions and cook over moderate heat for about 2 minutes. Add the garlic which has been crushed and chopped. Continue cooking slowly for about two more minutes. Add the ground pork and beef. Increase the heat to moderately high and brown the meat, breaking it up with a spatula. Season with salt and pepper. As the meat is browning, grind the cloves and cinnamon in a molcajete or grinder. Add the spices to the meat along with the raisins and chopped almonds. Stir the mixture together. Sprinkle the entire surface lightly with the two tablespoons of flour. Stir it in. Reduce the heat to moderate. Bring three or four inches of water to a boil in a small saucepan. Pierce the stem end of the tomatoes with a fork and dip each one into the boiling water for 10-15 seconds. Plunge into a bowl of cool water (to stop the cooking) and peel the skin with a small knife. Cut out the stem end with the knife and squeeze out the liquid and seeds. Chop the tomatoes and add them to the meat in the skillet. Cook the mixture about 10 minutes more or until most of the liquid has evaporated. Set picadillo stuffing aside.

To prepare the chilies:
8 chilies, poblanos
flour for dredging
4 eggs, separated
pinch of salt
oil for frying (3/4" deep)

Heat a griddle over high heat and roast the chilies on the griddle, turning to blister on all sides. As they are done, place in a warm, damp towel and let them stand for about 15 minutes. This helps to further loosen the skin and softens the chile a little. Slit one side of the chile; remove the seeds and veins. Peel off the outer skin. Stuff the chilies with the picadillo (seasoned meat) and pat completely. Dredge them one at a time in the flour to coat evenly and lightly on all sides. Set aside. Heat about 3/4-inch of oil in a skillet. Separate the eggs and place the whites in a large bowl along with a pinch of salt. Whip the egg whites until they form stiff peaks. Beat in the yolks one at a time. Holding each chile by the stem, dip them one at a time into the beaten egg batter, then place them gently into the hot oil. Fry them on all sides until they are evenly golden brown. Drain on absorbent paper.

Mary Nell Reck

CHILE RELLENOS GONZALEZ

1/2 medium onion, finely chopped
1 tablespoon shortening
1/2 cup water
4 large eggs, separated
1/2 teaspoon salt
2 cups tomato sauce
1/2 cup lard
4 California fresh green chilies, roasted and peeled
2 tablespoons flour
1/4 pound Monterey Jack cheese

Brown onion in shortening. Add water and tomato sauce. Bring to a boil. Reduce heat and simmer gently while preparing chilies. Add salt to egg whites and beat until stiff. Beat egg yolks slightly and add to stiffly beaten egg whites. Gently fold together. Heat skillet on low to medium heat. Melt lard in skillet. Remove seeds from chilies, being careful not to split the peppers. Cut cheese into slices 1/4" thick and 2" long. Stuff chilies with cheese. Sprinkle chilies with flour. Increase heat until lard is hot. Dip chilies in egg batter then place in skillet. Cover entire mixture with egg batter. Cook until browned on both sides. Serve covered with hot tomato sauce.

Gonzalez Family

CHILE RELLENOS

6 to 10 blistered and peeled fresh, long green chilies (canned whole chilies may be used).
1/2 pound Monterey Jack cheese, cut into strips
1/2 cup onions, chopped
3 egg whites, beaten stiff
3 egg yolks
flour
All-Purpose Chile Sauce or tomato sauce (see Sauces)
Flour tortillas (optional)

Cut a small slit into the chile; stuff with cheese and onions (do not overstuff). Dredge lightly in flour. Take beaten egg whites and gently fold in three egg yolks. Dip floured and stuffed chilies one at a time into egg batter and fry (both sides) in 1/4 inch of hot oil. Remove when lightly browned, drain on paper toweling and serve covered with a mild red sauce. They may also be wrapped up in a warm flour tortilla.

Efrien Rodriguez

MAIN DISHES

The following main dishes are not always offered in the average Tex-Mex restaurant. They make a delightful change of pace from standard fare and are truly "Texified" border cooking.

CARNE ASADA

1 flank steak
4 tablespoons tomato paste
1 cup strong black coffee
1/4 cup Worcestershire sauce
1 tablespoon sugar
1 tablespoon salt
1 teaspoon cayenne
1 teaspoon black pepper
2 tablespoons fresh lime juice
1/4 cup vegetable oil

Combine all the marinating ingredients in a small saucepan. Heat until the flavors are combined. Marinate the flank steak in the sauce 6-8 hours. Grill over charcoal, generously basting the meat frequently. When richly browned on the outside but still quite pink inside (about 4-5 minutes in all) remove from the coals. Allow the meat to rest for 5-7 minutes. To serve, very thinly slice on the diagonal, cutting across the grain of the meat.

Mary Nell Reck

MEXICAN-STYLE PORK CHOPS

6 (1-inch thick) pork chops
1/2 teaspoon salt
1/2 teaspoon black pepper
1/4 cup flour
2 tablespoons vegetable oil
1/2 to 1 cup chopped onion
1 minced garlic clove
1/3 cup chili sauce
2 teaspoons Worcestershire sauce
3 tablespoons vinegar
1-1/2 tablespoons brown sugar
3/4 cup boiling water

Trim fat from pork. Rub with salt, pepper and flour and pound lightly. Heat oil in deep skillet (with oven-proof handle) and brown chops. Add onion and garlic; cook about 5 minutes. Remove excess oil. Mix chili sauce, Worcestershire sauce, vinegar, sugar and water. Add to skillet, cover, and bake at 375° for 50 minutes, removing cover for the last 10 minutes.

Texas Department of Agriculture

SOUTH OF THE BORDER CHICKEN

2/3 cup flour
1/4 cup plus 2 tablespoons grated Parmesan cheese
1 teaspoon paprika
1/4 teaspoon black pepper
1 (3 pound) fryer, cut into pieces; reserve giblets
1/2 cup margarine
1 teaspoon oregano
1 teaspoon salt
1 (Number 303) can tomatoes
1 medium green pepper, diced
8 ripe olives, pitted and sliced

Cook giblets in water until tender, drain. Save broth; chop giblets very fine. Place flour, 1/4 cup cheese, paprika and pepper in paper bag. Shake chicken in bag until well coated; reserve remaining flour. Sauté chicken in margarine in large skillet until golden on all sides. Remove from skillet; place in 3 quart casserole. Stir salt, oregano and remaining flour into margarine left in skillet. Add tomatoes and giblet broth; cook over medium heat, stirring constantly, until thickened. Add remaining ingredients. Pour gravy over chicken; cover and bake at 350° for 40 minutes or until chicken is tender.

Mrs. E. A. Brinkoeter

CHICKEN LIVERS AND AVOCADO IN SOUR CREAM

1/4 cup chopped onion
1/4 chopped green pepper
1 clove garlic (optional)
1/2 pound chicken livers
2 tablespoons butter
1 ripe avocado, diced
3/4 cup sour cream
1/2 teaspoon Worcestershire sauce
1/2 teaspoon paprika
salt and pepper to taste

Sauté onion, pepper, garlic, and livers in butter until livers are just cooked, about 10 minutes. Remove garlic. Add diced avocado and cook gently until heated, about 1 minute. Stir in sour cream. Add Worcestershire, paprika, salt and pepper. Serve on hot buttered toast or flour tortillas.

Mrs. Max L. Crim

SPANISH DUCK

1 duck
flour
fat
1 green pepper, chopped
1 small hot pepper, chopped
1 large onion, chopped
1 small can tomatoes or 1 can tomato soup with one can water
salt
pepper
dash of chili powder

Dress and cut duck as you would a fryer. Roll in flour and fry in deep fat until brown. Take from frying pan. Pour out all fat and return duck to frying pan. Mix remaining ingredients; pour mixture over duck, cover and return to low heat. Cook 45 minutes to 1 hour, or until tender. NOTE: This can also be cooked in covered casserole at 350° for 45 minutes to 1 hour.

Mrs. Fred Flanagan

SOUR CREAM JALAPENO CHICKEN

2 pounds chicken, sectioned
1 jalapeno pepper, quartered and seeded
8 ounces sour cream
1 (10-ounce) can mushroom soup, undiluted
1 teaspoon paprika
salt
pepper
4 ounces fresh mushrooms, coarsely chopped

Combine everything in casserole. Bake at 350° for 1-1/2 hours. Serve over rice.

Bill Maxwell

CEVICHE

1-1/2 pounds fillet of sole, cut into bite-size pieces
8 ounces lime juice
8 ounces lemon juice
1 teaspoon oregano
1 teaspoon gumbo filé
1 teaspoon celery seeds
1/2 teaspoon black pepper
5 tablespoons cilantro
3 teaspoons salt
1 teaspoon vinegar
2 diced onions
4 large tomatoes, peeled and chopped
1/2 can Ro-Tel chilies
1 bottle Spanish olives, chopped
1/2 cup Bertoli olive oil
2 to 3 avocados, chopped
2 large jalapeno peppers, chopped

Cover fish with lemon and lime juice. Sprinkle with salt. Cover and marinate for 24 hours in a glass container. Drain off all juices. Mix all other ingredients together except avocado. Let stand in a covered container in the refrigerator for 3-4 hours. Add avocados before serving.

Susan Francis

HUACHINANGO A LA VERCRUZANA

2 (2-pound) red snappers
salt and white pepper to taste
2 tablespoons fresh lime juice
flour for dredging
2 eggs
4 tablespoons milk or water
4 tablespoons oil
4 tablespoons butter

Fillet the fish. Rinse and pat dry. Sprinkle with salt and white pepper. Sprinkle both sides with the lime juice and set aside for about 30 minutes to season. Shortly before serving the dish, dredge the fish in the flour to coat lightly. Heat about 2 tablespoons each of the butter and oil in a sauté pan. In a shallow bowl, combine the eggs and milk or water. Beat them lightly with a fork to combine. Dip the floured fish fillets into the eggs quickly to coat each side. Place them one at a time in the hot butter-oil mixture. Shake the pan to keep them from sticking and sauté until golden brown on each side. Remove the fish to a serving platter and keep warm until ready to serve. To serve, coat the fish with the sauce Vera Cruz.

SAUCE VERA CRUZ:
4 tablespoons olive oil
1 medium onion, thinly sliced
3 cloves garlic, peeled and crushed
3 large tomatoes, peeled, seeded and chopped
1 large bay leaf
1/2 teaspoon oregano
12 green olives, cut in half
2 tablespoons capers
2 jalapeno peppers, seeded and cut into thin strips
1/2 teaspoon salt
1/4 teaspoon black pepper

Heat the oil in a sauté pan. Sauté the onion and garlic slowly until they are soft but not brown. Stir in the chopped tomatoes, bay leaf, oregano, olives, capers, and jalapenos. Season to taste. Cook over medium-high flame for about 10 minutes or until some of the liquid has evaporated and the sauce develops a rich flavor.

Mary Nell Reck

HANGOVER SHRIMP

1 (32-ounce) can V-8 juice
1 can beer
3 to 6 chopped jalapenos
1 large onion
1 teaspoon salt
2 to 3 cloves garlic
3 to 5 pounds shrimp, peeled and deveined

Put all ingredients in a large pot and bring to a boil. Cook shrimp for 10 minutes. Turn off the heat and let shrimp marinate in the liquid for an additional 20 minutes. Drain shrimp and chill before serving.

Sam Asper

CAMARRONES AL AJO (GARLIC SHRIMP)

1 pound jumbo shrimp, washed, peeled and deveined
1 stick butter
3 cloves garlic, crushed
squeeze of fresh lemon

Make a mixture of the butter, garlic and lemon. Place shrimp in shallow broiling pan; spoon mixture over shrimp. Broil for 5 minutes on one side, turn, spoon additional butter mixture on other side and broil for another 5 minutes.

Mrs. John Runner

BROWNSVILLE SHRIMP

4-1/2 pounds fresh shrimp, shelled
1/2 teaspoon cayenne pepper
3 cloves garlic, crushed
paprika
filé powder
2 lemons, thinly sliced
1 pound butter
1/2 cup lemon juice
1/4 cup chives, chopped
1 teaspoon salt
2 ounces Tabasco sauce

In a large oblong baking dish arrange layer of shrimp, sprinkle cayenne evenly over surface, add half the garlic, dust with paprika and filé powder, and arrange half the lemon slices over surface. Add another layer of shrimp and repeat procedure with cayenne, garlic, paprika, filé powder, and lemon slices. Combine remaining ingredients in a saucepan and simmer slowly till butter is melted. Pour butter sauce over shrimp and bake at 350° for 20 minutes. Serve with plenty of hot Mexican or French bread to dip into the sauce.

Mary Yturria

CALABAZA MEXICANA

2 tablespoons butter or margarine
2 small calabazas or 3 medium zucchinis, thinly sliced
1 medium onion, finely chopped
2 cloves garlic, minced
1 (17-ounce) can whole kernel corn, drained
1 (4-ounce) can green chilies, drained, seeded and chopped
1/2 to 3/4 cup shredded sharp Cheddar cheese

Melt butter in a large skillet. Add squash, onion, and garlic; sauté about 8 minutes or until squash is crisp-tender. Stir in corn and chilies; spoon into a 1-quart casserole. Top with cheese; bake, uncovered, at 350° for 10 minutes or until cheese is melted.

Anita Cox

NOPALITO (CACTUS CASSEROLE)

2 quarts salted water
1 pound young cactus (packaged) washed and cut into strips
2 tablespoons shortening
1 onion, chopped
1 green bell pepper, chopped
2 tablespoons hot chili sauce
1/2 cup dried shrimp (packaged) soaked in hot water
3 eggs, beaten
salt and freshly ground pepper to taste

Bring water to full boil, cook cactus 20 minutes, and drain. In a heavy skillet melt shortening, add onion and bell pepper, and sauté over medium heat till tender. Add hot chili sauce, cactus, shrimp and stir thoroughly. Add eggs, salt and pepper to taste, and stir slowly till eggs have set.

Mary Yturria

GREEN CHILE CHEESE BAKE

5 eggs, slightly beaten
1/4 cup flour
1/4 teaspoon baking powder
1/2 teaspoon salt
1 (10-ounce) carton creamed cottage cheese
1/2 pound Monterey Jack or Cheddar cheese, shredded
1/4 pound butter, softened
1 (4-ounce) can chopped green chilies

Preheat oven to 350°. Mix ingredients together. Pour into 8-inch square cake pan and bake 40-45 minutes. Cut in squares.

Mrs. Harold (JoAnn) Shull

CHEESE AND GREEN CHILIES MINI QUICHE

2 (4-ounce) cans green chilies, seeded and split
1 pound white cheese (Jack or Gruyère), grated
1 pound sharp Cheddar cheese, grated
6 eggs
1 (5-1/2-ounce) can evaporated milk
dash Tabasco sauce

Preheat oven to 350°. Grease 9 x 13-inch pan with margarine. Place chilies on bottom of pan, distribute cheese over chilies. Beat eggs slightly, add milk and Tabasco and pour over cheese. Place in oven for 35-40 minutes. Cut in squares while still warm.

Mrs. William D. (Ursula) Deakins

JALAPENO PIE

1 (7-ounce) can jalapeno peppers, drained, rinsed and seeded
1/2 pound sharp Cheddar cheese, coarsely grated
4 eggs, beaten
salt to taste

Cut peppers into thin long slices and line bottom and sides of a 9-inch pie plate. Press grated cheese over peppers. Add salt to eggs, beat slightly again and pour over cheese. Bake at 350° for 25-30 minutes. Slice pie into small wedges and serve as finger food with cocktails, or slice into four to six equal size wedges to serve as a luncheon dish.

Mary Yturria

TACO-CHINNI

2 pounds fresh zucchini squash
1 pound ground lamb or beef
1 can taco sauce
1/2 cup finely chopped onion
1 cup grated cheese (Cheddar, Swiss or slices of American cheese)

Wash, slice and salt the zucchini squash. Brown the squash in fresh hot oil. Drain and place a layer in a 2-quart baking dish. Pour out oil, and in same pan, brown ground meat. Stir in onion. When meat is brown and the onion is transparent, add the small can of taco sauce. Heat through and spread layer over squash. Top with the sliced or grated cheese; add more squash and meat until all ingredients are layered in. Top with last of cheese and slide into preheated 350° oven. Bake about 30 minutes until cheese topping is melted and dish is hot through. This dish can be made with any cheese on hand and squash may be replaced with eggplant. It also freezes well to be used later.

Sue Simms

BEEF MEXICANA

3 pounds beef tenderloin
1 large onion, peeled, sliced
2 medium bell peppers, sliced
4 tomatoes, skinned, with seeds and juice removed
2 cloves garlic, crushed and chopped
salt and black pepper to taste
1 cup tomato puree
3 tablespoons sweet paprika
1 tablespoon seasoned chicken stock base
2 to 3 chilies, serranos

Cut the tenderloin into 2 inch cubes and sauté over very high heat in a little oil until the meat is browned on all sides but still rare in the center. Remove from the pan and keep warm. In the same skillet, add a little more oil and sauté the onions and bell peppers for 3-4 minutes until tender. Add the garlic; sauté about 2 minutes more. Add the tomatoes and sauté about 2 minutes. Stir in the tomato puree, paprika, and chicken stock base. Season to taste with salt and pepper. Thinly slice the peppers, removing the skin and seeds. Toss the mixture together and return the sauteed beef to the pan. The meat should be resting in a layer on top of the vegetables. Heat the mixture through for about five minutes more, covered. Serve immediately. Delicious with plain white rice.

Mary Nell Reck

JALAPENO CORN BREAD CASSEROLE

1 cup yellow cornmeal
1 cup milk
2 eggs
3/4 teaspoon soda
1/2 cup bacon drippings
1 (1-pound) can cream-style corn
1 pound ground meat
1 large onion, chopped
1 pound round cheese, grated
5 canned jalapenos

Combine cornmeal, milk, beaten eggs, salt, soda, bacon drippings and corn. Mix well and set aside. Brown meat until crumbly. Drain well on paper towels. Pour half of corn bread batter into well-greased cast iron skillet or baking dish that has been dusted with cornmeal. Sprinkle grated cheese evenly over batter. Sprinkle meat evenly over cheese, then sprinkle chopped onions and jalapenos over meat. Top with remaining corn bread batter. Bake at 350° for about 50 minutes.

Mrs. Chester L. Geuea

MEXICAN GREEN RICE CASSEROLE

1/4 pound butter
1 green bell pepper, chopped
2 Mexican poblano peppers
1 onion, chopped
1 small green chile pepper
1 cup sour cream
1/2 pound Monterey Jack cheese, grated
1-1/2 cups rice, cooked

Sauté peppers and onion in butter. When soft, put in blender and mush. Add sour cream. Preheat oven to 350°. In 1-1/2 quart casserole, layer 1/2 of rice, 1/2 of pepper mush, 1/2 of cheese. Repeat in same order ending with cheese. Place in oven uncovered until cheese melts. Can be frozen before oven cooking.

Mrs. Ben (Mi Mi) Hammond

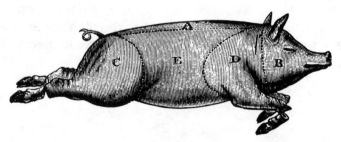

DESSERTS

Usually after a good Tex-Mex meal, there is no room for dessert. But for those with a sweet tooth, here is a sampling of the more popular "postres."

SOPAIPILLAS

4 cups flour
1-1/2 teaspoons salt
3 teaspoons baking powder
salad oil for deep frying
4 tablespoons sugar
3 tablespoons shortening
milk (about 1-1/4 cups)

Sift flour; measure and sift again with the salt, baking powder and sugar. Cut in the shortening, and add milk to make a soft dough just firm enough to roll. Cover bowl and let dough stand for 30 minutes; then roll 1/8 inch thick (no thicker) on lightly floured board and cut in diamond or triangle shaped pieces. Heat about 1 inch of oil in a frying pan to about 380-400° or cook in deep fryer. Add a few pieces at a time; turn at once so they will puff evenly, then turn back to brown both sides. Drain on paper toweling. Serve with butter. Makes 4 dozen.

Mrs. Sam Langford

BUNUELOS

2 cups all-purpose flour
2 tablespoons sugar
1/2 teaspoon salt
2 eggs
6 tablespoons milk
2 tablespoons melted butter
oil for deep frying

In a large mixing bowl combine the flour, sugar, and salt. In a small bowl combine the milk and eggs; beat them together lightly and drizzle in the melted butter while continuing to beat. Stir the egg mixture into the flour mixture with a fork until it barely holds together. Turn out onto a lightly floured surface and knead for three to five minutes. Divide the dough into 24 pieces. Roll each piece into a 5-inch round (tortilla shape). Drop the buñuelo into 375° oil and fry until golden brown. This should take about 2-3 minutes. Turn them over with tongs while cooking to brown them on both sides. Take them from the oil and place on absorbent paper. Drizzle lightly with cinnamon sugar syrup and serve. Cinnamon Sugar Syrup (recipe follows) and serve.

CINNAMON SUGAR SYRUP

1-1/4 cups sugar
1 cup water
2 tablespoons corn syrup
1 stick cinnamon

Place all the ingredients in a small saucepan. Bring to a boil and cook uncovered for 10-15 minutes. If you are using a thermometer, it should read 220°.

Mary Nell Reck

MEXICAN ORANGE CANDY

3 cups sugar
1/4 cup boiling water
1 cup evaporated milk
few grains of salt
2 teaspoons grated orange rind
1 cup chopped nuts

Slowly sift 1 cup sugar into hot, heavy frying pan, stirring constantly, to caramelize. Add boiling water. When sugar is melted, add 2 cups sugar, milk and salt, stirring constantly. Cook to 236° or until mixture forms a soft ball when dropped in water. Remove from heat; add orange rind. Cool at room temperature without stirring until lukewarm or until hand can be held comfortably on bottom of pan. Stir in nuts. Beat until candy holds its shape. Drop from teaspoon on waxed paper to form small patties. Cool. Makes about 3 dozen.

Mrs. B. W. (Margaret) Kempe

CACTUS CANDY

cubes of barrel cactus
water to cover cubes
sugar (equal to amount of cactus cubes)
1 tablespoon slaked lime to each quart of water used
(buy lime at drugstore)

First find a barrel cactus. Use a hatchet to chop off all the ribs and to remove green coating from the pulp. Cut the pulp into cubes. Let cubes stand overnight in water to which lime has been added. The next morning wash cubes thoroughly in several clear waters. Boil cubes in water until clear and transparent. Drain thoroughly. Measure equal amounts of sugar and cubes and boil gently until sugar is absorbed. Roll in graduated sugar.

MEXICAN TEA CAKES

2-1/4 cups all-purpose flour
1/4 teaspoon salt
1/4 teaspoon ground cinnamon
1 cup butter, softened
3/4 cup finely chopped pecans
1/2 cup sifted powdered sugar
1 teaspoon vanilla extract
powdered sugar

Combine flour, salt, and cinnamon in a large mixing bowl. Add butter, pecans, 1/2 cup powdered sugar and vanilla; stir until well blended. Shape dough into 1-inch balls, and place on ungreased cookie sheet. Bake at 400° for 10-12 minutes. Roll cookies in additional powdered sugar while hot. Remove to wire racks to cool completely, and reroll cookies in powdered sugar. Makes 5 dozen.

Maxine Cates

MEXICAN WEDDING RING COOKIES

1 cup butter
1/2 cup powdered sugar
1 teaspoon vanilla
2 cups flour, sifted
1/2 cup chopped pecans
powdered sugar

Preheat oven to 350°. Cream butter and sugar, add vanilla, flour and nuts. Blend well. Form in balls the size of a nickel, roll and shape like crescents or as desired. Bake 10-12 minutes on ungreased cookie sheet until just slightly browned. When cool, roll in powdered sugar or shake, a few at a time, in sack of powdered sugar. Makes about 4-5 dozen.

Mrs. R. P. (Snowie) Roberts

MANGOS FLAMEADOS

2 tablespoons butter
2 tablespoons sugar
juice and grated rind of one orange and one lime
4 tablespoons Triple Sec
2 mangos, cut into quarters
4 tablespoons tequila

Melt the butter in a chafing dish. Stir in the sugar. Add the orange and lime rind and then the orange and lime juice. Stir in the Triple Sec. Let the mixture cook over a low flame until it begins to thicken. Add the mangos; turn to coat in the syrup. When heated through, add the tequila and ignite. When the flames die down, serve on dessert plates or over vanilla ice cream in a sherbet glass. The fruit may also be served with Crema Fresca or lightly sweetened whipped cream.

Mary Nell Reck

CONGEALED MANGO MOUSSE

2 cups boiling water
8 ounces lemon Jello
15-ounce can mangos (including juice)
4 ounces cream cheese, softened
sour cream

Dissolve Jello in boiling water. In a blender, blend mangos, juice and cream cheese until smooth. Whisk mango mixture into dissolved Jello and mix well. Pour into a 1-1/2 quart mold, chill thoroughly and unmold on lettuce leaf. Garnish with sour cream.

Mary Yturria

MARGARITA ICE

2 cups fresh lime juice (reserve
 peels)
3 cups sugar
2 cups water
finely grated peel of 3 limes
3 egg whites
sugar
1 cup white tequila
1/2 cup Triple Sec
lime slices and mint sprigs for garnish

Pour lime juice into ice cream maker. Combine sugar, water and lime peel in heavy 3-quart saucepan. Bring to boil and cook without stirring until syrup reaches 234° (thread stage) on candy thermometer, about 5-7 minutes. Set pan in large bowl of ice water and stir syrup with wooden spoon until cooled to lukewarm. Blend into lime juice. Fill ice cream freezer with mixture of 8 parts ice to 1 part rock salt. Freeze lime mixture according to manufacturer's instructions until just partially frozen (this should take about 20 minutes). Meanwhile, beat egg whites in mixing bowl until stiff peaks form. Spoon over lime mixture and continue churning until firm, about 10 minutes. Remove container and transfer to freezer. To serve: Scoop Margarita Ice into glasses and top with small amount of tequila and Triple Sec.

Mary Nell Reck

MARGARITA PIE

1/2 cup butter, melted
1-1/4 cups pretzels, crushed
2 tablespoons sugar
14-ounce can condensed milk
1-1/2 ounces Triple Sec
1-1/2 ounces tequila
1/4 cup lime juice
1 pint cream, whipped
lime slices for garnishes

Combine first 3 ingredients and freeze in pie tin. Combine remaining ingredients, fill crust, garnish with lime slices and freeze (covered) 4 to 5 hours before serving.

Doriana Schmeltz

DRINKS

Water is probably the first thing the uninitiated reaches for, vainly trying to drown the fire found in some Tex-Mex food. It doesn't help; only the passage of time quells *that* burning sensation. Sweat it out and sip on one of the following drinks.

MEXICAN ICED TEA

3 quarts water
12 limes
6 lemons
6 Mexican lemonlimes (dark green), (if not available, use additional 3 lemons and 3 limes)
2 oranges, sliced
2 grapefruits
1/4 cup sugar

Cut lemons and limes in half and squeeze the juice into a large container. Throw the rinds in after squeezing. Do likewise with 6 lemonlimes or their substitutes. Squeeze the oranges and grapefruits, then slice before throwing the rinds in. Add sugar and lots of ice.

Frank Rivera

JALAPENO WINE

Jalapeno wine is one of those things destined to take its place right along with onion gum, trick white soap, and binoculars that leave black rings around the eyes. The wine is a novelty item most connoisseurs of the grape hope to encounter only in a fever dream. For the curious (or those who can't resist one more practical joke) we present Sam Lewis' wine recipe in its entirety: Take any white wine recipe and substitute one eighth of the grapes required with seeded and chopped jalapeno peppers . . . period.

Sam Lewis

SANGRIA

1 orange
1 lemon
1/3 cup sugar
1 bottle dry red wine
1 (20-ounce) bottle club soda
1-1/2 to 2 ounces cognac

Slice the fruit and put into a pitcher. Add sugar and a generous splash of wine. Let marinate for several hours at room temperature. When ready to serve, poke the fruit with a wooden spoon to extract juices. Add the remainder of the wine, soda and cognac.

Mary Eleanor Cartall

SPANISH SANGRIA

1 lemon
1 lime
1 orange
4 ounces brandy
1/4 cup sugar
1 bottle Spanish red wine
2 tablespoons lemon juice
ice cubes
soda water

Slice fruit and put in pitcher with brandy and sugar. Let stand 1 hour. Add wine and lemon juice and stir. Let sit 1 hour. Before serving, add ice cubes and fill pitcher with soda water to taste. Stir briskly.

Mrs. Charles W. (Joan) Robinson

FOYLAN'S MARGARITAS

1 ounce fresh lime juice
1 ounce Cointreau
2 ounces tequila
2/3 blender full of ice

Rub rim of champagne glass with lime and dip in salt. Combine ingredients in blender with ice until mushy.

Casa Tres Changos

SENOR MIGUEL'S SPECIAL MARGARITA

1 ounce Grand Marnier
1 ounce Triple Sec
2 ounces Herradura Tequila Gold
3 ounces simple syrup*
2 ounces fresh-squeezed lime juice (save some slices for garnish)
kosher salt

Rim a 16-ounce mason jar with a cut lime. Press rim onto a plate of kosher salt so that it's coated, but not to excess. Fill a cocktail shaker with liquid ingredients. Add ice, shake and strain into mason jar. Top off with ice cubes and garnish with a lime slice. *(To make a simple syrup, fill any container half full with sugar then pour in enough hot water to completely fill container. Stir until dissolved and let cool.)

Ralph and Susi Chacon

BRANDING IRON SUNRISE

1/2 ounce Cassis liqueur
1 splash lime juice
2 ounces tequila
club soda

Put these ingredients in 12-14 ounce Collins glass. Add ice, top with club soda and stir.

Branding Iron Restaurant

TRADITIONAL

Although chili and barbecue may be the most flamboyant stars attributed to Texas dining, Texans still reserve room in their hearts and stomachs for true down-home cookin', otherwise known as Lone Star Haute Cuisine. This style of cooking cannot be characterized by any one particular dish, but is instead distinguished by culinary contributions from a variety of ethnic cultures that settled Texas in the nineteenth century. The blending of Germans, Czechs, American Indians, Mexicans and over twenty other distinct nationalities is responsible for the wonderful array of foods eaten in Texas. Consequently, you'll find corn bread, coleslaw German sausages and sauerkraut spiced with Mexican chile peppers. Czechoslovakian kolaches may be offered at the same table right along with smoked jackrabbit glazed with Indian mesquite bean jelly. And traditional Texas bread puddings are in some cases made from day-old French baguettes.

As a result of this ethnic mishmashing, the "Magnificent Empire of Texas" harbors one of the most well-fed populations on the face of the earth; cantilevered guts are de rigueur, with food-oriented activities ranking second only in popularity to football as the national pastime (I say "national" because Texas has become a country unto itself — complete with a Texas passport and a time-honored movement to secede from the Union). When it comes to the subject of food, Texans are dedicated to it, to say the least. Thousands will gather weekly at Peach Jamborees, Turkey Trots, Watermelon Thumps, Rocky Mountain Oyster Fry Offs, Goat Burnings, Jalapeno

During the Revolution of 1836, Texas troops, fighting for their independence, quite often had to clothe and feed themselves. Uniforms were assembled from past campaigns or made from buckskins. Wild game made up the bulk of the soldier's diet. Pictured here is a large pot of chili (in this case armadillo chili) "the dish that defeated the Mexican Army." *Painting by Bruce Marshall, courtesy of the Institute of Texas Cultures.*

Eating Contests and — for the less adventuresome gourmands — an Oatmeal Boiloff, held yearly in (you guessed it) Oatmeal, Texas. All of these food "happenings" are done in good-natured fun and serve as a popular excuse for a social gathering. The festivals also serve as present-day reminders (to people who all-too-easily forget) that the availability of food should always be cause for celebration. This concept was something Texas pioneers were painfully aware of, and fortunately, that attitude is still prevalent among their descendants.

Necessity being the mother of invention, the first Texans had to make-do with what was available. The philosophy of "waste not, want not" was strictly adhered to. Early settlers survived hard times by mastering the technique of living off the land and by recycling leftovers and poor cuts of meat into simple but savory dishes that became the trademarks of Texas cookery.

For example: wheat flour and sugar were luxuries that, in the early 1830's, colonizers rarely had. Therefore, the raising of corn became a matter of survival (corn was chosen over wheat because it was a crop more easily harvested by hand). This versatile plant substituted for amenities lacking in the pioneers' diet. From the pith of the stalks came molasses. It was used instead of sugar as a sweetener (dessert recipes like pecan pie and praline candy were modified to accommodate this thick syrup). Kernels were fried, boiled, toasted, roasted and popped. When dried and ground into meal, corn became Texas flour, used in place of wheat to make breads, chess pies, johnnycakes and corn dodgers. Leftover corn bread was dunked into buttermilk and eaten as a favorite Texas dish called crumblin'. Stale corn bread was fed to the family cow, pig or chicken. In turn, these animals eventually found themselves on the dinner table — the end product of a favorite traditional recipe such as the popular dish called "Sunday Chicken." As with the corn, all parts of the animals were used; sweetmeats went into Son-of-a-Gun Stew, and meat scraps were ground up to make sausages or baked into bread loaves. And yes, any extra went back to feed the rest of the live- stock. The whole cycle continues.

Wild game like venison, turkey and doves made up the balance of the diet until the rounding up of stray longhorns became big business in the mid 1800's. Unfortunately, much of the beef was very tough so range cooks floured and pounded the meat into submission, frying it in rendered fat. Cream gravies made from drippings saved from other dishes were poured over the meat; this has become one of Texas' most well-known entrees — Chicken Fried Steak.

Since Texas spans such a great geographical region, encompassing many different climates and soils, a variety of foodstuffs could be grown in different parts of the state. In South Texas, the sandy soils and warm, humid climate easily supported fields of melons, gourds and squashes. Sorghum and various grains also proliferated in this fertile land. Along rich bottomlands, pecan groves thrived. Farther north, around Stonewall, peach orchards were planted and from these acreages Texans built a renowned reputation for scrumptious peach cobblers. And from the apple orchards in the Panhandle area, ingenious settlers made apple vinegar which was used instead of lemon juice or citrus fruits in making delicious vinegar pies.

Due to the unpredictable harshness of the Texas climate and environment, experience taught pioneers to grow hardy vegetables. In backyard gardens all across Texas, "keeper" vegetables were grown because of their resistance to insects and their enduring shelf-life. Black-eyed peas (Texas Caviar), okra, potatoes, cabbages and snap beans were favorites. Vegetables were always boiled in water until properly "cooked down." "Pot likker," the juice from the cooked vegetables, was poured over corn bread in a bowl. Canning food was a necessity since rural electrification (for refrigeration) did not come to most of Texas until the 1930's. It wasn't unusual for a family to put up 2000 jars during a season. Canned fruits, vegetables and relishes became staples incorporated into the style

of Texas cooking. This is one reason why most Texans aren't too keen on fancy, fresh salads. Having been raised on canned goods, many prefer the traditional "keeper" salads like sauerkrauts, and sugary fruit salads that won't spoil readily in the Texas heat.

The hardships and rigorous lessons of frontier life helped mold the culinary tastes and manners of most Texans. As a result, they have developed a very unpretentious attitude when it comes to the business of eating. When Texans go out to eat, it's done in an informally grand manner. Most traditional Texas restaurants debunk the conventional trappings normally associated with eating out and opt for relatively utilitarian decor and relaxed atmosphere. Although coats and ties are seen in the new, European-style restaurants of the big cities, a pair of clean jeans and shiny boots will get most people into any place worth going in. Dining, Texas Style, is a warm, friendly experience, not a stiff, stodgy affair.

The stereotypical bigness associated with the state is also reflected in its foods and food emporiums. Steak palaces, the most prevalent and popular dining establishments in Texas, are prime examples. "Zentner's Daughters" in San Angelo, accommodates up to a thousand hungry patrons in one sitting. Owner Betty Zentner says, "Texans want to come in, sit down, eat and git . . . jest a blowin' and a goin'. No fancy frills, just darn good food. And we serve them enough so there's always extra to take home. That makes them happy, and happiness is getting harder to find after visiting most American restaurants."

To insure that the formula works, Betty's 82-year-old father rises at 6:30 every morning to personally select the grain-fed beef that makes Zentner's so famous for its steaks. He is a firm believer in not cutting corners, which so many other restaurants do, and insists that the hindquarters are hung for 21 days to "age" until acquiring "wang." (Wang is a term for the natural mold that envelopes meat as it ages. It is a sign that the enzymatic process which tenderizes meat tissues is occurring. Of course, it is trimmed off before cutting the meat up into steaks.) This extra care and attention is what distinguishes the flavor of Texas meats from the rest of the country's high-priced cuts. Zentner's steaks are cooked to perfection in garlic and flour on seven grills that total 175 square feet. Onion rings and Texas fries come as side orders called blocks (a block is a french fry cage filled to the top and dumped into a basket). On the weekends, Zentner's sells literally a ton of these a day. The garlic flour-encrusted steaks are served in pyramid shaped mounds on huge platters (with doggie bags to take home the inevitable leftovers). The meat is so succulent, people fly in from Houston just to have Betty personally butcher their favorite cuts to take back home.

Now, if garlic and flour isn't your idea of eating steak, there is the "Big Texan" in Amarillo to satiate the diehard. Here 72-ounce steaks are grilled over mesquite wood and served gratis — providing you eat the whole thing (currently about one in every five people succeed) within one hour.

Texans respect and enjoy the privilege of eating quality foods. Whatever the dish, the most important aspect of Texas cooking is best summed up by restaurant owner Joan Stocks Nobles who says, "To put a frozen T.V. dinner or boxed-mix down in front of someone is like telling them to go to hell. With all the processed foods we eat, we're slowly embalming ourselves in preservatives. Real Texas cooking is made from scratch, with whatever is available. So if you are missing something — improvise! Never waste anything." This is the attitude that makes the taste of Lone Star cooking so unique.

Besides iced tea, beer is a Texan's favorite beverage. At cookoffs, Lone Star, Pearl or Shiners are carried in hip holsters (especially designed to accommodate beer cans) for a quick draw. Pictured are interior shots of Pearl Brewery in San Antonio shortly before re-legalization of beer in 1933. *Courtesy of the Institute of Texan Cultures.*

TEA

Texans love their tea — oceans of it — so much so that truck stops and cafes keep trays stacked full of iced tea instead of the customary glasses of water. In one Texas diner, we were first served a round of iced tea, and then were asked for our order. We politely told the waitress there must be some mistake because no one had ordered tea. Her eyes widened. Obviously miffed, she swept the iced tea glasses from our table without a word and never returned. Cowboys and truckers, hunched over their iced teas, shot menacing glances in our direction, muttering something about "damn northerners." It became uncomfortably obvious we had committed a culinary faux pas that should never be repeated again. The next time we sat down to eat and the inevitable glass of iced tea confronted us, we kept our mouths shut. We had learned our lesson.

After relentlessly questioning Texas tea drinkers about why they drink so much tea, we found the following three reasons most commonly cited: Reason One: "Tea has a way of slakin' your thirst better than water." Reason Two: "Texas water tastes terrible. You've gotta put somethin' in it to change the taste." Reason Three (the most common response): "I dunno . . . Ah jes' lahke it." Well they must, because if it wasn't for the "X" in Texas, the state would have been named after the drink.

BEANS

Beans are a staple Texans were raised on. Pinto beans (cowboys called them prairie strawberries, whistleberries or musical fruit) are the most commonly used bean. In conjunction with corn bread, beans made a nearly perfect food, supplying proteins necessary for survival when meat was scarce. Range cooks and housewives were intuitively aware of this nutritional fact and served beans relentlessly, day after day. Beans were boiled, baked, mashed, fried and refried until hapless recipients begged for mercy. This constant subjection to beans (the fruit of many disguises) may be over-exaggerated, but during the early days of Texas, it was "put up or shut up." As one story goes, a disgruntled range hand, after having been "fed up to here with beans," "accidentally" tipped over the day's pot of you-know-what. He had hoped the chuck wagon cook would replace the omnipresent beans with something more palatable. No such luck. The clumsy waddy somehow survived the endless oaths and wrath of the camp cook; he went to bed wiser and a bit hungrier (about a serving of beans' worth). His compatriots' growling stomachs during the night also made it clear to him that, the next day, "Don't spill the beans!" And he didn't — he valued his life! Today beans may be the butt end of a great many jokes, but they are gaining a greater acceptance in America's dietary habits, particularly in light of ever-spiraling meat prices.

CORN BREAD

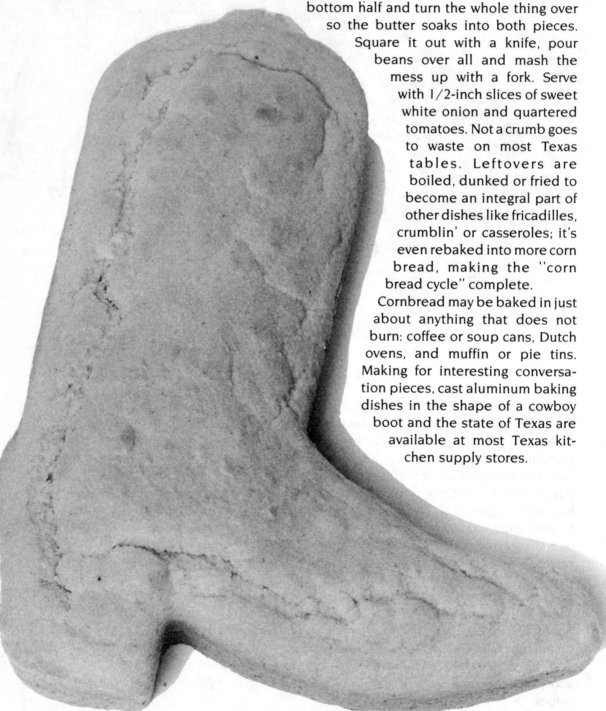

Corn bread is to Texas as tortillas are to Mexico. It can be found at breakfast, lunch and dinner where its fresh-baked aroma brings strong Texans trembling to their knees. It is usually eaten with a generous slathering of "cow grease" (butter) and a tall glass of cold buttermilk. Another favorite method is to slice a pan full of corn bread in half, the long way, and drown one half in butter. Place the top half on top of the bottom half and turn the whole thing over so the butter soaks into both pieces. Square it out with a knife, pour beans over all and mash the mess up with a fork. Serve with 1/2-inch slices of sweet white onion and quartered tomatoes. Not a crumb goes to waste on most Texas tables. Leftovers are boiled, dunked or fried to become an integral part of other dishes like fricadilles, crumblin' or casseroles; it's even rebaked into more corn bread, making the "corn bread cycle" complete.

Cornbread may be baked in just about anything that does not burn: coffee or soup cans, Dutch ovens, and muffin or pie tins. Making for interesting conversation pieces, cast aluminum baking dishes in the shape of a cowboy boot and the state of Texas are available at most Texas kitchen supply stores.

STEAK

When it comes "rat" ("rat" is a colloquial term meaning "right") down to it, Texans spell food: S-T-E-A-K. They love their meat, and for good reasons, too. Texas is, was and probably will forever be cattle country. Texans know how to raise meat, age it and cook it to perfection. When they want to sample this meaty art form weekly pilgrimages are made to any one of the thousands of steak palaces Texas is so famous for. The best places personally select their own beef and age the meat on the premises for up to three weeks. Steaks are cut large (five pounders are common) and prepared in a variety of styles. Probably the most popular are steaks grilled over a mesquite wood fire. Chicken fried steaks also have a loyal following, as do German fried steaks which are lightly floured and cooked on a grill sizzling with garlic, salt and rendered sweet suet. Meat emporiums cater strictly to the carnivorous diner, so take warning, you non-meat eaters; if you inadvertently stroll into one of these places, prepare to face what many call a vegetarian's nightmare.

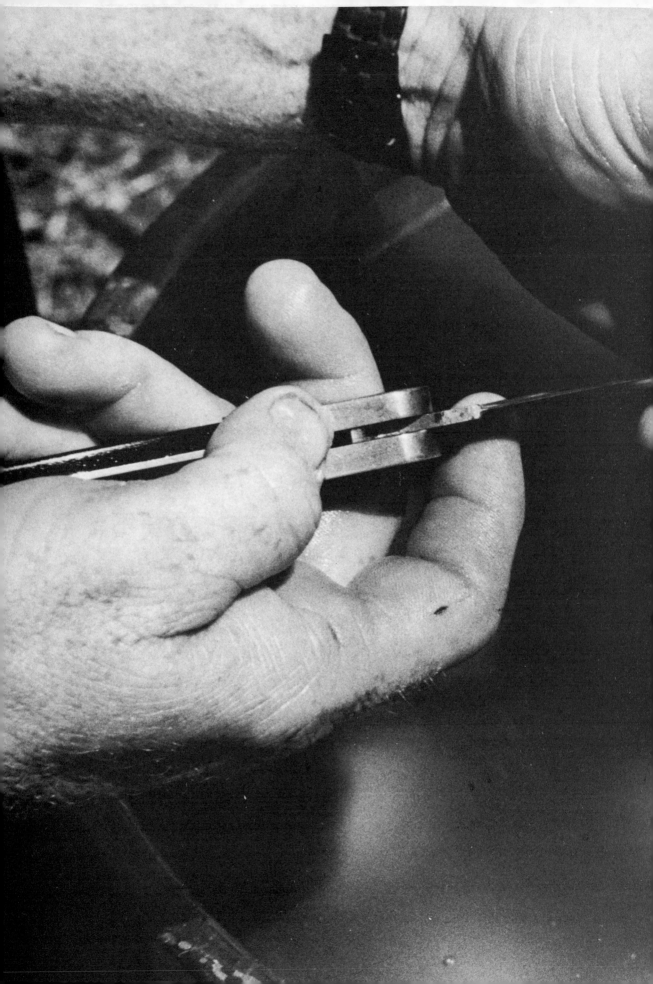

MOUNTAIN OYSTERS

Each year in San Angelo the same old jokes fly thick and fast: "Welcome to the World's Largest Testicle Festival . . . Yessireee, ladies and gentlemen, we have the situation well in hand . . . All you young bull-headed boys oughta steer clear of the area, please." A groan ripples through the crowd gathered around the ratchet-jawed announcer, Tex Schofield. He continues undaunted, "The mouth of the chili world is on the ball-eye today-eye, eh-eye???" (The addition of the sound "eye" is a particular tonal inflection the verbose Mr. Schofield is afflicted with.) Another collective groan and a pair of pinking shears glinting in the sunlight "help" Tex get on with the proceedings. "All right-eye . . . I can take a hint-eye. Those of you nuts, nuts enough to enter the Great Knee-Dimpling Contest, please step up to the stage. The Great Ejaculated Nicotine-eye Tainted Mucous Expectorant-eye Contest, otherwise known as the Tobacco Spitting Contest, will follow shortly." And so it goes at The Original World Championship Rocky Mountain Oyster Fryoff.

The brainchild of Sam Lewis, the fryoff is probably one of the world's weirdest, but most entertaining, events. It was originally devised in conjunction with the San Angelo Chamber of Commerce to attract attention to the city, and it has succeeded admirably. In 1981, over 5,000 people attended this oddball event. Cooks came from all over Texas to compete, frying up calf fries (bull testicles), sheep and turkey nuts (one zealot entered a plate full of little breaded BB's, claiming they were culled from the private parts of rattlesnakes). Visitors strolling the grounds had a chance to sample the "comestible digestibles" and view Oyster Shuckin' Texas Style firsthand. Eventually the moment of truth arrived, and the contestants were asked to "lay yer nuts on the table" for the purpose of judging the entries. For the judges, who had the most difficult job at this event, emergency stomach pumps were available, as well as taste bud neutralizing agents (that would be anything from 7-Up to Shiner). Sam Lewis made it clear "that anything goes here, the judges can be bought!" Apparently they were; because of some snafu, first place was never awarded. "But winning isn't everything," as one man with two propellers (whirring crazily) stuck onto his head told us. "People are here to have a good time and make friends." The flyer advertising the event had put it this way: Thank you, have a ball and come again." And that's precisely what we did.

Background photo — The hands of "Bugger Red" Anderson remove the tough outer skin from a calf fry. Red came to the cookoff as a spectator, but was recruited by the "Brownwood Ball Team" when their head cook imbibed to freely from a case of light beer.

COUNTRY FRIED RATTLESNAKE

If you have the stomach for it, snake meat is delicious. It's been described as tasting somewhere between finger lickin' good chicken, frog legs and fish. The only problem you'll run into cooking rattlesnake is catching it. Be careful. Consult a professional snakearoo (that's a buckaroo who catches snakes instead of cows) before you go foraging for this unpredictable dinner dish. The best place to educate yourself on the subject is at the Sweetwater Rattlesnake Roundup, held in the second week of March in Sweetwater, Texas. Each year, up to 5000 Nile Perch (rattlesnakes) are harvested. They are milked for venom, sent to research labs, eaten, and/or made into hatbands, belts and wallets. The head cook at the Roundup is Mama Doris Ransberger. In 1959, when the Roundup got its official start, snake meat was barbecued. The meat turned out to be tough. Mama Doris stepped in to help and deep fried it. At first, no one would eat snake meat, but after her own children stepped up and popped succulent morsel after succulent morsel into their innocent mouths, leery ranchers and farmers formed long lines to taste the delicacy. Today, the snake-eating ritual is one everybody willingly participates in. Here is Mama Doris' recipe from the

Rattlesnakes in America book. Get yourself a rattlesnake. Skin and clean it. Cut the snake up into three-inch lengths. Bread the meat in flour, salt and pepper, and deep fat fry in oil at 450° until browned. Serve garnished with cholla cactus segments, small rocks, sand and beer. For dessert, pop open a cold can of jackrabbit milk. From tip to tail, the Western Diamondback Rattlesnake may grow to a length of seven feet and weigh up to ten pounds. Pictured here is "Angie," one of the author's "Do Not Touch!" souvenirs from Texas (who, by the way, won't find herself as the main ingredient in Doris' recipe).

APPETIZERS

Appetizers are kind of an anomaly on the Texas table. They "just kinda get in the way of the main dish." If you *do* find "appetizers" served, they are curious, to say the least.

TEXAS CAVIAR — PICKLED BLACK-EYED PEAS

2 (Number 2) cans black-eyed peas
3/4 cup salad oil
1/4 cup wine vinegar
1 clove garlic or garlic seasoning
1/4 cup thinly sliced onion
1/2 teaspoon salt
cracked or freshly ground black pepper

Drain liquid from the peas. Place peas in pan or bowl; add remaining ingredients and mix thoroughly. Store in jar in refrigerator and remove garlic bud after one day. Store at least two days and up to two weeks before eating. Drain before serving.

Mrs. James Liberman

DR. PEPPER CHEESE PECAN BALL WITH DRIED BEEF

1/2 pound processed American cheese, grated
1 (3-ounce) package cream cheese
3 to 4 tablespoons Dr. Pepper
2 teaspoons lemon juice
1/2 teaspoon salt
1/4 teaspoon garlic, minced
1/16 teaspoon crushed, dried red pepper
1/2 cup pecans, chopped
1-1/2 cups chopped dried beef

Blend cheeses and Dr. Pepper in electric mixer until light and fluffy. Add remaining ingredients except for beef. Shape into 2 balls and chill about 20 minutes. Roll in the chopped dried beef. Make sure all areas are covered. Place in a plastic bag and chill thoroughly. Serve with cheese knife for spreading on party rye slices or crackers.

M.A. Pepper

QUICK HORS D'OEUVRES

bacon
pickled watermelon rind, chunked

Wrap bacon slices cut in thirds around bite-size pieces of pickled watermelon rind and secure with a toothpick. Bake in 400° oven until bacon is crisp. Drain and serve hot.

Ann Stool

TEXAS TRASH

3/4 cup bacon grease (or oleo)
1-1/2 sticks oleo
3 tablespoons Worcestershire sauce
3 tablespoons garlic salt
1-1/2 teaspoons Accent
2 tablespoons Tabasco
1 large can mixed nuts
1/2 box Cheerios
2 boxes pretzels
1/2 box Wheat Chex
1/2 box Rice Chex
oyster crackers (optional)

Mix first 6 ingredients together in a saucepan and pour over the next 6 ingredients. Bake 1-1/2 hours at 225°. Stir every 15 minutes. Place in coffee cans or covered containers and serve for snacks.

Mary Ann Smallwood

TEXAS HOT PEPPER PECANS

1/4 cup butter
2 cups pecan halves
4 teaspoons soy sauce
1 teaspoon salt
12 dashes Tabasco

Melt butter in baking pan. Spread pecans evenly in pan and bake at 300° for 30 minutes. Combine soy sauce, salt and Tabasco and toss with pecans. Spread on paper towel to cool.

Mrs. Jack Williams

BEST BAR-NONE BEAN DIP

4 cups pinto beans
2 cups chopped onions
3 cloves garlic, chopped
2 tablespoons ground cumin seeds
2 tablespoons bacon drippings
6 tablespoons chili powder
salt to taste
1/2 cup butter
1/2 pound sharp Cheddar cheese, grated
dash of Mexican hot sauce

Soak beans overnight. Cook in soaking water with onions, garlic, cumin, chili powder and bacon drippings. Simmer 3 to 4 hours. When beans are soft, add salt. While beans are warm, add butter, cheese and hot sauce. Blend in blender until smooth. Serve warm.

Mrs. J. L. (Marie) Renick

BAVARIAN DIP

1 (3-ounce) package cream cheese
2 tablespoons lemon juice
1 (8-ounce) package Braunschweiger
1 envelope dried onion soup mix
1 tablespoon horseradish
1 teaspoon Worcestershire sauce
dash of Tabasco
2/3 cup evaporated milk

Combine first two ingredients in small bowl of electric mixer or blender. Add the rest of the ingredients. Blend at high speed until completely smooth. Chill before serving.

Margy Hulings

SAUCES & CONDIMENTS

Fancy gourmet sauces and delicate salad dressings are not a major part of the culinary program. You will find little bottles of Tabasco just about everywhere. Most sauces are used on meats and fish. As for condiments relishes, chow-chows and preserves help spice up any meal. In the old days, it was not unusual for a Texas family to put up a thousand jars of fruits and vegetables during a year.

JEFFERSON SAUCE

2 gallons green tomatoes
1-1/2 to 2 cups green hot peppers
1/2 cup salt (not iodized)
1 tablespoon black pepper
1 gallon onions
5 cups sugar
1/2 gallon white vinegar

Quarter the tomatoes; slice the onions round and chop the peppers. Mix all ingredients and boil 25 to 30 minutes. Pour in sterilized jars and seal. This sauce recipe came from Jefferson Parish in Louisiana. It was served with catfish, but is good with all meats.

Dickie Davis

STEAK SAUCE

1 medium-sized can button mushrooms
1 medium-sized can sliced mushrooms
1/2 cup red wine
2 tablespoons browned flour
1 teaspoon Accent
1/4 teaspoon garlic powder
1 tablespoon lemon juice
salt and pepper to taste

Sauté mushrooms in butter. Brown flour in iron skillet, stirring constantly. Add equal parts juice from mushrooms and red wine. Thicken with browned flour sifted in gradually. Next, stir in the seasonings. Cook over medium heat about 10 minutes, stirring occasionally. Pour over prepared steaks.

Dr. F. M. Sporer/Donor: Mrs. H. H. Niehuss

MINT SAUCE

1/2 cup vinegar
1/4 cup sugar
1/4 cup water
dash salt
1/2 cup finely snipped mint leaves

In saucepan combine vinegar, sugar, water and salt. Bring to boil, reduce heat and simmer uncovered 5 minutes. Pour immediately over mint leaves; let steep 30 minutes. Strain or serve as is, hot or cold, with lamb. I usually store it with mint leaves still in and strain into serving pitcher.

Mrs. Robert (Lo) McCauley

CHOW CHOW

12-1/2 pounds green tomatoes
8 large onions
18 green peppers
3 tablespoons salt
6 hot peppers
1 quart vinegar
1 tablespoon cinnamon
1 head cabbage
1 tablespoon allspice
1/4 teaspoon cloves
3 tablespoons mustard leaves
1-1/4 cups sugar
1/2 cup horseradish

Chop tomatoes, onions and peppers together and cover with the salt. Let stand overnight. Drain. Add the hot peppers, which have been chopped, and add vinegar and spices. Allow to boil slowly until tender, about 15 minutes. Pack tightly in jars and seal at once.

Mrs. Jim McCarty

SLANG JANG

1-2/3 cups chopped ripe tomatoes
1 cup chopped bell pepper
2 cups chopped onions
2 tablespoons salad oil
1/3 cup sugar

1/2 cup vinegar
3 teaspoons Accent
salt and pepper to taste

Combine vegetables and toss with the oil. Add all other ingredients and mix well. Place in covered jar or bowl and let stand several hours. A delicious relish served with cream peas or black-eyed peas.

Cherokee Club Kitchen

WATERMELON RIND PRESERVES

rind of one watermelon - juicy, "snappy" and sliced thin (5 quarts)
5 cups sugar
1/2 cup water (no more than that)
1 lemon

Separate the rinds, sugar and water into two pots. Add 1/2 lemon to each pot (sliced paper thin). Cook for about 1 hour, uncovered. If there is lots of juice, use a fairly high flame; if no juice, start with low flame and increase heat as juice cooks out. After first hour, combine both pots together and cook over low flame until rind is waxy and juice is thick and syrupy — usually about 3-1/2 to 4 hours. Serve chilled over corn bread which is dripping in butter.

Marion Bennett

PICKLED OKRA

okra
2 quarts water
1 cup canning salt
1 quart apple cider vinegar
1 jalapeno pepper
1 clove garlic
head of dill

Boil water and salt together for 10 minutes, then cool. Add the vinegar. In the bottom of your jars, cut the remaining spices, then pack in raw okra, pour the brine over okra and seal.

Rosa Slawson

JERUSALEM ARTICHOKE PICKLES

Jerusalem artichokes
small hot peppers
garlic cloves
3 quarts water
1 quart vinegar
1/3 cup canning salt
1 tablespoon mustard seeds
1/2 cup sugar
dill (optional)

Wash and scrub with a stiff brush the amount of artichokes you have. Slice in 1/8"
slices (you can leave the small ones whole). They will darken if left uncovered so slice
them into cold water. In each sterilized quart jar, put 1 small hot pepper, 1 or 2 cloves
garlic and fill jar with artichoke slices. Combine in pan water, vinegar, salt, mustard
seeds and sugar. Boil 5 minutes. Pour boiling liquid over artichokes and seal at once.
Let stand 4 to 6 weeks before using. It takes approximately 2 cups liquid per quart of
artichoke slices, so if you have just a pint or so, decrease the amount of liquid you
prepare. Too, if you like dill, you can add a small head of fresh dill or 1/2 teaspoon
dill seeds to each quart.

Mrs. John (Nancy) Greenway

CUCUMBER PICKLES

9 quarts small cucumbers
1 gallon vinegar
1 cup sugar
1 cup salt
1/2 cup dry mustard
small piece alum

Wash cucumbers. Boil vinegar, sugar, salt and mustard. Drop in a small piece of alum.
Pour over cucumbers and seal jars.

Joan Stocks Nobles

BREAD & BUTTER PICKLES

12 to 15 sliced cucumbers
2 sliced onions
saltwater
3-1/2 cups vinegar
2 cups water

1-1/2 cups sugar
4 teaspoons mustard seeds
1 teaspoon tumeric seeds

Soak sliced cucumbers and onions overnight in weak saltwater in crock. Boil together the rest of the ingredients. Let cucumbers and onions drain and add to the boiling ingredients and quickly bring back to a boil. Boil for a few minutes. Pour into jars and seal.

Joan Stocks Nobles

CREAMY GARLIC DRESSING

2 cups mayonnaise
1 cup buttermilk
1 teaspoon Accent
1-1/2 teaspoons garlic salt
1 teaspoon onion salt
1 teaspoon parsley flakes
1 teaspoon oregano
1/8 teaspoon celery salt
1 teaspoon dried chives

Mix all ingredients well. Refrigerate. This will keep for a month. Great on salad or baked potato.

Mrs. C. W. (Maxine) Talley

LONE STAR SALAD DRESSING

1-1/2 cups salad oil
1 cup Lone Star beer
1 tablespoon Worcestershire sauce
2 (10-3/4-ounce) cans condensed tomato soup
1 small onion, grated
1 large clove garlic, minced
1 tablespoon sugar
2 tablespoons salt
1 tablespoon prepared horseradish

Combine all ingredients in a bowl and beat until well blended. Chill until ready to serve. Beat again just before serving.

Donny Jacobson

MAYONNAISE

2 egg yolks
pinch of salt
1/4 cup lemon juice
1-3/4 cup Wesson oil
cayenne pepper

In a small crock that has been chilled, beat lightly the egg yolks. Add a pinch of salt. Alternate a little at a time, beating steadily, the lemon juice with the Wesson oil. Garnish with cayenne. Use as a topping with: 1) tomatoes stuffed with cottage cheese seasoned to taste with salt and pepper, 2) pineapple or pear halves stuffed with cottage cheese 3) or use with any type sandwich.

Joan Stocks Nobles

MESQUITE BEAN JELLY

4-3/4 cups mesquite bean juice
1/4 cup lemon juice
1 box Sur-Jel
7-1/2 cups sugar

Select mesquite beans that are juicy and filled out well. Green ones are all right if not too green. To prepare: wash, snap and place in large container. Add enough water to nearly cover beans. Cook for 30 minutes at 15 pounds of pressure. Drain juice and pour back into pressure cooker. Add another batch of beans and enough water to nearly cover. Cook same as first time. Drain off juice and set aside. Repeat above method until you have 4-3/4 cups bean juice. Place bean juice and lemon juice in a large container. Add one box of Sur-Jel. Stir until it boils. Add sugar, stirring constantly, and bring to a full rolling boil. Boil hard for one minute, stirring constantly with a metal spoon. Remove from heat. Skim off foam. Pour into glass jars leaving 1/2 inch at top. Seal.

Mrs. Cathy Walker

ON THE SIDE

Texans have never been real "keen" on soups. Instead hearty soup/stews, the ones that'll put meat on your bones, are more characteristic of Texas cooking. Vegetables also take second billing in this "meat and potatoes"-oriented culture. "Keeper" vegetables like the aforementioned beans, potatoes, carrots and onions are boiled, baked and fried into oblivion, to the horror of most vegetarians.

PAETZEL'S PINTO POT

10 pounds pinto beans, well washed
5 onions, chopped
1 or 2 teaspoons comino
1 (6-ounce) pack mild chili powder
6 jalapenos, finely chopped
4 cloves garlic, smashed
black pepper to taste
salt to taste
1 pound thick bacon, cut in pieces

Start soaking beans about 5:00 P.M. Then leave and go somewhere and indulge in Pearl Beer until 2:00 A.M. Come home if you can, and start cooking. (Must continue to drink Pearl Beer while cooking.) Drain beans, put in large iron pot, and add the rest of the ingredients. Cover with water. Cook beans until 7:00 A.M. Turn off at 7:00 A.M. and go to sleep until 10:00 A.M. 10:00 A.M. — Time for Chili Cookoff to begin! Get up!

Ed Paetzel

COWBOY BEANS

2 pounds pinto beans
2 pounds ham hocks or salt pork
2 onions, chopped
4 tablespoons sugar
2 green chilies or to taste
1 can tomato paste
salt

Wash beans and soak overnight. Cover beans with water and cook with above ingredients over low heat (simmer) until done. Sample the beans while cooking so you can add salt to taste. Add water as needed.

Sharon Blackmore

RED CALDWELL'S BEANS-R-BEST

2 pounds pinto beans
1 pound salt pork, cubed 1 x 1 x 1/4"
1 teaspoon chili powder
2 medium onions, chopped
2 cloves garlic, minced
2 jalapenos, sliced
1/2 teaspoon cayenne
1 teaspoon black pepper
salt to taste after beans are cooked

Soak the beans overnight, then drain off soak water. Fill with water to cover beans, add onions, garlic, peppers, salt pork and spices except the salt. Cook damn slow four to six hours on a very low heat — just enough to move the liquid around. Add salt to taste when beans are done. Serve with corn bread or flour tortillas and beer.

Red Caldwell

TEXAS RANGER BEANS

1/2 cup brown sugar
1/2 cup tomato catsup
2 teaspoons vinegar
2 teaspoons chili powder
dash Worcestershire sauce
1/2 teaspoon salt
1/2 teaspoon pepper
2 cans beans with pork
1 large onion, sliced

Mix sugar, catsup, vinegar, chili powder, Worcestershire sauce, salt and pepper to a paste. Add to beans and onion. Bring to a boil. Bake in 325° oven for 1 hour or until sauce is thick.

Mrs. O. R. Langford

HOT PANTS BEANS

1 pound of pinto beans, well washed
2 medium onions, chopped
6 thick slices bacon, chopped
1 tablespoon salt
1 can of tomatoes or tomatoes and chilies, if you like 'em hot (optional)
1 teaspoon sugar (optional)

Put the beans in a big pot filled with water and soak them overnight. Add the onions, bacon and salt and let boil for 2 hours. Taste-test after 1 hour. Add optional ingredients if desired. In Texas we don't put beans in our chili, but they're great as a side dish. All you foreigners go ahead and dump them in if you must; but cook them this way *first*. SECRET: A teaspoon of Bicarbonate of Soda in the water the beans cook in will take the acid effect out. And then you'll have the Bicarb handy in case you need it for your stomach!

Allegani is one of those Texans willing to 'fess up to liking beans with her chili. Hot Pants Beans are the perfect accompaniment to her Hot Pants Chili which appears in the Chili section.

Allegani Jani

STUFFED BAKED POTATOES

potatoes (per person)
2 tablespoons butter
1/8 teaspoon salt
1 tablespoon half-and-half
sliced Cheddar cheese

Bake potato 1 hour at 400° or until done. Cut in half while still hot. Spoon out potato leaving a little "meat" in the shell. Mix butter, salt and half-and-half with mashed potato meat and spoon mixture back into the shell. Top with sliced Cheddar cheese. Heat in 400° oven until cheese melts.

Joan S. Nobles

HOME FRIES

6 boiled potatoes
1/2 cup shortening
1-1/4 teaspoons salt
1/8 teaspoon pepper
paprika

Peel potatoes and slice or dice. Heat shortening in a large skillet. Place potatoes in skillet over medium high heat. Sprinkle with salt, pepper and a dash of paprika. Fry until golden brown, turning occasionally.

Virginia Scott

ONION RINGS

20 large white onions, sliced 1/2-inch thick (use nothing smaller than a half dollar)
1 tablespoon sugar
1/2 gallon buttermilk
1 teaspoon soda
vegetable shortening or beef tallow
flour

Make a batter from the sugar, buttermilk and soda. Dip onion rings in batter, then in flour, then in batter and again in the flour. Deep fry in vegetable shortening or beef tallow at 350° until golden brown.

Dorothy Buckalew

GARLIC GRITS

8 cups boiling salted water
2 cups grits
1 stick butter
2 rolls garlic cheese
3 teaspoons sherry
1 tablespoon Tabasco
1 tablespoon Worcestershire sauce
2 eggs, well beaten

Preheat oven to 300°. Cook grits in boiling water, stirring constantly. Cook until done, but not dry. While hot, add butter and cheese. Stir until melted. Add sherry, Tabasco and Worcestershire sauce. Mix well. Add eggs. Pour into oblong baking dish, brush with melted butter and bake 1 hour.

Mrs. Bob (June) Grundy

BIG TEX CARROTS A LA ORANGE

5 cups cooked sliced carrots
6 tablespoons brown sugar
2 tablespoons flour
salt to taste
3/4 cup Big Tex orange juice

Place carrots in baking dish and sprinkle with mixture of brown sugar, flour and salt. Pour orange juice over all. Bake at 350° for 20 to 30 minutes.

FRIED OKRA

3/4 pound okra
1 cup buttermilk
1/2 teaspoon garlic salt
1/2 teaspoon onion salt
flour in a bag
oil for deep frying

Cut okra into half-inch slices. Season buttermilk with garlic and onion salt. A few at a time, soak okra slices in buttermilk until well coated. Shake okra in bag of flour. Keep slices separated. Deep fry in hot oil until golden brown. Drain on paper towel. Repeat operation until all is cooked. Freezes well.

Mrs. Wilburn (Fran) Oatman

TEXAS CORN

corn on the cob (per person)
1/4 cup margarine, melted
1 tablespoon chili powder
1 teaspoon paprika
salt and pepper

Wash and silk corn. Combine margarine, chili powder and paprika. Brush each ear of corn with mixture; sprinkle with salt and pepper. Wrap each ear in foil with a "drugstore wrap" to seal. Place on cookie sheet; bake for 1 hour at 350°. Corn may also be cooked on a grill.

Mrs. Bill Garrison

SUCCOTASH

1 cup boiled corn
1 cup lima beans
1/3 cup milk
1/8 teaspoon black pepper
1/2 teaspoon salt
2 tablespoons butter or margarine
1/2 teaspoon sugar

Combine all ingredients and cook 10 minutes.

Sallie Hill

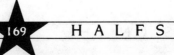

HOPPING JOHN

1 cup dried black-eyed peas
1/4 pound salt pork, diced
1 medium green pepper, chopped
1 medium onion, chopped
1 cup rice
1 tablespoon butter or margarine
pinch cayenne pepper
salt and pepper to taste

Soak peas overnight; drain. Add salt pork, green pepper and onion. Cover with water and simmer for 2 hours or until peas are tender. Cook rice according to package directions. When peas are done and water has cooked very low, add rice and remaining ingredients. Cover and cook over low heat until all liquid is absorbed. Serve hot.

Cookbook Committee

FRICADILLES

1 jackrabbit
1 sage chicken
sow-bosom (salt pork)
1 onion
pepper to taste
2 eggs
flour
vegetables - any on hand

Dress the game, cut meat off the bones, grind the meat along with the salt pork, onion and pepper to taste. Mix well. Fry as sausage. Take bones with meat removed and boil. When bones are boiled clean, remove them and add any vegetables to the broth (as carrots, potatoes, beans, etc.). Take the mixture of ground meat, prepared to fry. Add 2 eggs and enough flour to make mixture stick together and drop mixture by the teaspoon in the broth. Boil for 20 minutes or until fricadilles are done.

Edward H. Gould

MYRLE GREENWOOD'S SON-OF-A-GUN STEW

Son-of-a-Gun Stew, originally dubbed Son-of-a-Bitch Stew, is a favorite cowboy dish. Everything but the hooves, hair and horns go into it. The dish's unique taste comes from the margut, the intestinal tube that contains partially digested milk solids in unweaned calves. The stew received its name when an inquisitive cowhand, looking into the pot full of "this and that," asked the cook, "what the hell is in there?" The cook stirred up a few of the more biological-looking chunks and replied with a straight face, "It's a son of a bitch."

suet
1 calf heart
1 piece calf liver 1/3 the size of the heart
2 calf kidneys
the sweetbreads
the marrow gut*
the brains
6 pods garlic, minced
1 large onion, chopped fine
1 tablespoon ground comino seeds
salt
chopped hot green peppers (optional)

*If you don't know where the marrow gut ends and other things begin, find someone who does and let them SHOW you!

Cut the heart, liver, kidneys and marrow gut into bite-size pieces. Sear this on top of the stove in a roaster in which you have melted suet. Mash the brains and add them. (This is the thickening.) Add the onions, garlic, cominos, salt to taste and, if you like, a few finely chopped hot green peppers. Put cover on roaster and place in 300° oven until done. This will take an hour or an hour and a half. Stir once or twice, but not too often or you'll have mush.

Murle Greenwood

ROMAINE LETTUCE SOUP

2 tablespoons butter
1 small onion, minced
1 quart chicken broth
2 quarts chopped romaine
salt and pepper to taste
4 egg yolks
1 cup heavy cream

Sauté onions in butter until tender. Add broth and bring to boil. Add romaine, salt and pepper and cook over low heat 10 minutes. Beat egg yolks and cream together. Stir into soup and cook over low heat until thickened. DO NOT BOIL.

Mrs. Thomas E. (Jo) Zion

BIRD STEW

6 to 8 birds
3 quarts cold water
1 onion
1 can tomatoes
4 medium potatoes
1/2 apple
2 tablespoons butter
1 bay leaf
pinch of sage
whole cloves
whole allspice
salt and pepper
red pepper to taste
1/3 bottle catsup
Worcestershire sauce to taste
1/2 pint cream

Put birds in stewing kettle; add water and bring to boil. Add onion. Boil 1 hour; add tomatoes, potatoes, apple and seasonings. Simmer for 2 hours. Add catsup and Worcestershire sauce. Simmer 30 minutes to 1 hour. Before serving, add cream. Add more water during the cooking as needed.

Mrs. W. C. Smith

FIVE MINUTE SOUP

This soup is a fine example of Texans recycling leftovers.

4 or 5 leftover biscuits
1-1/2 cups milk
1/4 cup of butter
salt and pepper

In a heavy cast-iron skillet, melt 1/4 cup of butter. Crumble (coarsely) leftover biscuits into melted butter. Stir constantly until biscuits are a golden brown. Add milk and heat. Do not boil. Add salt and pepper and serve.

Viola Shepherd

HOPKINS COUNTY STEW

4 slices bacon, diced
2 tablespoons butter or margarine
3-1/2 to 4 pound stewing chicken, cut into pieces
6 medium onions, chopped
1 green pepper, chopped
1-1/2 cups chopped celery
3 (1-pound) cans tomatoes
2 (12-ounce) cans kernel corn
3 pounds potatoes, peeled and diced
1-1/2 cups water
1 tablespoon salt
1/4 teaspoon paprika
1/4 teaspoon curry powder
1/4 teaspoon pepper

Fry bacon in large kettle; add butter or margarine and chicken and sauté until well browned. Add remaining ingredients, bring to a boil, and simmer. To expedite cooking indoors, cook covered at least 4 hours, stirring occasionally. After about 1 hour, remove chicken; bone. Dice meat and return to kettle.

Mrs. J. Linton Clark

ALLEGANI'S OKRA GUMBO

2 tablespoons bacon drippings
3 cups okra, chopped
3 tomatoes, chopped
2 cups sliced zucchini
1 teaspoon garlic salt
1/2 teaspoon pepper
1 teaspoon chili powder
1 tablespoon Tabasco
3 cups water

In a heavy pot, sauté okra in drippings (this helps rid okra of its "sliminess"). Add remaining ingredients. Simmer for one hour. Serve with corn bread.

Jani Schofield

CHICKEN GUMBO

1 (3-pound) frying chicken
1 teaspoon salt
1 bay leaf
6 to 8 cups chicken broth
1 small can tomato sauce
1/2 can Ro-Tel tomatoes with chilies
1 green pepper, chopped
2 large onions, chopped
2 stalks celery, chopped
1 package frozen sliced okra

Boil chicken until very tender in broth to which you have added salt and bay leaf. Cool in broth. Bone and save broth. Add broth to all other ingredients and simmer for 1-1/2 hours to develop flavor.

ROUX:
1/4 cup margarine
1 cup water
2 to 3 tablespoons flour

Add flour to melted margarine and cook, stirring constantly until very dark brown. Add water and blend. Stir this into above mixture and add chicken. Heat and serve over rice.

Lilla B. Rimel

BREADS

Breads are an important staple in any culture's diet. In the early days of Texas, corn was more widely cultivated than wheat (it was easier to harvest by hand) so most breads were cornmeal based; hence the abundance of corn bread recipes.

LIGHT WHITE BREAD

Handed down in my family who have been ranch owners in San Angelo area since 1880's. Women made their own bread and from this basic recipe developed *many* kinds of rolls.

4 cups milk
8 tablespoons Crisco
3/4 cup sugar
2 packages dry yeast
10 to 12 cups flour
2 tablespoons salt

Scald together the milk, Crisco and sugar. Remove from heat and put in large bowl. Cool to room temperature and add the yeast. Beat in about 6 cups of flour, then add and "work in" with your hands approximately 4 to 6 more cups of flour to make a stiff (yet soft) dough. Do not knead on board. Let rise one hour covered with a cloth. Punch holes in top of dough, sprinkle salt over and work in again. Let rise one hour. Butter 4 loaf pans, fill with dough and let rise 45 minutes. Bake at 325° until golden brown.

Variations:

Rolls — Melt 3 tablespoons oleo on cookie sheet. Roll out dough 1/2" thick, cut with biscuit cutter, dip in oleo and fold over. Let rise 45 minutes. Bake at 400°.

Cinnamon Rolls — Melt 8 tablespoons oleo on cookie sheet. Roll out dough 1/4" thick, sprinkle with melted butter, sugar, brown sugar and cinnamon and drizzle with white Karo syrup. Roll up and cut rolls 1/2" thick. Let rise 45 minutes. Bake at 400°.

Potato Bread or Rolls — Use basic recipe and add 1 or 2 cups mashed potatoes with first rise.

Egg Rolls — Use basic recipe but substitute butter for Crisco and beat in 4 whole eggs with first rise.

Bran Rolls — Use basic recipe but substitute 1/2 bran flour for 1/2 white flour.

Joan Stocks Nobles

BASIC YEAST DOUGH

2 packages dry yeast
1/4 cup warm water
1-3/4 cups milk
1/4 cup cooking oil
1/4 cup sugar
1 tablespoon salt
5 to 6 cups flour
1 egg, beaten (optional)
1/4 cup additional sugar (optional)

Sprinkle yeast into water and let stand about 5 minutes. Scald milk, oil, sugar and salt. Let cool to lukewarm. Add yeast. Add flour and mix to a soft dough (it may take more or less flour). Knead until smooth, place in a greased bowl, set in a warm place (out of draft) and let rise until double. Punch down and allow to rise again. Replace 2 cups white flour with 2 cups whole wheat flour and use honey to sweeten for a delicious difference.

Venetia Hartley

FOOLPROOF BREAD

3 cups flour
1 package dry yeast
1/2 cup cooking oil
1/2 cup water
1/2 cup milk
1/3 cup sugar - less if desired
1 tablespoon salt
2 eggs
2 one pound coffee cans to bake in

Sift flour and yeast together. Heat over low heat the milk, oil, water, sugar and salt. Stir to blend — do not boil — just scald. Mix well together the warm (not hot) liquid and eggs. Blend in a little at a time the flour-yeast and stir well. Divide dough in half and put in well-greased coffee cans. Cover with lids and let rise until dough is about 1/2 inch from top. Remove lids and cook at 375° for 30 minutes. Let stand in cans about 15 minutes before removing.

Mrs. Ira Connaway

WHITE BREAD

1/2 cup warm water
2 packages dry yeast
1-3/4 cups lukewarm milk
2 tablespoons sugar
1 tablespoon salt
2 tablespoons soft shortening
7 cups flour

Add part of sugar to water before adding yeast. Measure 1/2 cup warm water in large mixing bowl and add yeast, stirring to dissolve. Set bowl in pan of very hot water until yeast starts to work and foam. Stir in milk, sugar, salt, shortening and then start adding flour and stir. Add flour until it handles easily and doesn't stick. Put dough on floured board and knead until it is smooth and elastic and no longer sticks to board. Round up in greased (butter) bowl. Turn to bring greased side up. Cover with damp cloth and put in oven with a pan of hot water on lower shelf. Let dough rise until doubled in bulk, approximately 1-1/2 hours. Punch down and turn dough over; cover with damp cloth again and let rise for about 30 minutes. Divide dough into 2 equal parts. Let rest on board (covered with dry tea towel) for 10 minutes; knead again and shape into loaves and put in greased bread pans. Put in oven; cover pans with dry cloth. Put pan of hot water on bottom rack of oven and let rise for 45 minutes to 1 hour. This will make the loaves rise until almost to top of bread pans. Turn oven on after removing towel and pan of water, to 375°. Starting in a cold oven lets the loaves rise a little more as the oven heats. Bake approximately 35 minutes. Take out of pans, put on rack and brush tops of loaves with butter.

Kathleen Ellison Loomis

MONKEY BREAD

1 stick melted butter
1 cup scalded milk
1 package yeast dissolved in 1/2 cup warm water
2 whole eggs
1/2 cup sugar
1/2 teaspoon salt
3 cups flour
1 stick butter

Beat eggs. Add sugar, salt, milk, one stick of melted butter and 1-1/2 cups flour. Beat again. Add yeast last. Let rise one hour, then add another 1-1/2 cups flour and blend well. Cover and refrigerate overnight. Take out 2 hours before cooking and let rise. Melt the other stick of butter. Pour half of the butter in deep pan. Put batter in pan, pour remaining butter on top and bake at 350° for 30 minutes.

Sue Sims

SOURDOUGH STARTER & SOURDOUGH BREAD

Sourdough bread is a Western bread; it was used when we didn't shop every day for groceries and will last a very long time if it is used and water and flour is added to the starter. The cowboy cooks used this.

SOURDOUGH STARTER
2 cups flour
2 cups water
2 tablespoons sugar

Mix ingredients together and let stand in a warm place 2 or 3 days or until fermented. The kitchen cabinet is a good place to let it stand.

SOURDOUGH BREAD
1 package dry yeast
1-1/2 cups warm water
1 cup sourdough starter
6 cups flour
2 teaspoons salt
2 teaspoons sugar
1/2 teaspoon soda

Dissolve yeast in warm water; add starter, 4 cups flour, salt and sugar. Stir vigorously for 3 minutes, let rise 2 hours or until double in bulk. Mix soda with 1 cup flour. Add to dough. Knead with remaining flour. Shape into loaves, place in loaf pans. Let rise until double in bulk. Brush top with a small amount of water. Bake in 400° oven for 45 to 50 minutes. This can also be rolled and cut for dinner rolls instead of loaves.

Pap Mack Buckalew

RED CHILI BISCUITS

2 cups all - purpose flour
1 tablespoon sugar
1 tablespoon baking powder
1 teaspoon salt
1/3 cup lard or shortening
1 tablespoon chili powder
1/2 cup shredded Cheddar cheese
1-1/2 cups sourdough starter (see recipe following)

Cut lard into dry ingredients until mixture resembles a fine meal. Add the cheese and sourdough starter and mix until flour is moistened. Place mixture on a floured surface. Knead lightly and pat to 1/2-inch thick. Cut with a 2-1/2-inch cutter. Put biscuits in a greased pan and bake in a 400° oven for 20-25 minutes.

1 quart lukewarm water
1 package dry yeast
2 teaspoons sugar
4 cups all-purpose flour

Put water in crock, add yeast and sugar to soften, stir in flour. Cover with a clean cloth. Let rise until mixture is light and slightly aged, about 2 days. Mixture will thin as it stands; add flour as needed. As you use sourdough from the crock, replace it with equal amounts of flour and water.

Philip Morris

BOURBON BREAD

1 package dry yeast
1 cup flour
1/4 cup light brown sugar
1/2 cup lukewarm water
2-1/4 cups unsifted flour
2 eggs, plus 1 white, beaten
1 teaspoon salt
1/3 cup melted butter
1/2 cup warm milk
1/4 cup bourbon

Combine the first 4 ingredients in a large bowl. Beat the mixture well and set the bowl in a dishpan of warm water. Cover with a towel. Let the dough rise for approximately 1 hour. Beat the eggs and the egg white until light. Then beat the eggs and all the remaining ingredients into the yeast mixture. Beat this mixture hard, using your hands, for approximately 4 minutes. The dough should be light, but with a good body. Add up to 3/4 cup more flour if needed. Place the dough in the bowl, and then in the pan of warm water. Cover. Let rise for approximately 45 minutes to 1 hour. Beat hard again. Then place in a greased bread pan. Set the pan in the warm water again and cover with a towel. Let the dough rise until it reaches the top of the pan. Place the pan in a cold oven. Set the temperature at 400° and bake for 15 minutes. Turn the oven down to 325° for another 25 minutes. Turn the bread onto a wire rack to cool, and cover lightly with a cloth. Freezes well.

Kirsten Sonne Felker

CAMP BREAD

5 pounds flour
1-1/2 cups Crisco
2/3 cup sugar
1 tablespoon salt
4 tablespoons baking powder
3 quarts buttermilk

Heat the lid on the fire until you just about can't touch it with your fingers. Leave it there. Get one large bowl. Cream all dry ingredients together with your hands — it's better that way. Then add buttermilk, making sure the dough is thick. Knead until elastic. Make "slugs" the size of grapefruits or larger and roll out into 1-inch thick pancake shapes. They should be large enough to fill the bottom of the Dutch oven. Place in greased even, cover with warmed lid and set oven in coals to cook. Cook until the top of the bread is browned.

CAMP BISCUITS
5 pounds flour
2-1/2 cups Crisco
2/3 cup sugar
1 tablespoon salt
5 tablespoons baking powder
3 quarts buttermilk

Cream all dry ingredients together with hands — it's better that way. Then add buttermilk, making sure dough is thick. Knead until elastic. Roll out into 1/2" pancake and with biscuit cutter cut out biscuits. Put into greased Dutch oven — crowd biscuits. Make sure lid is hot.

Euel Stribling

DILL BREAD

1 package yeast
1/4 cup warm water
1 cup small curd cottage cheese
2 tablespoons sugar
1 tablespoon minced onion
1 tablespoon butter
2 teaspoons whole dill seeds
1 teaspoon salt
1 egg
2-1/4 to 2-1/2 cups flour, sifted
1/4 teaspoon soda
butter
seasoned salt

Soften yeast in warm water. Combine cottage cheese, sugar, onion, butter, dill seeds and salt in saucepan. Heat but do not boil. Let cool; add dissolved yeast and egg. Combine flour and soda. Add the liquids to the flour and stir. Let set until dough has doubled in size. Turn dough out on floured board and knead for 1 minute. Divide into 2 loaves and let double in size again. Bake at 350° for 40 to 50 minutes. Butter top of loaves and sprinkle with seasoned salt.

Mrs. David M. Bandy, Mrs. C. P. Sterns, Mrs. Martin Graef

SPOON BREAD

1-1/4 cups cornmeal
1 teaspoon salt
1 cup boiling water
3 tablespoons butter, melted
1 cup milk
1 cup flour
3 teaspoons baking powder
3 eggs, separated
1/4 cups shortening, melted

Preheat oven to 350°. Pour boiling water over cornmeal and salt, add melted butter and milk. Set aside to cool. Sift flour and baking powder. Beat egg yolks and stir into cornmeal mixture. Add flour. Beat egg whites until stiff and fold into mixture. Add melted shortening. Pour into buttered 2-quart casserole and bake 30 to 35 minutes.

Mrs. J. B. (Mary Jane) Mallard

MAMA'S ROLLS

1/2 cup sugar
1/2 cup Crisco
1 teaspoon salt
1 package yeast
1 beaten egg
flour

Pour 1-1/2 cups hot water over sugar, salt and Crisco. Cool to lukewarm. Put 1 package yeast in 1/2 cup warm water. Dissolve. Add 1 beaten egg and mix all ingredients together. Add flour to make a good dough as heavy as you can beat with a wooden spoon. Put in a greased pan and refrigerate. When you want to make buns, take out enough dough and work it down. Put rest of dough back in refrigerator. Bake on medium till done.

Marion Bennett

CORN BREAD

1 cup flour
1 cup cornmeal
1/2 cup sugar
2 tablespoons baking powder
1 teaspoon salt
1 well-beaten egg
2 tablespoons melted lard
1 cup sweet milk

Mix well. Grease pan and sprinkle with cornmeal. Cook until well done.

Mrs. A. L. Coffman

HOT WATER CORN BREAD

6 cups white cornmeal
2 teaspoons salt
2 to 3 cups boiling water
1/4 cup milk
Crisco or cooking oil

In large bowl combine cornmeal and salt. Pour over enough boiling water to mix meal. Add 1/4 cup milk. Wet hands with cold water, pat dough into patties approximately 3/4" thick and 3" long. Fry in hot Crisco or oil until golden brown.

Joan Stocks Nobles

ALAMO CORN PONES

1/2 cup boiling water
1 cup white cornmeal
2 tablespoons shortening
1 teaspoon baking powder
1/2 teaspoon salt
1/4 cup cream or milk

Pour boiling water over cornmeal and chill for one hour. When time is up, start oven at 400°. Put the 2 tablespoons shortening in heavy skillet and heat until fat melts. Now pour one tablespoon melted shortening into cornmeal mixture. Add other ingredients. Mix well. Drop by tablespoons into hot skillet. Flatten with back of spoon. Bake 20 to 30 minutes until nicely browned.

Cora Margaret Wardlaw

SKILLET CORN BREAD OR MUFFINS

2 cups white cornmeal
1-1/2 tablespoons flour
1 tablespoon sugar
1 teaspoon salt
1 teaspoon baking powder
1 teaspoon soda
2 eggs
1 cup milk
1 teaspoon vinegar
4 tablespoons oleo or butter

Mix cornmeal, flour, sugar, salt, baking powder, soda, eggs, milk and vinegar. Put 4 tablespoons butter in skillet (or in 12 muffin tins). Melt in 400° oven until it "pops." Pour in batter and cook until golden brown.

Joan Stocks Nobles

CRUMBLIN'

Crumblin' is a traditional Texas dish/drink characteristic of the Texan's penchant for "waste not, want not." In the early days of Texas statehood, cornmeal flour was more readily available than wheat flour. Consequently, corn bread was a prevalent dish in most households. There was always leftover corn bread, and since most Texans had a family cow, buttermilk from the cow was mixed with the bread into an interesting "drink." It's not for everyone, but those who grew up during the Depression remember the concoction well.

buttermilk
corn bread

Pour buttermilk to fill a large glass 2/3 full. Then take fresh-made or day-old corn bread and crumble into glass of buttermilk. Let soak to desired consistency and drink. One variation includes a tablespoon of finely minced sweet white onions.

Frank Mullins

HOECAKE

2 cups cornmeal
very hot water
1 teaspoon salt

Mix cornmeal and salt in bowl. Moisten with water. Let stand for one hour. Shape with hands into flat cakes about 1/2″ thick. Fry on hot, greased griddle until brown. Turn gently and brown on other side. Serve piping hot.

Patsy Henderson

DALLAS CADDO CLUB HUSH PUPPIES

2 cups cornmeal
1 cup flour
1/4 cup sugar
1/4 teaspoon soda
3 teaspoons baking powder
2 teaspoons salt
1 teaspoon black pepper
1 teaspoon poultry seasoning
1 teaspoon Accent
1/4 cup parsley flakes
1 onion, chopped
2 eggs
1 cup buttermilk
1 tablespoon butter, melted

Combine all ingredients. Drop in hot oil from a tablespoon making one-inch balls. Cook until brown. Mixture will keep for several days in the refrigerator.

Mrs. Jon B. (Nancy Blakely) Ruff

LADY BIRD'S POPOVERS

1 cup sifted flour
1 cup milk
2 eggs, beaten
1/4 teaspoon salt
2 tablespoons shortening, melted

Preheat oven to 450°. Mix and sift flour and salt. Combine eggs, milk and shortening. Gradually add to flour mixture, beating about 1 minute or until batter is smooth. Fill greased, sizzling hot muffin pans 3/4 full and bake in very hot oven (450°) about 20 minutes. Reduce to moderate heat (350°) and continue baking for 15 to 20 minutes. This is one of my favorites for ladies' luncheons (in spite of calories).

Mrs. Lyndon B. (Lady Bird) Johnson

SOURDOUGH PANCAKES

1/4 yeast cake
1 teaspoon sugar
1-1/2 cups water
flour to make a soft sponge
2 cups water
2/3 cup sugar
1 teaspoon salt
flour to make pancake-like batter
2 eggs
1 tablespoon baking powder
1 teaspoon soda

Mix 1/4 yeast cake, 1 teaspoon sugar, 1-1/2 cups water and enough flour to make a soft sponge. Let set a day in a stone crock or plastic bowl (not metal). At night, add 2 more cups water, 2/3 cup sugar, 1 teaspoon salt and enough flour to make pancake-like batter. Let set overnight. The next morning, save out all the batter except 1-1/2 cups. Put what you saved (Sourdough Starter) in a glass jar with a "not-too-tight" lid. Refrigerate. Use at least once a week to keep it at its best. Add to the 1-1/2 cups of starter still in the bowl 2 eggs, 1 tablespoon baking powder and 1 teaspoon soda. Don't have it too thick and don't cut down on sugar as that is what makes it good.

Joan Menzies

SALADS

To most of the United States, the word "salad" conjures up visions of crisp lettuce and fresh vegetables. In Texas, salad can mean anything *but* that, as the following collection illustrates.

CHERRY 7-UP SALAD

2 (3-ounce) packages cherry Jell-O
20 ounces 7-Up
1 can mandarin oranges, drained (optional)
3 bananas, sliced
1-1/2 cups boiling water
1 (20-ounce) can crushed pineapple, drained (reserve juice)
1 cup chopped pecans
1 cup pineapple juice from crushed pineapple
3 tablespoons flour
1 egg
1/2 cup sugar
1 cup whipping cream, whipped

Dissolve Jell-O in water and put in 13 x 9" Pyrex dish. Add 7-Up and let cool. When cool mix pineapple, nuts, bananas and oranges in Jell-O. Chill until firm. For topping, mix pineapple juice, flour, egg and sugar and cook until thick. Cool. Add 1 cup of whipping cream, whipped. Cover Jell-O mixture with topping and refrigerate to set more firmly.

LeRuth Stewart

COCA-COLA SALAD

1 package lemon Jell-O
1 tablespoon plain gelatin
1 small can pineapple
1 small can black sweet cherries, chopped
1 cup nuts, chopped
1 Coca-Cola

Take juice from pineapple and cherries and finish filling with water to 2 cups; add Jell-O. Add 1 cup nuts. After it begins to jell, add the Coca-Cola. Jell in individual servings.

Mrs. Cullis King

ROYAL CROWN CHERRY SALAD

1 (Number 2) can Bing cherries
1 (8-ounce) can crushed pineapple
water
2 (3-ounce) packages cherry gelatin
1-1/2 cups Royal Crown Cola
1 cup chopped pecans
sour cream
strawberries
salt

Drain and reserve juice from Bing cherries and pineapple. To the combined juices, add enough water to make 2 cups. Place in a saucepan and bring to a boil. Pour over gelatin. Cool and add drained cherries and pineapple, along with Royal Crown Cola and chopped pecans. Top with sour cream and strawberries with a dash of salt.

Pat Brown

SPRING SALAD

1 package lemon Jell-O
1/2 teaspoon salt
1/2 cup shredded carrots
1 tablespoon chopped pimientos
1 tablespoon sugar
2 tablespoons chopped sweet pickles
2 tablespoons vinegar
1 tablespoon chopped onion
1-2/3 cups boiling water
1/2 cup diced celery
1/2 cup cooked asparagus

Dissolve Jell-O in boiling water. Let cool and add other ingredients. Pour into mold and let set.

Mrs. Sam Mason

SEA FOAM SALAD

1 (Number 2) can pears
1 package lime gelatin
2 small packages cream cheese
2 tablespoons salad dressing
1 cup whipping cream

Drain pears and heat one cup of juice. Dissolve gelatin in hot juice. When cool and slightly set, add cream cheese and salad dressing, which have been softened together. Mash the pears with a fork or strain and add to the gelatin. Whip the cream and fold into salad. Chill in a mold or cake pan.

Mrs. Jeff Davis

TEXAS SALAD

2 packages lemon or lime gelatin
1 (Number 2) can crushed pineapple
1 small can pimientos
1 cup nuts, chopped
1 pound cottage cheese
1 cup heavy cream, whipped

Bring pineapple to a boil; add gelatin and stir until dissolved. When mixture begins to congeal, fold in remaining ingredients. Pour into mold and chill until firm.

Mrs. F. A. Boutwell

EIGHT-HOUR SALAD

1 large head lettuce, shredded
1/2 cup celery, cut fine
1/2 cup green pepper, chopped fine
1/2 cup green onions with tops, chopped fine
1 package frozen green peas (cooked and drained)
1 cup mayonnaise
8 slices bacon, fried crisp and crumbled
1 cup shredded Cheddar cheese

Layer all ingredients in order given. Do not mix. Cover tightly and refrigerate at least eight hours. Put in crystal bowl that you will serve in. Will keep for days.

Janie Cunningham

24-HOUR FRUIT SALAD

1 large can fruit cocktail, drained and cut up
1 small can pineapple, drained and cut up
16 marshmallows, cut in bits
a few cherries
3 sliced bananas
1 pint whipped cream

Mix fruit and sauce together. Fold in whipped cream. Let set in refrigerator for 24 hours.

Mrs. Jas. D. Sumrall

SWEET 'N' SOUR BLACK-EYED PEA SALAD

1 (Number 2) can fresh black-eyed peas
2/3 cup cooked, diced carrots
1 medium onion, chopped
1 medium bell pepper, chopped
1 small can pimientos, chopped
1 button garlic, minced
1/4 cup sugar
1/4 cup white vinegar
1/4 cup vegetable oil
2 tablespoons Worcestershire sauce
1/3 can condensed tomato soup

While carrots are cooking, chop remaining ingredients and combine. Dice carrots and mix together with other ingredients. May be served chilled or hot. Keeps well in icebox.

Marjorie Luckenbach

WILTED LETTUCE SALAD

1 head romaine lettuce
9 green onions and tops
9 slices bacon
4 hard-cooked eggs
salt and pepper
vinegar
2 teaspoons sugar

Chop lettuce and onions; fry bacon, reserving drippings. Add salt and pepper and toss. Crumble bacon and slice 3 eggs; add to mixture. Add enough vinegar to drippings to make 1 cup; add sugar. Mix well and heat. Pour over salad and garnish with remaining egg.

Mrs. T. W. Rodgers

SWEET AND SOUR RED CABBAGE

1 medium red cabbage, shredded
3 tablespoons butter
1 tart apple, thinly sliced
5 whole cloves
salt to taste
1/4 cup vinegar
2 tablespoons sugar

Rinse cabbage in water and drain. Melt butter in large, heavy skillet; add cabbage, apple, cloves and salt to taste. Cover and cook slowly for 25 minutes or until cabbage is tender. Add vinegar and sugar and simmer 5 minutes. Taste and add more sugar, vinegar and salt if desired.

Mrs. B. C. (Betty) Garnett

24-HOUR SLAW

Sauce:
4 tablespoons vinegar
4 tablespoons sugar
2 egg yolks, slightly beaten
4 tablespoons butter

Cook vinegar, sugar and egg yolks until thickened, adding butter last.

1 large head cabbage, shredded
1 large or medium white onion, sliced and separated into rings
3/4 cup sugar
1 cup white vinegar
2 generous teaspoons mustard
1 tablespoon sugar
1 teaspoon celery seeds
1-1/2 teaspoons salt
1/4 cup salad oil

Sprinkle 3/4 cup sugar over cabbage and onions and mix well. Use your hands to mix. Bring to a boil the remaining ingredients. When dressing is cold, pour over cabbage. Let stand overnight. This is good for days.

Belle Garner

OUTLAW COLESLAW

1 quart cabbage, grated
1/2 cup carrots, grated
1/2 cup green peppers, grated
3 tomatoes, quartered

Dressing (pour over vegetables and toss well):

1/2 cup mayonnaise
4 tablespoons vinegar
1/2 teaspoon salt
1/2 teaspoon pepper
1/2 teaspoon sugar
1 tablespoon onion, minced

Mrs. W. J. Stroman

BARBECUE SLAW

1 small head cabbage
2 stalks celery
1 medium green pepper
1 medium onion
3/4 cup catsup
1/4 cup vinegar
2 tablespoons sugar
1 tablespoon Worcestershire sauce
1 tablespoon prepared mustard
1 teaspoon salt
dash cayenne pepper

Grate, chop or grind cabbage, celery, green pepper and onion. Combine catsup and remaining ingredients. Mix with vegetables. Chill several hours.

Mrs. Robert Nelson

CABBAGE SLAW

3 cups cabbage, finely shredded
1/2 cup celery, minced
1/2 cup onion, minced
1 bell pepper, finely cut
1/2 cup salad dressing
3 tablespoons vinegar
3 tablespoons sugar
1 teaspoon salt
1/2 teaspoon celery seeds
pepper to taste

Combine cabbage, celery, onion and bell pepper and mix well. Combine remaining ingredients and pour over slaw.

Mrs. Julia Keese

CHICKEN SALAD

3 to 4 pounds dressed chicken
1 medium onion
2 to 3 stalks celery
1 tablespoon gelatin
1/4 cup cold water
1 cup mayonnaise
1/4 cup chopped celery
1/2 cup ripe olives, chopped
1/4 pimiento, chopped
1/2 cup chopped pecans (optional)
stuffed olives, sliced
parsley

Wash and clean chicken. Season chicken and fill cavity with onion and celery. Boil until done. Let set in broth several hours or overnight. Bone chicken and chop in bite-size pieces. Soak gelatin in cold water, place in top of double boiler and heat until completely dissolved. Add mayonnaise to gelatin mixture; fold in 2 cups chicken, celery, olives, pimiento and pecans. Turn into mold and chill until firm. Garnish with mayonnaise and stuffed olives and parsley.

Mrs. Grady Evans

POTATO SALAD

4 large potatoes, unpeeled and cut in thirds
1/2 cup chopped bell pepper
4 hard-boiled eggs, chopped
6 green onions, minced
1/4 cup minced celery
1/4 cup drained pickle relish
1/4 cup chopped parsley
1 to 2 tablespoons chives
1 (2-ounce) jar pimientos, drained
1 cup Hellmann's mayonnaise
1 to 2 tablespoons mustard
1 to 2 tablespoons sugar
salt and black pepper to taste
1/2 pound chopped crisp bacon

Cook potatoes until done but not squishy. Let cool and peel. Dice in large pieces (they will break up) then mix all together. Sprinkle bacon over top.

Claire Smith Foster

PLAIN GERMAN POTATO SALAD

4 medium potatoes
1/2 teaspoon salt
1/8 teaspoon pepper
3/4 teaspoon sugar
1 small onion, chopped
1/4 cup mild white vinegar
1/2 cup boiling water
3 tablespoons vegetable oil

Boil and peel potatoes. Set aside to cool. Put salt, pepper, sugar, onion and vinegar in mixing bowl and add boiling water. Cool for 10 minutes. Slice cold potatoes in mixture. Set aside for 30 to 40 minutes, stirring occasionally. If all liquid is not absorbed, spoon it off. Add oil and stir. Refrigerate. Stir before serving. This will keep 3 to 4 days.

Mrs. Floyd (Hanna) Mockert

COLD STEAK SALAD

2 pounds boneless sirloin, cut in 1/2-inch cubes
1/2 cup butter
3/4 pound mushrooms, sliced
1 (9-ounce) package frozen artichoke hearts, cooked and cooled (may use fresh or canned)
1 cup diced celery
1 pint small cherry tomatoes
2 tablespoons chopped chives
2 tablespoons chopped parsley
2 cups dressing (below)
2 teaspoons hot mustard

In a large skillet over high heat, sauté the meat cubes in butter until browned on all sides. Transfer to a large bowl and cool. Quickly sauté the mushrooms in butter remaining in the skillet and add to bowl with artichoke hearts, celery, tomatoes, chives and parsley. Mix lightly.

Dressing:
2-1/2 cups oil
3/4 cup wine vinegar
6 shallots, finely chopped
1/3 cup chopped parsley
1/3 cup dill weed
salt and pepper to taste
1/8 teaspoon Tabasco

Combine all ingredients in a jar and shake. Mix 2 cups of dressing with the mustard and pour over the salad. Toss, cover and marinate overnight.

Mrs. Eugene W. (Nancy Green) McWhorter

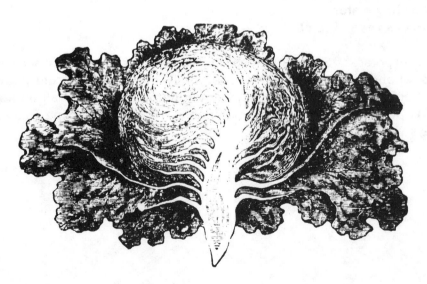

MAIN DISHES

Hailing from a proud and independent heritage, Texans learned to fend for themselves; wild game still figures on the menu but above all, beef is the favorite dish, followed by cabrito (young goat) and pork.

JOHNNY KNOWS IT!

1 pound ground meat
1 clove garlic
1 green pepper, chopped
1 can tomato soup
1 large can tomato sauce
1 can tomato paste
1 large onion, chopped
1 cup celery, chopped
1 small jar stuffed olives
1 package large egg noodles
1/2 pound grated American cheese

Brown meat, pepper, onion, celery and garlic in butter. Cook and drain noodles. Add chopped olives. Add to meat mixture, put cheese on top and cook in 325° oven until cheese melts.

Sue Sims

TEXAS HASH

2 to 3 tablespoons shortening
1 pound ground beef
2 large onions, sliced
2 large green peppers, chopped
1 teaspoon chili powder
2 cups canned tomatoes
salt and pepper to taste
1/2 cup uncooked rice
1/2 cup water

Melt shortening in skillet; add ground meat, onions and peppers. Cook 5 to 10 minutes. Add seasonings and tomatoes. Sprinkle with uncooked rice and 1/2 cup water. Put top on skillet and cook slowly for 45 minutes or until rice is done.

Mrs. Stella Sheppard

DIRTY RICE

2 bell peppers
2 onions
4 stalks celery
1/2 pound chicken livers and gizzards
1 clove garlic
1/2 pound ground beef
2 to 3 tablespoons bacon fat
Tabasco
Worcestershire sauce
salt and cayenne pepper
2 cups cooked brown rice

Grind peppers, onions, liver, gizzards and garlic together. Sauté this plus ground beef in bacon fat for about 20 minutes or until done. Stir this mixture into hot cooked brown rice.

N. Wilkinson

GREEN RICE

3 cups cooked rice
1 can cream of chicken soup
2 green onions, chopped
1 large bell pepper, chopped
3 tablespoons margarine
1 egg, well beaten
1 package frozen chopped broccoli
1 tablespoon Worcestershire sauce
salt and pepper to taste

Melt margarine and add onions, peppers and broccoli. Cook until broccoli is thawed. Add soup, egg and other seasonings to rice. Add broccoli mixture and mix well. Put in buttered baking dish and bake at 350° for 30 minutes.

Mrs. W. P. Taliaferro

GREEN BEAN WHIRLIGIG

1 (Number 2) can green beans
1 can evaporated milk
2 tablespoons butter or margarine
2 tablespoons flour
1/4 teaspoon salt

2 tablespoons pimientos, diced
1 cup prepared biscuit mix
1-1/2 cups luncheon meat or cooked ham, ground

Drain beans; measure liquid. Add evaporated milk to make 1-1/2 cups liquid. Melt butter; add flour and salt. Stir to a smooth paste. Add liquid gradually and cook until mixture thickens and comes to a boil. Add beans and pimientos; heat. Turn into small shallow baking dish. Prepare biscuit dough; roll into a rectangle 8 x 12 inches. Spread with meat; roll tightly as possible. Cut in 1-inch pieces. Place on top of bean mixture. Bake at 425° for 25 minutes.

Mrs. Spearman R. Pool

KING RANCH CHICKEN

3 to 4 pound hen
1 onion
1 or 2 stalks celery
salt and pepper
1 large bell pepper, chopped
1 large onion, chopped
1 can mushroom soup
1 can cream of chicken soup
1/2 pound Cheddar cheese, grated
chili powder
garlic salt
1 package frozen tortillas
1 can Ro-Tel tomatoes and chilies, undrained

Boil hen until tender in water seasoned with onion, celery, salt and pepper. Cut chicken into bize-size pieces and reserve all stock. Chop onion and bell pepper, combine soups and grate cheese. Just before putting casserole together, soak the frozen tortillas in boiling chicken stock until wilted. Start layering casserole in a 9 x 12-inch baking dish in this order: tortillas "dripping with stock," chicken, onion, bell pepper (sprinkling to taste with chili powder and garlic salt), soup mixture and cheese. Repeat the layers, being sure the tortillas are oozing with the stock. Cover the casserole with the Ro-Tel tomatoes and all the juice. Juices in the casserole should be about half the depth of the dish; if not, add a little more stock. May be made and frozen several days ahead, but always make at least one day ahead and refrigerate so that the flavors will blend. Bake uncovered at 375° for 30 minutes.

Mrs. Dee Smith

RANCH CHICKEN

12 corn tortillas
1 can cream of mushroom soup
1 can cream of celery soup
1 can cream of chicken soup
1 can Ro-Tel tomatoes with chilies
2 small cans chopped green chilies
1 chicken, boiled and chopped bite size
1 pound grated cheese
chicken broth
salt and pepper to taste

Cut tortillas in fourths and put in soup mixture until soft. Remove and put in casserole dish. Layer with chicken, cheese, onions and broth. Pour remaining soup over top and top with grated cheese. Bake at 250° for 1 to 1-1/2 hours. Reheat later.

Joan Stocks Nobles

PORK SAUSAGE PIE

1 pound pork sausage
1 cup chopped onion
1 cup chopped celery
1 cup pared, diced potato
2 tablespoons flour
1/4 teaspoon salt
1/4 teaspoon mace
1 cup water
pastry for 9-inch double crust pie

Cook sausage until lightly browned. Drain off excess fat. Add onion, celery and potato; stir and heat thoroughly. Stir in flour, salt and mace. Add water; cook until thickened, stirring constantly. Cover and simmer 15 minutes. Uncover and simmer to thicken, if needed. Cool. Divide pastry in half. On lightly floured board, roll out half the pastry into a circle about 1/8 inch thick. Fit crust into 9-inch pie plate. Trim crust. Roll out remaining pastry. Cut small slits for vents. Fill lined pie plate with sausage mixture. Moisten edge of crust. Cover with top crust. Press edges together; trim crust. Seal and flute edges. Bake in 400° oven until crust is brown and filling is bubbling, 30 to 35 minutes. Let stand 10 to 15 minutes before serving. Cut into wedges.

Texas Department of Agriculture Pamphlet

TANGALINA

1 pound hot pork sausage
1 pound ground beef
1 (12-ounce) can whole kernel corn
1 (14-1/2-ounce) can tomatoes
1 (16-ounce) can English peas, drained, reserve juice
1 (4-ounce) can drained mushrooms
1 package onion soup mix
1/2 cup chopped stuffed olives
1 (16-ounce) can bean sprouts, drained (optional)
1 (10-ounce) package wide egg noodles
1/2 cup grated sharp Cheddar cheese
dash paprika

Preheat oven to 350°. Fry pork sausage, drain and put into main cooking container. Fry beef, skim off excess grease. Add to pork. Add corn, tomatoes, peas, olives and mushrooms. Dissolve soup with pea juice, add to mixture. Add bean sprouts. Cook noodles until done, drain and add to above mixture. Mix lightly together. Cover with cheese, sprinkle with paprika. Bake in oven for about 15 minutes.

Mrs. Bob (Sybil) Johnson

CREAMED SWEETBREADS

1 pound sweetbreads
2 eggs, hard cooked
2 cups sweet milk
5 tablespoons flour
4 tablespoons butter or margarine
1 teaspoon salt
1/4 teaspoon pepper (black)
1 tablespoon lemon juice

Gently cook sweetbreads (about 20 minutes) until tender. Allow them to cool and separate the sweetbread from the membrane that binds it together. This can best be done after the meat is cooked. It will not come apart in the uncooked stage. Set the sweetbreads aside for later use and discard the membrane. In a double boiler, make a white sauce of the milk, butter, flour, salt and pepper. When this is thick and smooth, add the lemon juice. Then add the sweetbread meat and the chopped hard-cooked eggs. Allow this to heat and serve on toast for breakfast or lunch.

Henrietta Harrison

TEXAS STYLE PIZZA

1/2 lb. ground beef
1 envelope (1-3/4-oz.) French's Chili-O Seasoning Mix
1 can (about 16-oz.) tomatoes
1 can (15-oz.) kidney beans, drained and rinsed
1 package active dry yeast
3/4 cup warm water
2-1/4 cups biscuit mix
1/2 cup cornmeal
Shredded Cheddar or American cheese

Brown ground beef in large skillet, stirring to crumble; pour off excess fat. Stir in seasoning mix, tomatoes, and beans; simmer, uncovered, ten minutes. Sprinkle yeast over warm water in large mixing bowl; stir to dissolve. Add biscuit mix and cornmeal; stir until smooth. Knead 25 strokes on floured surface. Divide in half, roll or pat each to a 14-inch circle on greased pizza pans or baking sheets. Spoon filling on top of crust; sprinkle with cheese. Bake at 425° for 15 to 20 minutes, until crust is golden brown. 6-8 servings.

Mrs. Bennie Radford

CALF'S HEART

calf's heart
bread stuffing
salt and pepper
fat for frying
flour

Wash the calf's heart, remove veins, arteries and clotted blood. Stuff with bread stuffing and sew. Sprinkle with salt and pepper. Roll in flour and brown in hot fat. Place in covered pot, half cover with boiling water and bake slowly about 2 hours at 300°, basting regularly. (It may be necessary to add a little more water.) Remove heart from pan and slice. Thicken liquid with flour, season with salt and pepper and pour over heart before serving.

Mrs. Louis Strohacker

JAMBALAYA

1 pound cured ham, cubed
3 slices bacon, cut in small pieces
1/2 cup chopped green onions and tops
flour

1 (16-ounce) can tomatoes, chopped
1 (10-ounce) can tomato puree
1/2 cup chopped celery
2 or more cloves garlic, minced
1 teaspoon sugar
2 to 3 bay leaves
1/2 cup chopped green pepper
Accent
Savory salt
red pepper
salt
1/4 cup chopped parsley
1 (8-ounce) can mushrooms
3 pounds shrimp, peeled and cleaned
2 (17-ounce) cans whole kernel corn, drained
a few oysters (optional)
butter (optional)

Brown ham, bacon and onion together; stir in enough flour to absorb fat. Brown lightly; add tomatoes, puree, celery, garlic, bay leaves, green pepper and season to taste with seasonings. Cover and let cook until vegetables are tender. Add parsley, mushrooms, shrimp and corn, and cook until shrimp are done. Thicken with flour and add oysters which have been browned in butter, if desired.

Bess Vallery Topp

MEAT LOAF

2/3 cup dry bread crumbs
1-1/2 pounds ground meat
1/4 cup grated or chopped onion
1 cup sweet milk
2 eggs, well beaten
1 teaspoon salt
6 tablespoons brown sugar
2 teaspoons dry mustard
1/2 cup catsup

Soak bread crumbs in milk. Add meat, onion, eggs and salt. Put in baking dish. Make a topping by mixing the sugar, mustard and catsup. Pour over meat loaf and bake at 350° for 45 minutes.

Mrs. W. Bruner Smith

ROCKY MOUNTAIN OYSTERS ON THE HALF SHELL

1-2 pounds bull testicles aka: calf fries, Rocky Mountain Oysters (sheep or turkey testicles may be used also)
1 cup flour
1/4 cup cornmeal
1 cup red wine
salt, pepper, garlic powder
Louisiana Hot Sauce
cooking oil (pure hog lard is the best, but a mixture of 60% peanut oil and 40% vegetable oil will do)

With a very sharp knife, split the tough skin-like muscle that surrounds each "oyster." Remove the skin. Set "oysters" into a pan with enough saltwater to cover them for one hour (this takes out some of the blood). Drain. Transfer "oysters" to large pot. Add enough water to float "oysters" and a generous tablespoon of vinegar. Parboil, drain and rinse. Let cool and slice each "oyster" into 1/4 inch thick ovals. Sprinkle salt and pepper on both sides of sliced "oyster" to taste. Mix flour, cornmeal and some garlic powder to taste in a bowl. Roll each "oyster" slice into this dry mixture. Dip into milk. Dip into dry mixture. Dip into wine quickly (you may repeat the procedure if a thicker crust is desired). Place each "oyster" into hot cooking oil. Add Louisiana Hot Sauce to cooking oil (go wild with it, but watch out for repercussions — hot splashes). Cook until golden brown or tender, and remove with a wire mesh strainer (the longer they cook, the tougher they get). Serve in one of those cardboard beer cartons that four six-packs come in, layered with paper towels. Eat 'em, don't wait for nothin'! Chase with beer. Variations include serving cooked "oysters" on a real oyster half shell with a sprig of parsley and a few drops of lemon juice.

Ted Karkoska

RESAPEE REBELS MOUNTAIN OYSTERS

1/3 cup soy sauce
1/2 cup dry red wine
1 teaspoon salt
1 tablespoon brown sugar
1/2 onion, chopped
juice of 1 lime
1/8 teaspoon cayenne pepper
calf fries

Marinate calf fries in other ingredients for 2 hours.

Bisquick batter
finely chopped onions
finely chopped jalapenos
flour

hot grease
frog tails (optional)

Dip calf fries in batter then roll in onions and jalapenos. Roll in flour and fry in very hot grease. For prize-winning results, add finely chopped frog tails to the onions and jalapenos.

Cary Tomerlin

THE BEST CHICKEN-FRIED STEAK SOUTH OF OMAHA

Bill Maxwell, former Texas restaurateur, originally claimed his chicken-fried steak was the "best found south of the Rio Brazos." Subsequent chicken-fried steak contests proved him truthful, so he extended his claim to include all lands south of the Arkansas River. In another conversation with Bill, we found his "boundary" had crept north to Omaha, Nebraska. Well, eventually he's gonna have to stop at the North Pole . . . we hope.

1 (6-ounce) round steak cutlet, machine tenderized
flour
4 eggs
1 can flat beer
1 tablespoon Adolph's meat tenderizer
salt, pepper and garlic salt to taste
white cream sauce

Sprinkle salt, pepper and garlic salt on both sides of tenderized steak to taste. Put steak onto a tray that is well-covered with flour. Then "pound the hell out of it (the steak) with stiff fingers, working from the center out, until it reaches the size of an L.P. record." Flip several times and repeat pounding. Mix eggs, beer, 1 teaspoon salt and Adolph's meat tenderizer in a shallow bowl. Add enough flour to make a thin, watery batter. Beat mixture smooth. Dip meat into batter. "Flop" back onto flour tray and cover with flour. Pound again with fingertips until moisture is absorbed. Cook in deep fat at 350° until golden brown. Serve with French fries and cover with a white cream sauce.

Bill Maxwell

MISS PIGGY'S WHITE GRAVY

1/2 cup meat grease (chicken fried pour-off with goodies left in is best)
1 to 1-1/2 cups flour
garlic salt
pepper
1 (8-ounce) can evaporated milk
1 cup water

Heat grease until smokey hot, stirring constantly, and add enough flour until heavy. Add garlic salt and pepper to taste (sparingly). Brown sauce then turn to lower heat and add evaporated milk and water, continuing to stir constantly to get rid of lumps. Cook to desired thickness.

Hickory Hut/Barb's Mom

HILL COUNTRY FRIED STEAK

2 pounds round steak or 8 cube steaks
1/2 cup flour
1 teaspoon salt
1/4 teaspoon pepper
1/2 cup vegetable oil

Pound steak and cut into 8 pieces. Combine flour, salt and pepper and coat steaks on both sides. In a heavy skillet heat oil and sauté steaks 5 minutes on each side. Keep warm while making gravy.

PAN GRAVY:
4 tablespoons pan drippings
3 tablespoons flour
2-1/4 cups milk
1 teaspoon salt
1/4 teaspoon pepper

Pour off all but 4 tablespoons of pan drippings. Blend in flour, stirring constantly, until bubbly. Stir in milk, salt and pepper. Continue cooking and stirring, scraping cook-on juices from bottom and sides of skillet, until gravy thickens and bubbles for 1 minute.

Cookbook Committee

SOURDOUGH STEAK

1 (3-pound) round steak
1 cup all-purpose flour
2 teaspoons onion salt
2 teaspoons paprika
1 teaspoon black pepper
1 cup Sourdough Starter (see Breads)
3/4 cup lard or shortening

Using a meat tenderizing mallet or knife, pound steak to 1/2 inch thick. Cut into serving pieces. Combine flour and seasonings. Dip pounded steak in Sourdough Starter, then in flour mixture. Fry in 1 inch of hot lard in heavy skillet.

Philip Morris

ZELMA KESSLER'S GERMAN STEAK

2 pound round steak
1 large dill pickle
1 cup water
3 slices bacon
2 tablespoons Worcestershire sauce

Cut steak into serving pieces. Salt, pepper and flour each piece. Place 1/2 piece of bacon on each piece of steak. Lay slice of pickle on bacon, roll and fasten with toothpick. Brown in hot oil. Place in casserole, pour water and sauce over meat. Cover and bake 1-1/2 hours at 350°.

Zelma Kessler

JACK LEMMON'S STEAK MARINADE

1 cup beef broth
1/2 cup soy sauce
2 jiggers (3 ounces) Bourbon
1 clove pressed garlic
1/2 teaspoon ground ginger
1/4 cup Worcestershire sauce
2 tablespoons mesquite honey

Combine ingredients in a glass jar, shake, pour over a 3 to 4-pound, 2-inch thick sirloin and let marinate several hours, at room temperature, turning several times. Broil over mesquite, or charcoal with mesquite chips.

STEAK FLAMBÉ

1 flank steak (1-1/2 to 2 pounds)
3/4 cup maple-flavored syrup
2 tablespoons soy sauce
1/4 cup red wine vinegar
2 teaspoons dry mustard
1 teaspoon salt
1/2 teaspoon black pepper
1 clove crushed garlic

Score steak and place in shallow glass baking dish or cooking bag. Combine remaining ingredients and pour over scored steak. Refrigerate 24 hours, turning several times. Remove from pan and place on broiler pan. Broil 5 inches from fire for 5 minutes on each side.

Patsy Henderson

RANCH STYLE MINUTE STEAKS

1 cup corn flakes, crushed
1 tablespoon chili powder
1 egg
1 tablespoon water
4 minute steaks
2 tablespoons fat
1/2 cup onion, chopped
1/2 cup green pepper, chopped
1 can tomato sauce

Combine corn flakes and chili powder; beat egg with water. Dip steaks in egg; coat with corn flakes. Brown in hot fat. Remove from skillet; sauté onion and pepper until golden. Add steaks and tomato sauce. Cover and simmer 45 minutes.

Miss Merlene Patterson

SPIKE STEAK

2-inch thick sirloin steak (about 3 pounds)
1 tablespoon black peppercorns
2 cloves garlic, minced
4 cups coarse salt
3/4 cup water

Trim excess fat from steak. Crack peppercorns coarsely and mince garlic. Press peppercorns and garlic into both sides of steak and let stand at room temperature for I hour. Make a thick paste of salt and water; cover top side of peppered steak with half the mixture. If cooking steak over coals, cover salt side with a wet cloth or paper towel and place salt side down on the grill. (Cloth or paper holds the salt in place; will char as the steak cooks, but this does not affect the taste.) Cover top side with remaining salt mixture and another piece of wet cloth or paper towel. If broiling, put salt side up, 3 inches from heat. Put salt on other side of steak when it is turned. Cook 15 minutes on each side for rare, 25 minutes for medium rare. Remove salt before serving. Serve with One Shot Sauce.

Philip Morris

ONE SHOT SAUCE

1 pound butter
1/2 cup finely chopped onion
2 cloves garlic, minced
1/2 cup whiskey
1/4 cup Worcestershire sauce
1 tablespoon pepper
1-1/2 teaspoons dry mustard
1 teaspoon salt
1/4 teaspoon Tabasco

Melt butter in saucepan; add onion and garlic and cook slowly until onion is soft. Add remaining ingredients and beat to mix.

Philip Morris

LAMB STEAKS

leg of lamb
salt and pepper
flour
oil or shortening

Cut steaks from a leg of lamb about 1/2-inch thick. Chop with a mallet, season with salt and pepper, roll in flour and fry in hot oil or shortening until tender and browned. Turn onto a hot platter and serve immediately. Pass mint jelly or pickled fruit with the steaks.

Marie Schmidt

LAMB WITH SAUCE

2 pounds lean lamb, cut in 1-1/2 inch cubes
1 teaspoon salt
1/4 teaspoon pepper
2 teaspoons butter
2 large onions, sliced
4 scallions or green onions, sliced
2 egg yolks
1/2 tablespoon lemon juice
1/4 cup flour
1/4 cup chopped parsley
1/2 teaspoon dill weed
3 cups chicken broth or stock
1 small head iceberg lettuce, cut in 6 wedges
2 tablespoons water
1/4 cup sliced pimiento-stuffed olives

Coat lamb with mixture of flour, salt and pepper; brown in butter in Dutch oven or deep pot. Add onions, half of parsley, dill weed, chicken broth; mix well. Bring to a boil, reduce heat. Cover and simmer 1 hour and 30 minutes, or until lamb is tender, stirring occasionally. Add lettuce and scallions to lamb, spooning liquid over lettuce; cover and cook slowly 5 minutes. Remove lamb and lettuce, being careful to keep lettuce whole, and arrange in serving dish.

SAUCE:
Beat egg yolks with 2 tablespoons water and lemon juice. Stir into lamb stock and cook, stirring constantly until slightly thickened. Add remaining parsley and the olives. Heat to serving temperature. Pour over lamb and lettuce in serving dish. Serve with rice.

Mrs. Jack L. Groff

BAKED HAM WITH APPLE DOUGHNUTS

cured ham
whole cloves
brown sugar

Cut as much as possible of the rind from the top of the ham. Cut criss-cross pattern gently through the fat layer. In each corner of the criss-cross pattern, insert a whole clove. Cover the top of the ham with brown sugar. Bake at 300° thirty minutes for every pound of meat.

APPLE DOUGHNUTS:
5 medium apples
2 teaspoons baking powder

1 cup flour
1 egg
1/2 cup milk
1/4 teaspoon salt
2 tablespoons sugar
cinnamon
deep fat

Combine baking powder, flour and salt; add beaten egg and milk and heat until smooth. Peel and core apples; slice in 1/4-inch rings. Dip each ring in batter and fry in deep fat, turning rings gently until golden brown. Sprinkle with a little sugar and cinnamon, if desired, while still hot.

Joan S. Nobles

WILD GAME & SEAFOOD

Because of Texas' proximity to the Gulf of Mexico, shrimp, oysters and fish add to the abundance of other wild game. These are some of the finest traditional dishes for which Texas is famous.

VENISON STEAK

1-1/2 cups water
2 slices lemon
1 teaspoon whole black pepper
1/2 tablespoon poultry seasoning
1/4 teaspoon mace
2 tablespoons salt
1 cup vinegar
1/2 medium onion
6 whole cloves
3 to 4 sprigs parsley
2 to 2-1/2 pounds venison steak
flour
oil
2 cloves garlic, divided
1 tablespoon butter
3 tablespoons oil
1 small onion
1 cup consommé
1 scant cup thick tomato juice
1 cup dry red wine (claret)
1/2 teaspoon rosemary
1 tablespoon chopped parsley

Simmer first 10 ingredients 30 minutes and cool. Pour over steak and marinate 5 to 6 hours, then dry with cloth. Roll lightly in flour and brown in oil with 1 garlic clove. Drain and place meat in roasting pan; combine remaining ingredients and pour over venison. Cook at 350° for 1 hour.

Mrs. Frank Dana

RAGOUT OF VENISON

1/3 cup vinegar
2/3 cup red wine, claret or Burgundy
1 large onion, chopped
salt and pepper to taste
2 bay leaves, crushed
2 pounds venison

Combine marinade ingredients; bring to a boil. While warm, pour over meat. Store in a crock or enamel pan. Cover and refrigerate several hours or overnight, turning occasionally. Drain meat; reserve marinade.

4 tablespoons hot fat
1 onion, finely chopped
1 pinch of thyme
1 bay leaf
1/2 teaspoon black pepper, freshly ground
1 teaspoon salt
1 tablespoon bacon, finely chopped
beef stock
12 small whole onions
12 to 15 mushrooms
butter, melted
parsley

Brown meat in hot fat; add chopped onion, thyme, bay leaf, pepper, salt, bacon and wine marinade. Cook covered over low heat for 1 hour. If more liquid is needed, add beef stock. Add whole onions; cook 1 hour longer. Sauté mushrooms in butter, serve over meat. Sprinkle with parsley.

Mrs. B. L. Giddens

FRIED YOUNG SQUIRREL

1 squirrel, cut in serving pieces
1 clove garlic, chopped
1/2 cup olive oil
flour
salt and pepper

Soak squirrel overnight in saltwater in the refrigerator. Sauté garlic in olive oil. Roll squirrel in flour, salt and pepper; fry in garlic mixture, turning only once, until well browned.

Mrs. Allie W. Baugh

WILD TURKEY WITH ONION-CORN BREAD STUFFING

2 cups minced onion
1 cup diced celery
1/2 cup butter
2 teaspoons salt
5 teaspoons ground sage
1/4 teaspoon pepper
7 cups toasted bread crumbs
4 cups corn bread crumbs
3/4 cup turkey stock or hot water
3 eggs, beaten
12 to 15 pound turkey

Sauté onion and celery in butter until onions are limp and transparent. Add seasonings, bread crumbs, stock and eggs. Mix lightly. Rub inside of bird with salt and fill loosely with stuffing. Bake turkey as usual, removing 20 to 30 minutes before serving.

Marion Bennett's Mother

WILD DUCK

1 brace of wild ducks
1 pint sherry wine
2 bottles onion juice
1 wine glass olive oil
1 cup water
1/4 pound butter, melted
1/2 teaspoon cayenne pepper
1 teaspoon black pepper
1 teaspoon salt
1 tablespoon parsley, chopped
bay leaves

Stick bay leaves on breasts of ducks with toothpicks, about 3 to a duck. Place in roaster, breasts up. Mix sauce and pour over ducks. Start in 400° oven, cook 20 minutes, then turn heat down to 300° and simmer until tender, about 2 hours. Use gravy as is.

Mrs. B. E. Wallace

PHEASANT IN HERB GRAVY

1 (2 to 3 pound) pheasant
1/2 cube margarine or butter
1 can mushroom soup
1 soup can water
1 teaspoon salt
pepper to taste
1 tablespoon dried marjoram
1/4 teaspoon garlic powder
2 teaspoons minced dried onion
1 cube chicken bouillon (optional)

Sauté pheasant in margarine. Mix remaining ingredients; pour over pheasant. Simmer slowly 1 hour or until pheasant is fork-tender. Gravy may be increased if necessary during cooking by adding water to which 1 cube chicken bouillon has been added.

Mrs. T. F. Voiles

QUAIL BAKED IN WINE

2 shallots, chopped
2 cloves garlic, finely chopped
1/2 bay leaf or 2 pieces
1 teaspoon peppercorns
2 cloves
butter
6 quail
4 tablespoons flour
1 pint white wine
1/2 teaspoon salt
1/8 teaspoon pepper
few grains cayenne
1 teaspoon chives

Slowly cook shallots, garlic, bay leaf, peppercorns and cloves in 1/2 cup butter for 8 minutes, stirring constantly. Sauté quail until well browned. Add wine; simmer for 30 minutes. Remove quail; strain sauce into a container. Melt 4 tablespoons butter in a saucepan; blend in flour. Slowly stir in reserved sauce; cook until thick. Add remaining seasonings and quail. Cover and heat to boiling.

Mrs. Douglas Buchanan

CAJUN DOVE DELIGHT

12 doves, dressed, with hearts and gizzards
salt and pepper
onion salt
garlic salt
1/2 stick margarine
2 medium or large onions, minced
paprika and parsley, garnish

Sprinkle moist doves with salt, pepper, onion salt and garlic salt. Melt margarine in heavy cast aluminum or cast-iron pot with tight-fitting lid. Brown doves on back, breast and sides. Place browned doves on their backs and cover with minced onions. Put lid on pot and let smother very slowly for 45 minutes. Turn doves over on breast, allowing onions to drop into gravy. Replace lid and cook on a very low fire; simmer for 2 hours. If fire is too high, natural gravy will boil away and you will have to add water. When done, doves will be a beautiful dark brown and so tender that meat will separate from bone readily. The thin dark brown gravy with onions and giblets is best served over steaming hot rice. Place steamed rice on platter, place doves around rice, breast side up and garnish with paprika and parsley. The secret of Cajun cooking is using the proper type of pot and very little fire. The slow, slow cooking allows ample time for proper blending of flavors and retains the natural juices for gravy.

Harley Berg

DUTCH OVEN DOVE

24 doves
6 strips bacon, cut in half
salt and pepper to taste
6 tablespoons flour
2 cans beef bouillon
4 (4-ounce) cans mushrooms
1 bay leaf
2 whole cloves
1/2 cup sherry
parsley, chopped

Sauté strips of bacon in Dutch oven. Take out and reserve. Brown doves slowly in bacon drippings and season with salt and pepper. Remove doves. Brown flour in drippings and add bouillon. Stir constantly until thickened. Add mushrooms. Return doves to pan. Add bay leaf and cloves. Put bacon on top. Cover and simmer 1 hour. Add sherry and sprinkle with parsley. Cook 15 minutes longer. Before serving, remove bay leaf and cloves.

Mrs. Jon (Sherrie) Vogler

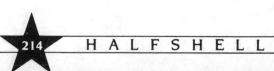

POTTED DOVES

6 doves
1/2 to 2/3 cup chopped onion
1/2 cup fresh mushrooms or 4 ounces canned mushrooms
1 tablespoon parsley
1/2 to 1 cup heavy cream or sour cream
salt and pepper to taste
1 cup white wine

Wash birds, dry, rub with salt and flour and sauté lightly in butter. Remove and place in a casserole. Sauté onions, mushrooms and parsley in remaining butter. Pour over the birds with 1 cup white wine. Bake until the doves are tender, basting several times during the cooking. Add more wine or water if needed. Just before serving, add heavy cream or sour cream and heat. Add salt and pepper to taste.

Mrs. John Runner

ROAST DOVE WITH WILD RICE DRESSING

6 doves, cleaned and dressed
1/2 cup green pepper, chopped
1/4 cup onion, chopped
butter or margarine
2 cups cooked wild or brown rice
1/2 cup olives, chopped
1/2 cup mushrooms
paprika

Split doves. Cook green pepper and onion in butter until tender. Add the rice, olives, mushrooms and paprika. Add more butter or margarine if necessary to make mixture moist. Stuff the doves. Place in an uncovered roasting pan; roast at 300° for 1 hour. Baste frequently with 2 tablespoons butter or margarine in hot water.

Mrs. Joe W. Caldwell

BEER BATTER FOR DEEP-FRYING FISH

Down in Texas, fish frys are popular events. They usually get started when a mess of Texans decide "it's time to go fishin'." Weekend fishing trips down the Rio Grande or on the Gulf of Mexico bring back yeller cat, red snapper or ocean trout, three favorite fish. They are usually breaded, deep fried in coconut oil and chased — with lots of beer.

1 (12-ounce) can light beer
1 cup sifted all-purpose flour
1 tablespoon salt
1 tablespoon paprika

Sift flour, salt and paprika together. Sift into beer, lightly beating with wire whisk until light and frothy. This mixture may be used at once or after standing several hours. When using batter, stir from time to time to keep it thoroughly mixed. Flour fish and dip into batter. Let fish rest several minutes before frying so it will not be too "drippy." Fry at about 400° in oil until golden brown. This batter is also ideal for onion rings and other vegetables.

Mrs. Max (Martha) Euwer

PEDERNALES BATTER FOR FRYING FISH

1 cup yellow cornmeal
1 teaspoon salt
1/2 teaspoon pepper
1-1/2 teaspoons paprika
1/2 teaspoon celery salt
1/4 teaspoon dry mustard
1/4 teaspoon onion powder

Combine ingredients and roll fish in mixture. (Fish or fish fillets should be cleaned, washed and patted dry.) Fry in shallow, moderately hot oil (370°) for about 5 minutes on each side, or until fish flakes easily when tested with a fork.

Cookbook Committee

STUFFED BAKED TROUT

6 (10-ounce) trout
3/4 pound sole fillet
3/4 pound crab meat
1/2 cup sauterne
1/4 cup minced shallots
2 egg whites
salt
pepper
half-and-half cream
seasoned flour (salt and pepper)
oil for frying
cherry tomatoes
parsley sprigs

Bone trout; leave head attached. Grind sole and crab meat using medium grinding blade or chopper. Mix sauterne and shallots in small pan and boil until reduced by 1/2. Add wine mixture to ground fish. Beat egg whites until frothy and blend gradually into fish mixture. Season to taste with salt and pepper and add just enough cream to make moist, but firm, dough. Fill trout cavities with mixture and close with small skewers or toothpicks. Dip trout in cream, then in seasoned flour. Preheat oven to 350° while sautéing trout in hot oil until golden, turning carefully once. Drain fish and arrange side by side in shallow baking dish. Bake 20 to 25 minutes. Arrange fish on heated platter and garnish with cherry tomatoes and parsley.

Harold H. Petrauschke

JEZZ'S OYSTER CHOWDER

8 to 12 oysters, medium sized
2 cups water
2 cups milk
1/2 cup onion, finely chopped
1/2 cup celery, finely chopped
3 tablespoons butter
1 tablespoon parsley, finely chopped

Put butter in a medium-sized pot and sauté onions and celery. Add milk and water, bring to a near boil, stirring to prevent burning. Lower heat. Clean and 'gut' oysters. Wash thoroughly to remove sand. Cut oysters into quarters ("for women and children") or leave them whole ("for men"). Add to pot with parsley. Simmer for five to ten minutes. Serve with oyster crackers.

Ted Karkoska

A TEXAS ROUX

1/2 cup flour
1/2 cup oil
water
salt (optional)

Mix the flour and oil and brown this in iron skillet until very dark, stirring constantly. Be careful not to burn it. Remove from heat, let cool, stir in a little water, and mix well. Add more water to make a thick paste. Now stir this into your gumbo. Cook until the stew is thickened, and you're ready to serve it over rice. (You may decide to add a little more salt at this point.)

You might like to use a dry roux instead. Here's how: In a heavy iron, dry skillet, add the flour — nothing else. Cook dry flour over low heat stirring constantly until it gets as dark as cocoa. Then stir a little of this at a time into your gumbo and simmer 'til thickened. When serving, sprinkle with gumbo filé.

Tina Tskieti

SHRIMP CREOLE

1 pound cooked shrimp
1/2 pound margarine
1 clove garlic, mashed (or 1/4 teaspoon garlic powder)
2 medium onions, chopped
1 cup diced celery hearts and leaves
1 cup chopped green pepper
1 bunch fresh green onions, chopped
1 bay leaf
1 (1-pound) can tomatoes, mashed after draining, reserve juice
1/4 teaspoon paprika
salt
pepper
2 tablespoons grated Cheddar cheese
1/4 teaspoon powdered ginger

Melt margarine in large skillet. Sauté garlic, medium onions, green pepper and celery. Turn heat down. Add green onions, tomatoes and remaining ingredients, except shrimp. Simmer over medium-low heat for 25 to 30 minutes, stirring occasionally. Add shrimp the last 5 minutes of cooking time. Add tomato juice during cooking only if mixture becomes too thick and there is likelihood of scorching. Remove bay leaf. Serve over rice.

Linda Van Horn

TEXAS GUMBO

3/4 cup oil
1 cup flour
4 tablespoons bacon drippings
2 cloves garlic, minced
1 green pepper, chopped
3 large onions, chopped
8 stalks celery, chopped
1/2 cup parsley, chopped
2 quarts hot chicken stock
2 quarts hot water
1/2 cup Worcestershire sauce
Tabasco sauce to taste
2 large ripe tomatoes, chopped
1/2 cup catsup
3 tablespoons salt
6 slices cooked crisp bacon, broken up
1/4 teaspoon thyme
1/4 teaspoon rosemary
red pepper flakes to taste
2 cups chopped cooked chicken breast
2 pounds crab meat
4 pounds boiled, cleaned shrimp
1 tablespoon brown sugar
3 tablespoons lemon juice
2 tablespoons water
2 teaspoons filé

Make a dark roux using oil, flour and bacon drippings. To make a dark roux, use medium heat and cook about 45 minutes, using a wooden spoon and stirring constantly. Add garlic, green pepper, onions, celery and parsley to roux and stir constantly 1 hour. This is what makes it good! Add hot chicken stock, hot water, Worcestershire sauce, Tabasco, tomatoes, catsup, salt, bacon, thyme, rosemary and red pepper flakes. Simmer 3 hours. Thirty minutes before serving time, add chicken, crab, shrimp, brown sugar and lemon juice. Simmer 30 minutes. Do not boil. Put 2 tablespoons water in cup, add filé and stir until it combines. Add to hot gumbo just before serving. Freezes well. Freeze only the gumbo as it is, before adding the chicken, crab. shrimp and filé.

Undeé Sonsat Ewell

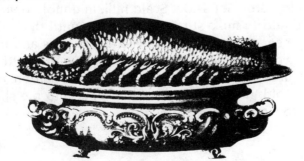

DESSERTS

Texans love their desserts. Cakes, pies, puddings and candy are always available to help fill the "chinks" in a hungry stomach. However, beware, the word "calorie" has yet to appear in print anywhere in Texas!

VINEGAR PIE

1 cup sugar
1 cup cold water
4 eggs, beaten
2 tablespoons flour
3 tablespoons butter
5 tablespoons vinegar
unbaked pie shell

Mix all ingredients well. Simmer until thickened. Pour into a pie shell and brown in oven.

Mrs. John Blakely,Sr.

BOURBON PIE

1 envelope unflavored gelatin
1/2 cup cold water
1-1/2 cups milk
3/4 cup sugar
3 tablespoons cornstarch
3 eggs, well beaten
1 tablespoon butter or oleo
1/4 cup bourbon
1/2 teaspoon vanilla
1/2 pint whipping cream, whipped
1 pie shell, baked
ground nutmeg

Soften gelatin in cold water. Set aside. Scald milk in double boiler, combine sugar and cornstarch and add to milk, stirring constantly, until thick. Cook 15 minutes, stirring often. Add a small amount of this custard to eggs and mix well. Add egg mixture to remaining custard and cook 1 minute longer. Add butter and gelatin and chill mixture 30 minutes in refrigerator, but do not let it harden. Add bourbon and vanilla; blend well. Fold in whipped cream and pour into pie shell. Sprinkle with nutmeg and chill 4 to 6 hours before serving.

Dolores Lanford

GREEN TOMATO PIE

green tomatoes
scalding water
lemon juice or vinegar
1 cup sugar
1 tablespoon flour
1 teaspoon cinnamon
butter
2 unbaked pie crusts

Slice enough green tomatoes real thin to fill the size pan you use. Pour scalding water over the slices and let stand about 15 minutes. Drain while you make the pie crust; then proceed almost like making an apple pie. Add some lemon juice, or if you are like the old-timers and don't have any, use a little vinegar. Add sugar, flour and cinnamon. Mix well and put into the pastry lined pan, add pieces of butter to top and cover with top crust. Bake just like an apple pie.

Mrs. Paul Huntley

GERMAN SWEET CHOCOLATE PIE

1 (4-ounce) package German chocolate
1/4 cup margarine
1 large can evaporated milk
1-1/2 cups sugar
4 tablespoons flour
1/8 teaspoon salt
2 eggs
1 teaspoon vanilla
1 cup shredded coconut
1/2 cup chopped pecans
1 unbaked pie crust

Melt chocolate and margarine over very low heat. Remove from flame and gradually blend in milk. Combine sugar, flour and salt. Beat in eggs and vanilla. Fold in chocolate mixture and add coconut and pecans. Pour into unbaked pastry shell, fluted high. Bake at 375° for 50 minutes.

Virginia Archer

TEXAS MOLASSES PECAN PIE

9-inch uncooked pie shell
3/4 cup pecans
3 eggs
2 tablespoons butter, melted
1 cup sugar
1 cup molasses
1 tablespoon flour
1/8 teaspoon salt

Preheat oven to 450°. Beat eggs slightly, add melted butter, sugar, molasses, flour and salt. Place pecans in uncooked pie shell. Pour mixture over pecans. Bake in 450° oven for 10 minutes, then 300° for 30 minutes.

Pearl Glazner Anderson

BUTTERMILK PIE

1 stick butter
2 cups sugar
3 eggs
3 rounded tablespoons flour
1 cup buttermilk
nutmeg
1 teaspoon vanilla
unbaked pie shell

Cream together butter and sugar. Add eggs and flour, mixing before adding buttermilk, a dash of nutmeg and the vanilla. Pour into the unbaked pie shell and bake at 350° for 45 minutes. These pies freeze well.

Sue Sims

OLD-FASHIONED CHESS PIE

Chess pie is a generic term applied to pies usually made with cornmeal and buttermilk instead of wheat flour. They were "keeper" pies that did not spoil easily and were kept in an unrefrigerated food chest. The food chest was a common fixture found in most Texas homes before the days of refrigeration. Whenever Gramps wanted a treat, he'd point to the food chest and say, in his best Texas drawl, "Git me one of them ches' pies." Through the years the "t" was dropped in the Texas vernacular and chest became chess, as in pie.

2 cups sugar
1 tablespoon cornmeal
3 eggs, beaten
2 teaspoons vanilla
2 tablespoons flour
1 stick butter, melted
1/2 cup buttermilk

Mix and pour into shell and bake. Lemon flavoring or coconut may be added if desired.

Mammie Phillips

CHOCOLATE CHESS PIE

4 egg yolks
1 whole egg, slightly beaten
1-1/2 cups sugar
1/2 cup melted butter
1 teaspoon vanilla
1/4 cup cocoa
1/2 cup boiling water
1 unbaked pie crust

Beat egg yolks and egg with sugar. Bring water and butter to boil, add cocoa and mix. When cool, add to egg mixture. Pour into crust. Bake at 350° on lowest rack in oven until set. If pie gets too brown, turn oven temperature down.

Sue Sims

LEMON CHESS PIE

4 eggs, beaten slightly
2 cups sugar
1 tablespoon cornmeal
1 tablespoon flour
1/4 cup buttermilk
1/4 cup lemon juice
1/4 pound butter
1 unbaked pie crust

Mix all ingredients and pour into unbaked pastry shell. Bake at 325° on lowest rack of oven for 30 to 40 minutes or until brown and set.

Sue Sims

7-UP CAKE

3 sticks butter
3 cups sugar
5 eggs
3 cups flour
2 teaspoons lemon extract
3/4 cup 7-Up

Preheat oven to 325°. Cream butter and sugar together for 20 minutes; add eggs, beating in one at a time. Add flour 1/2 cup at a time; add lemon extract and fold in 7-Up. Pour into well-greased 12-cup bundt pan. Bake 1 hour and 10 minutes. Remove from oven and cool on wire rack for 10 to 15 minutes before removing from pan.

Mrs. Charles A. (Dee) Olsen

COCA-COLA CHOCOLATE CAKE

1 cup butter
3 tablespoons cocoa
1 cup Coca-Cola
1/2 cup buttermilk
1 teaspoon baking soda
1 teaspoon vanilla
2 eggs
2 cups flour
1-1/2 cups tiny marshmallows
2 cups sugar

Heat butter, Coke and cocoa together until boiling. Cool slightly. Combine buttermilk, soda, vanilla and marshmallows. Add to chocolate mixture. Combine sugar and eggs; stir in flour and add to above. Pour into greased 9 x 13-inch pan and bake at 350° for 55 to 60 minutes. Pierce hot cake with fork and let frosting run into holes.

FROSTING:
1 cup butter
3 tablespoons cocoa
6 tablespoons Coca-Cola
1 box powdered sugar
1/2 cup chopped nuts

Bring first 3 ingredients to a boil. Add sugar and beat well. Add nuts.

Gig Harlow

STIR CRAZY CAKE

2-1/2 cups all-purpose flour
1-1/2 cups sugar
1/2 cup cocoa
2 teaspoons soda
1/2 teaspoon salt
2/3 cup cooking oil
2 tablespoons vinegar
1 tablespoon vanilla
2 cups cold coffee (or cold water)
1/4 cup sugar
1/2 teaspoon cinnamon

Put flour, 1-1/2 cups sugar, cocoa, soda and salt into an ungreased 13 x 9 x 2-inch metal baking pan. Stir with a fork to mix; form 3 wells in flour mixture. Pour oil into one well, vinegar in one and vanilla in one. Pour cold coffee over all ingredients and stir with folk until well mixed. Do not beat. Combine remaining sugar and cinnamon; sprinkle over batter. Bake in 350° oven for 35 to 40 minutes.

R. J. Reynolds Tobacco

TEXAS GRAPEFRUIT CAKE

ORIGIN: Because they had no money to buy sugar, the poor housewives of Mexico's Rio Grande Valley border towns originated the Grapefruit Cake. According to tradition, the formula also included the shredded rind, but the more modern recipe has eliminated that and added sugar. In the early 1900s, a rare delicacy in the peasant's home of sun-dried bricks and thatched straw featured the cake and a small gourd of pulque, an intoxicating liquor made of the fermented sap from the maguey plant.

1 package white cake mix
2 packages unflavored gelatin
3/4 cup cooking oil
3/4 cup grapefruit juice
4 eggs
1 cup sectioned grapefruit

Combine cake mix, gelatin, oil and juice in a mixing bowl. Add one egg at a time, beating after each egg. Add sectioned grapefruit to batter and beat half a minute. Pour into a greased and floured tube pan. Bake 1 to 1-1/4 hours at 300°.

Patsy Henderson

CHOCOLATE KRAUT CAKE

1 (8-ounce) can sauerkraut
3/4 cup butter or margarine
2 cups sugar
2 eggs
1 teaspoon vanilla
2-1/4 cups flour
2 teaspoons soda
1/2 teaspoon salt
1/2 cup cocoa
3/4 cup buttermilk
1 cup boiling water

Rinse kraut well with cold water, drain, then put in blender and chop fine. Set aside. Cream butter with sugar, add eggs and vanilla and beat well. Sift together dry ingredients and add alternately with buttermilk. Add kraut and mix well. Last, fold in boiling water. Bake in greased and floured 13 x 9 x 2-inch pan for 25 minutes. Ice with your favorite chocolate icing.

Mrs. Ralph (Thelma) Platzer

YOUR FAVORITE CHOCOLATE ICING

1 stick margarine
6 ounces Philadelphia cream cheese
1/4 cup cocoa
2-1/2 cups powdered sugar
1 teaspoon vanilla

Combine all ingredients.

Barbara Bennet

MISSISSIPPI MUD CAKE

1 cup oleo
1/3 cup cocoa
1 cup coconut
1-1/2 cups flour
1 cup chopped nuts
4 eggs
2 cups sugar
1 jar Marshmallow Creme

Melt oleo; stir in coconut, cocoa, pecans, eggs, sugar and flour. Mix well. Pour into greased pan (16 x 11 x 1-inch) and bake at 350° for about 20 minutes. Remove from oven and spread Marshmallow Creme over top. Cover topping with the Final Topping.

FINAL TOPPING:

1 stick oleo, melted
1/3 cup milk
1 teaspoon vanilla
1 cup pecans
2 cups powdered sugar

Mix in order given. Spread over cake and let cool. Cut into small squares. Makes 36 squares.

Alice Tanner

PRUNE CAKE

1 cup sugar
1/2 cup butter
2 beaten eggs
1 teaspoon soda dissolved in 2 tablespoons hot water
2 cups flour
1/2 cup buttermilk
1 teaspoon vanilla
3/4 cup cooked chopped prunes

Cream together the sugar and butter then add the beaten eggs and soda. Add flour and buttermilk alternately, then add the vanilla and prunes. Bake at 350° in two layer cake pans until done.

FILLING:
1 cup sugar
1/2 cup flour
1 egg
1 cup buttermilk
3/4 cup cooked chopped prunes
1 cup chopped pecans
1 teaspoon vanilla
1 tablespoon butter

Cook first five ingredients in saucepan until thick. Add butter and vanilla, cool, then add pecans. Fill cake and cover top and sides with filling.

Joan S. Nobles

PUMPKIN POUND CAKE

2 cups sugar
4 eggs
1-1/2 cups oil
2 cups flour
1 teaspoon salt
2 teaspoons soda
3 teaspoons cinnamon
1-1/2 cups canned pumpkin

Preheat oven to 350°. Blend together sugar, eggs and oil thoroughly. Sift together dry ingredients and add alternately to first mixture with pumpkin, mixing well after each addition. Bake in greased and floured 1-inch tube pan for 1 hour. Cool 20 to 25 minutes in pan. Frost, when cool, with favorite icing.

Mrs. Eleanor MacMillan

FOURTEEN CARAT CAKE

2 cups flour
2 teaspoons baking powder
1-1/2 teaspoons soda
1 teaspoon salt
2 teaspoons cinnamon
2 cups sugar
1-1/2 cups oil
4 eggs
2 cups grated raw carrots
1 (8-3/4-ounce) can crushed pineapple, drained
1/2 cup chopped nuts

Preheat oven to 350°. Sift together first 5 ingredients. Add sugar, oil and eggs and mix well. Stir in carrots, pineapple and nuts. Turn into 3 greased and floured 9-inch layer cake pans or a 13 x 9-inch pan and bake 35 to 40 minutes, until top springs back when lightly touched with a finger. Cool a few minutes in pans, then turn out onto wire racks to cool. Frost with favorite icing.

Mrs. Robert (Flo) Buchenau

GRANDMOTHER'S PECAN RAISIN CAKE

1/2 pound butter
3 cups sugar
1 cup sour cream
3 cups cake flour
1/2 teaspoon baking powder
1/2 teaspoon salt
2 teaspoons vanilla
1 teaspoon butter flavoring
6 eggs
1 cup raisins
1 cup pecans

Beat sugar, butter and sour cream until fluffy. Sift together flour, baking powder and salt. Beat eggs well; alternate with flour into sugar mixture. Add vanilla and butter flavoring. Flour nuts and raisins before adding to mixture. Bake 1 hour in 325° oven in well-greased and floured pan.

Vangie Norris

ALMOND ICEBOX CAKE

1/2 cup butter or margarine
1/2 cup sugar
1 cup cake flour
1 teaspoon vanilla
4 tablespoons milk
4 egg yolks
1 teaspoon baking powder
pinch of salt
4 egg whites, beaten until stiff but not dry
1 cup sugar
3/4 cup slivered, blanched almonds
1 cup whipped cream
marshmallows

Mix first 8 ingredients as for any cake. Then divide batter into two 9-inch square pans. Beat 1 cup sugar into the stiff egg whites until dissolved. Spread this mixture on the batter, then sprinkle with 3/4 cup slivered, blanched almonds. Bake 30 minutes in moderate oven. Remove from pans and cool. Then invert one layer, meringue side down and put filling of 1 cup whipped cream and cut marshmallows between, placing top layer meringue side up. Place in refrigerator until ready to serve.

Mrs. Len Mertz

TEXAS PECAN COFFEECAKE

1-1/4 cups sugar
1 cup sour cream
1/2 cup butter
2 eggs
1 teaspoon soda
1 teaspoon baking powder
2 cups sifted flour
1 teaspoon vanilla
1 teaspoon cinnamon
1 cup chopped pecans

Cream 1 cup sugar, sour cream, butter and eggs. Add soda, baking powder and flour sifted together, and vanilla. Mix well; pour half the batter into a 9-inch greased, floured tube pan. Combine remaining sugar, cinnamon and pecans; sprinkle 2/3 of mixture over batter. Cut the topping into the batter; pour in remaining half of batter and sprinkle with remaining topping. Bake at 350° for 35 minutes. Toasting pecans before using in topping gives cake an elegant taste.

Mrs. Arlan L. Fenner

"UNDER THE TABLE" GINGERBREAD

1/4 pound butter
2 cups molasses
1 cup sugar
3 eggs, beaten
1 cup hot water
2 teaspoons soda
3 cups flour
1 tablespoon ginger
1 tablespoon cinnamon
1 teaspoon allspice
1 teaspoon cloves
1 teaspoon salt

Preheat oven to 325°. Melt butter, add molasses, sugar and beaten eggs. Add hot water. Mix well. Dissolve soda in 1 tablespoon water. Add to mixture. Mix flour, spices and salt. Add to mixture. It will be a very thin batter. Bake in large, flat pan with 3-inch sides for 45 minutes. Serve with Whiskey Sauce.

WHISKEY SAUCE:
1 tablespoon cornstarch
1 cup sugar
1-1/2 cups milk
1 tablespoon vanilla

3 beaten egg yolks
3 tablespoons whiskey (bourbon)

Combine cornstarch and sugar. Add milk and vanilla; stir. Add egg yolks. Heat to simmer. Add whiskey.

Mrs. William A. (Dorothy) Castille

DAM-FI-NO

This recipe is from the Bishop family of Electra, Texas. During the Depression it was the only dessert that could be afforded. Since it was created from a rather humble array of ingredients, no one could come up with a name for it. Hence, the perplexed answer became the recipe's title.

1 cup sugar
1/2 cup flour
1/3 teaspoon salt
2 cups evaporated milk
4 tablespoons oleo (colored with amber-colored capsule to give rich color)
3 egg yolks
1 teaspoon vanilla

Blend sugar, flour and salt. Pour in milk and egg yolks which have been beaten until smooth. Add oleo. Cook and stir like crazy until it thickens. Let cool and add vanilla. If you want a different taste treat, add cocoa, then 1 tablespoon less flour. Top with "calf-slobbers," otherwise known as meringue.

Bernice Bishop Nichol

OUT-OF-SEASON PEACH COBBLER

1/2 cup margarine
1 cup sugar
1 cup flour
2 teaspoons baking powder
3/4 cup milk
1 (29-ounce) can peaches

Preheat oven to 375°. Melt margarine in Pyrex dish. In mixing bowl mix sugar, flour and baking powder. Add milk. Pour mixture on top of melted butter, but do not mix. Add peaches, juice and all. Bake 40 minutes.

Mrs. T. L. (Isabel) McMillan

FRESH PEACH COBBLER

12 ripe peaches
1 egg
1 cup sour cream
3/4 cup sugar
2 tablespoons flour
1/2 teaspoon cinnamon
1/2 teaspoon nutmeg
1/4 teaspoon salt

Preheat oven to 350°. Peel, pit and halve or slice peaches. Place in casserole. Beat egg slightly, mix with sour cream, add sugar mixed with flour, cinnamon, nutmeg and salt. Bake 15 minutes.

TOPPING:
1/4 cup brown sugar
3 tablespoons flour
2 tablespoons butter
1/2 cup chopped pecans (optional)

Mix topping and sprinkle over peaches and bake 15 minutes longer at 350°.

Miss Mary Anderson

JAMBOREE PEACH COBBLER

1/2 cup margarine or butter
1 cup flour
2 cups sugar
1/2 teaspoon salt
3 teaspoons baking powder
1 cup milk
3 cups fresh peaches, peeled and sliced
1 teaspoon cinnamon

Preheat oven to 350°. Melt margarine in 8 x 12-inch baking dish. Sift together flour, 1 cup of sugar, salt and baking powder, and blend with milk. Pour mixture over melted margarine. Spread peaches over this and sprinkle with other cup of sugar mixed with cinnamon. Bake 1 hour. Crust will magically appear and cover entire surface of cobbler.

Mrs. Edwin A. (Berta) Thayer

FRUIT COBBLER

3 cups flour
2 tablespoons sugar
3 teaspoons baking powder
5 tablespoons butter
1/2 cup milk
3 to 4 cups fruit
3/4 cup sugar
3 tablespoons butter, melted

Mix flour, baking powder, 2 tablespoons sugar; work in 5 tablespoons butter and add milk. Grease pan with melted butter. Cover bottom of pan with fruit. Cover fruit with part of pie crust. Mix the balance of the fruit, sugar, butter and pour on top. Then top with the balance of the pie crust. Bake in oven 15 minutes at 450°; reduce heat to 350° for 25 to 30 minutes longer.

Joe Propps

BREAD AND BUTTER PUDDING

1/3 cup raisins
5 slices day-old bread
1/4 cup butter, melted
2 eggs
2/3 cup sugar
2 cups milk
1/2 teaspoon vanilla

Line bottom of well-greased oven-proof casserole with raisins. Cut bread in 1-inch strips; dip each strip in melted butter and arrange buttered bread strips in layers over raisins. Beat remaining ingredients together and pour over bread. Set dish in pan of hot water. Bake in 375° oven until bread is browned and a knife blade inserted in center of pudding comes out clean. Serve plain or with whipped cream.

Christine Guadarrama

CHERRY PUDDING

1 can sour pitted cherries (or other fruit)
3/4 cup sugar
1 cup flour
1 teaspoon baking powder
1 egg, unbeaten
3/4 teaspoon salt
1/2 cup sugar
1/3 cup oleo

Heat cherries and sugar and pour in bottom of baking dish. Mix flour, baking powder, egg, salt and sugar until crumbly and sprinkle over cherries. Melt and cool oleo and pour over all. Bake 20 minutes in 350° oven. Serve warm or cool, plain or with whipped cream.

Mrs. Tex Lucas

TEXAS FRENCH BREAD PUDDING

Mary Nell Reck taught Tex-Mex cooking at her cooking school in Houston, Texas, for years. She now runs "The Cafe Moustache," which features this delicious bread pudding hybrid; part traditional Texas cooking, part French haute cuisine.

1 quart boiling milk
1 pint whipping cream
8 eggs
2 egg yolks
2/3 cups granulated sugar
1 teaspoon almond extract
1/4 cup dark rum
1 to 2 loaves stale French bread
1/4 cup toasted, sliced almonds
1/4 cup raisins soaked in rum
1 cup sliced apples tossed in: 1 tablespoon lemon juice, 1 tablespoon brown
  sugar, 1/2 teaspoon cinnamon

Combine cream, eggs, yolks and flavorings in a very large bowl. Dissolve sugar in boiling milk and stir into cream mixture. Cut French bread into 2- to 3-inch chunky pieces (about 8 cups worth). Trim off crusts. Slice 2 loaves of bread into diagonals (leave on crusts). Butter a metal oval pan or deep dish pie pan and coat with granulated sugar. Dip trimmed bread pieces into custard mixture and pack into pan. Mound slightly and cover with a layer of sliced apples. Dip diagonal slices into custard mixture and arrange in overlapping layer on top. Carefully fill dish with remaining custard mixture. Place dish in a large pan of hot water and bake at 325° for 1-1/2 hours. Remove from oven and brush with hot glaze. Sprinkle edges with almonds and center with raisins, serve warm with creme anglaise.

GLAZE:
1 cup strained apricot preserves
3 tablespoons dark rum

Heat strained preserves. Stir in rum and brush, while hot, over cooked bread pudding.

CREME ANGLAISE:
6 egg yolks
3/4 cup sugar
1-1/2 tablespoons cornstarch
1 tablespoon vanilla extract
2 cups hot milk
1/2 cup very cold cream

Beat egg yolks until lemon colored. Gradually beat in sugar and cornstarch. Add hot milk and mix thoroughly. Cook in saucepan on very low heat, stirring with wooden spoon. Have a cold bowl ready containing the cold cream. When foam subsides from custard, pour immediately into the bowl to stop the cooking.

Mary Nell Reck

MRS. JOHNSON'S LACE COOKIES

1/2 cup flour
1/2 cup coconut
1/4 cup Karo syrup (red or blue label)
1/4 cup brown sugar, firmly packed
1/4 cup Mazola or margarine
1/2 teaspoon vanilla

Preheat oven to 325°. Mix flour with coconut. Cook over medium heat, stirring constantly, Karo syrup, sugar and margarine until well blended. Remove from heat and stir in vanilla. Gradually blend in flour mixture. Drop by teaspoonfuls 3 to 4 inches apart on ungreased cookie sheet. Bake 8 to 10 minutes until lightly browned. Cool 1 minute and remove. Cool on racks.

Mrs. Lyndon B. Johnson

TEXAS MILLIONAIRES

50 caramels
2 tablespoons butter
2 tablespoons water
3 cups pecans, halved or whole
8-ounce chocolate candy bar
2 to 3 ounces paraffin

Melt caramels, butter and water in double boiler. Add pecans. Drop by teaspoonfuls on foil-covered bread board or back of jelly-roll pan. Cool. Melt chocolate bar and paraffin together. Stick ice pick in cooled caramel-nut drops and dip through warmed chocolate mixture. Cool on foil. More or less paraffin may be used for firmness desired.

Gerald Pruitt

PRALINES

3 cups granulated sugar
1-1/2 cups buttermilk
1/2 teaspoon baking soda
2 tablespoons unsalted butter
2 teaspoons vanilla
2 cups pecans halves

Place the sugar, buttermilk and soda in a large, heavy saucepan. Stir only once. Bring to a boil. Reduce heat and boil gently for about 29 minutes, without stirring, or until the candy forms a soft ball when tested in a small bowl of cool water. As the sugar cooks it will caramelize and become a rich, amber color. When the candy has finished cooking, remove from the heat. Add the butter and stir vigorously with a wooden spoon until it begins to lose its shine and thicken a little. Add the vanilla and pecan halves. With the addition of the pecans, the candy will firm up almost immediately. Drop the candy by spoonfuls on buttered aluminum foil or waxed paper. Allow to cool and harden. Makes about 36.

Mary Nell Reck

DRINKS

Texans love their teas and beers, but also have an incredible ability to conjure up some exotic combinations. Cheers!

YANKEE TEA

hot water
milk
sugar
lemon extract (optional)
vanilla (optional)

Half and half hot water and milk sweetened with sugar and sometimes a drop or two of lemon extract or vanilla (these last usually being held in reserve for special occasions or company).

Joe De Yong

SPICED TEA

2 sticks cinnamon
10 whole cloves
grated rind of 1 orange
grated rind of 1 lemon
3 quarts water
2 tablespoons black tea
juice of 4 lemons
juice of 6 oranges
4 cups sugar

Put spices and rinds in cheesecloth bag. Cover with cold water, bring to boil. Remove from heat; add tea tied in a bag and steep for 5 minutes. Add strained juices and sugar; heat to boiling point. Remove spices and tea. Serve hot.

Mrs. J. L. Terrell

TEXAS SUICIDE

Mix any three available sodas together. Plus a pint of 151 if you're of age!

Unknown

SOCK COFFEE

1 clean white sock
coffee
water

Stick coffee inside sock and immerse in pot of boiling water (1 heaping tablespoon of coffee for each cup of water). Cook to desired strength or until the color of the sock matches the one you used yesterday morning. This recipe ain't no joke!

"Smokey"

COFFEE PUNCH

4 quarts double strength coffee
1 quart cold milk
1 tablespoon vanilla
1 cup sugar
2 quarts vanilla ice cream

Chill coffee; blend in other ingredients, adding ice cream last.

Mrs. Hugh Busby

TWO HUNDRED PUNCH

4 ounces citric acid
5 pounds sugar
ice and water to taste
2 cans frozen orange juice
1 can frozen lemon juice
1 can frozen pineapple juice
cherries, red or green (optional)
pineapple chunks (optional)

Soak citric acid overnight in tightly closed pint jar of water. Dissolve sugar in citric acid solution, adding as much water as necessary (probably several quarts). When ready to serve, add fruit juices, crushed ice and desired amount of water. Red and green cherries or chunks of pineapple may be added to dress it up.

Claire Abbett

GUARANTEED BEST BLOODY MARY IN TEXAS

11 ounces vodka
2 lemons (juice)
3 teaspoons Worcestershire sauce
12 dashes Tabasco
14 dashes celery salt
8 dashes salt
tomato juice (cold)

Combine first six ingredients into a liter bottle. Finish filling with tomato juice. Shake to mix. Serve over whole ice cubes.

Ray Moore

"THE" MILK PUNCH

1-1/2 cups sugar
3 cups water
1 fifth brandy
1/4 cup white creme de menthe
3/4 cup creme de cacao
whole milk to make a gallon of liquid
nutmeg for garnish

Make simple syrup by bringing to a boil 1-1/2 cups sugar and 3 cups water. Mix 1-1/2 cups simple syrup with remaining ingredients and freeze. Serve with nutmeg garnish.

Dorothy Turner Clendenen

PINK ARMADILLO

grapefruit juice
pineapple juice
cherry juice
1 ounce gin or vodka (optional)
cherries for garnish

Mix equal parts of grapefruit and pineapple juices. Add a lesser amount of cherry juice and the alcohol. Pour over ice cubes in a glass and garnish with a cherry.

Howard Johnson